Stain Removal

Stain Removal

Ethics and Race

⸺⊶⟨●⟩⊷⸺

J. REID MILLER

OXFORD
UNIVERSITY PRESS

Oxford University Press is a department of the University of Oxford. It furthers
the University's objective of excellence in research, scholarship, and education
by publishing worldwide. Oxford is a registered trade mark of Oxford University
Press in the UK and certain other countries.

Published in the United States of America by Oxford University Press
198 Madison Avenue, New York, NY 10016, United States of America.

Library of Congress Cataloging-in-Publication Data
Names: Miller, J. Reid, author.
Title: Stain removal: ethics and race / J. Reid Miller.
Description: New York, NY : Oxford University Press, 2017. | Includes
bibliographical references and index. | Description based on print version
record and CIP data provided by publisher; resource not viewed.
Identifiers: LCCN 2016015919 (print) |
ISBN 9780190280970 (hardcover) | ISBN 9780190055875 (paperback) Subjects: Ethics and race
—The everlasting stain—The secret of the mark—Cursed inheritance—Criminal suspicions.
LC record available at https://lccn.loc.gov/2016015919

Your Stain Removal kit includes:

    —instruction manual
    —patented removal solution (dry packet and activator)
    —mixing tub
    —mixing spoon
    —cleansing pad

Always begin with mildest treatment; increase strength as necessary.
(Note: Heavy stains may require repeat applications.)

Caution: Use only in well-ventilated areas

Contents

Acknowledgments

I AM FORTUNATE to have had a great deal of support during the production of this book.

My appreciation to those who contributed to the content of the manuscript at various stages: David Hoy, Jocelyn Hoy, Joel Yurdin, Aryeh Kosman, James Gulick, Naomi Koltun-Fromm, David Marriott, Ravi Sharma, Keith Bolton, and Lewis Gordon. My deepest thanks as well to those who provided support and encouragement during this time: Andrea Morris, Lisa Jane Graham, Darin Hayton, Rajeswari Mohan, Juno (Rheana) Salazar Parreñas, Rhacel Salazar Parreñas, Andrew Friedman, Bethel Saler, Erica Cho, Chiming Yang, Gus Stadler, Matthew Budman, Farid Azfar, Noah Tamarkin, David Sedley, Wendy White, Chiou-Ling Yeh, Stephen Sohn, Juliana Chang, and Richard T. Rodriguez. Special thanks to Alison Wittenberg, Tilden Broemser, Charles Easley, Melanie Boyd, E.B., Irene Miller, the inner circle, and especially to Bill Bellone for years of hot tea and shocking embellishments that kept me alert and skeptical. Cristina Beltran's friendship and generosity was instrumental to the publication of this book. Danielle Macbeth's guidance through the process of writing sustained my belief and focus on the project. Sometimes one needs a room of one's own; other times a borrowed one is what's called for—special thanks to Teresa de Lauretis for providing this room, intellectually and geographically, during the production of this work. And finally, for everything and everything, then now and to come, thank you Celine Parreñas Shimizu.

Convention holds that I include here the caveat that, despite the contributions of those above, any and every mistake of the book is solely mine, although, honestly, I don't see why I should have to take all the blame. How is it that those who receive credit for the success of a venture bear no responsibility for its failure? But here the argument of the book itself defeats me, for one of the consequences of rethinking value through the metaphor of the "stain" is a disabling of the fantasy of such reciprocal equations. Even my own work is against me.

This is not entirely true: yes, this book will seek its revenge on me; again, however, I hold little pretense of its being my own. Any half-witted analysis will show that everything in this book worth saying has been said before, inherited from writers more nimble and canny, more deserving of historical and intellectual recognition. The claims herein should not lose credibility because of this; indeed, their persuasiveness depends precisely on this familiarity—if anything is managed here it is not the forging of dangerous new ground but a redirection to what has previously been stated repeatedly and exhaustively, the crooked arc of the book's finger pointing readers to well-worn grooves that trace and retrace established circuits. This book does not survey uncharted territory but roots its nose in the most beaten treads of theoretical and folk wisdom regarding bodies and value. I guarantee that you have heard all of this many times before.

As it is with the best told stories.

Stain Removal

Introduction

SETTING THE STAIN

*A man's character greatly takes its hue and shape from the
form and color of things about him.*
FREDERICK DOUGLASS, *My Bondage and My Freedom*

THIS BOOK, as the title indicates, is about ethics and race. The conjunction
may confuse—would not the phrase "ethics *of* race" be more accurate? The
grammatical modification, though minor, is meant to capture an endeavor
distinct from the application of a metric to a concept. A short discussion of
the latter formulation—of what an "ethics *of* race" designates—will help to
distinguish the approaches.

An "ethics of" may be said to denote an assessment of the value, contingent or absolute, of any number of possible representational "objects," including but not limited to phenomena, deeds, states of affairs, affects, and beliefs.
This "ethical" assessment is conventionally distinct from ontological determinations of "what something is," those apperceptive processes by which objects
are said to appear to consciousness. An "ethics of," then, implies the coming
of some object into consciousness prior to and independent of an "ethical"
process to which it is subsequently subjected. Representational identity, in
other words, is taken as initially nonevaluative; "what exists" serves thereby
as the object upon which "ethics" enacts its effects. Accordingly, only a small
set of representational objects would appear for us as ethical objects; solely
those matters that pose significant and practical problems—that rattle what
we think of as the smooth exercise of daily life, or that explode in ways that
make anything like a "daily life" impossible—would comprise the primary
material for these critical if optional evaluative reflections. On this understanding, to engage in an "ethics of" is to bring the question of value, as if for
the first time, to phenomena definable without reference to value.

At its most rudimentary, an "ethics *of*" thereby connects two elements: a distinct "ethical object" (i.e., an action, quality, belief, or state of affairs capable of being put into question)—an account, that is, of "what is now going on" that calls for rethinking—and a mode of evaluative interpretation (i.e., a system, formula, or hierarchy of principles in light of which the value of the ethical object, of "what is now going on," is disclosed). Without a distinct object an "ethics of" has nothing—or rather too many things—to evaluate, leading to overly formless imperatives. General agreement may exist, for example, that "technology" raises important ethical questions, yet as an ethical object "technology" reasonably includes information gathering systems, molecular gastronomy, autotuning, and perhaps, as Jacques Derrida contends, language itself.[1] An "ethics of technology" at this panoramic scope could furnish little more prescriptive insight than cautious support of "good" rather than "bad" technologies—in effect, unhelpful restatements of the original question. Conversely, the absence of a coherent mode of evaluation easily trivializes the ethical object, creating contradictory or banal prescriptives. Applying an intuitive or "common sense" approach to a particular state of affairs, for instance, implies an ethical object that requires no special exercise of thought; moreover, it overlooks the possibility that this state of affairs may be itself the expression of contradictions internal to that "common sense." Sartre's account of the student torn between caring for his mother and fighting for his country illustrates how "common sense" core values like "family" and "patriotism" can generate the dilemmas they are then invoked to resolve.[2]

On these conditions an "ethics *of* race" would appear a prime or at least serviceable philosophical project. "Race," though difficult to define, certainly expresses a linguistically distinct notion that no other term replicates in its knotty mix of genealogical meanings and associations. Moreover, that race remains resiliently and controversially significant for descriptions of "what is now going on"—globally, psychologically, politically, and economically—suggests that it presents a legitimate and urgent object for ethical interrogation. It would appear as well that any number of evaluative theories might be harnessed to yield an ethics of race: communicative ethics, contract theory, natural or human rights discourse, virtue ethics, etc. The availability of plausible models of application suggests an ethical examination of race is not only feasible but also well overdue. Despite this, no ethical analyses of race exist.[3] To be sure, the topic of race surfaces occasionally in contemporary cultural and political theory, fields of discourse that frequently employ the prescriptive language of ethics but for which that language and the conditions of value are not themselves primary matters for reflection. In these interventions—often examining some aspect of multiculturalism, postcoloniality, hybrid identities, or transnational movements—the nature of the good (as freedom, equality, self-expression, etc.) and of the ethical subject (as a discrete possessor, giver, and arbiter of value), on which ethical claims about race necessarily depend, tend to be presented as self-evident, and thus escape precisely the critical attention that an evaluative study would generate. As a result, most cultural and political theory waggingly presented under the auspices of "ethics" has little to no ethical analysis to recommend it.

Take, for instance, the common presupposition in discourses of race that the qualitative assessment or "prejudgment" of embodied racial appearance constitutes a discriminatory practice. The broader evaluative principle invoked here is that ethical worth be determined independently of physiological appearance. It is a dualism that, in effect, holds that the *object* of ethical analysis and the *object* of material analysis be separate and non-intersecting. Most interventions of ethics and race start from this premise, yet it is far from decisive. For one, it presumes that an evaluative apperception of the body is a kind of "doing" or practice distinct from and subsequent to a value-neutral perception. This would mean we first "see" embodied subjects as sets of ethically unmediated physiological features to which we then, from some private internal reserve, affix (false) qualitative judgments. Relatedly, a principle that "one should not judge people based on appearance" imagines ethical subjectivity as what can be grasped apart from material "appearance." If so, what precisely would be the genuine, non-material substance of subjectivity being grasped here? Lastly, there is the metaethical problem of the exclusion of phenomena like bodies from the set of proper ethical objects, insofar as any such prohibition against ethics would itself be an ethical proposition. From where, other than ethics, could such a dictate come? Do bodies not have to fall under the auspices of ethical judgment in order to be deemed off limits to ethical analysis? How could ethics be expected to oversee itself in this way?

These are only a handful of the questions that an ethical examination of race would be obliged to address, questions that, notably, do not reduce to whether "racialization" is "good" or "bad" but place under negotiation the very parameters of ethics and thus the nature and function of value. It should not be expected, then, that the results of such an intervention will lend theoretical legitimacy to what is now being said about ethics and race, grounding conventional patter. On the contrary, they will indicate the relation of ethics and race as conducting an ongoing logic that Western modernity has long tried to disown, that of the genealogical inheritability of embodied value.

The disclosure and tracing of this logic begins by way of the briefest explanation that an "ethics of race" of the type described above has not taken place because, in short, it is not possible. This impossibility is not a consequence of "race" being too diffuse a notion to serve as an ethical object or of the lack of an appropriate ethical formula to which it could be submitted but of the overlapping discursive functions of ethics and race such that to speak of one is already to invoke the other.

The impossibility of an "ethics *of* race" should create some worry for any imagined application of ethics (inclusive of "justice" and "rights") to either racial strategies or ends, as it will affirm that race is not the kind of thing to which ethics could *apply*. Correlatively, it should be emphasized that "race" is not here *the* problem—as if the conceptual logic of value were not deeply implicated in this simultaneity of signification. As the book will show, one will be misled from the start by imagining ethics as innocent or impartial and thus as what displaces all responsibility for incoherence, contradiction, and paradox onto the delinquencies of "race." It may even turn out that, in the historical fight against racial hierarchies, "ethics" has always—perhaps necessarily—been playing both sides.

The Descent

So why is an "ethics *of* race" not strictly possible? Why, that is, is the relation of ethics and race not amenable to the guise of form and content, method and data, or theory and practice? The answer begins with the standard model of ethical theory, operative for any "ethics of X" as explained above, as what contains, in essence, three sequential steps: the presentation of an ethical object for evaluative assessment, the submission of that object's qualities to evaluative scrutiny, and the securing of that assessment to the object through the metaphor of "attachment" or "disclosure." This standard model of ethical theory, Bernard Williams writes, "implies a general test for the correctness of basic ethical beliefs and principles."[4] Williams also gestures, however, toward the existence of ethical objects that defy the operation of that standard model, not because they are "bad objects" but because, in some fashion, they corrupt or disable the model itself such that "there cannot be such a test" of the object's value. This standard model or "test" thus has two possible outcomes: either the revelation (or confirmation) of the object's proper worth or the disabling of the test by the object that incapacitates the very procedure of ethical evaluation.

This object for which can there be no test—that implodes it or elicits compromised and tainted results—is, for Williams, the "prejudicial" object. As he explains, when "prejudices" are held about an object, for instance, a type of person, ethical theory cannot conduct a proper evaluation, for what that theory would encounter is not that type itself but an already *prejudged* kind of entity. Accordingly, to properly evaluate an object ethical theory must encounter it as what has no known worth; for ethics to give an *unprejudiced* assessment value cannot have previously infiltrated and distorted that upon which it is to pass authoritative judgment. Even if value were intrinsic to the object, ethical analysis would need to approach it as having an as yet undetermined and thus unknown worth. Ethical theory on this account must be *other* than that which it assesses, something *external to and outside of* the object's definition and representational possibility; the object, for its part, must not have value as constitutive of or "attached" to its definitional identity but must instead be available to consciousness as ethically *unmarked*. In the matter of "race," then, the efficacy of the standard model depends upon ethics demonstrating its externality to race such that race as a possible ethical object be conceptually available prior to and outside of any value that may later characterize it.

In those instances, however, in which race *does* arise as a theoretical problem—the kind of problem that an ethics *of* race might be summoned to treat—value seems already "insinuated" in advance of its application through a formal model. That is to say, race names a difference that emerges precisely in the context of evaluative hierarchies. For example, when Immanuel Kant catalogues the "genuine races" in the following manner

First race, very blond (northern Europe), of damp cold.
Second race, copper-red (America), of dry cold.
Third race, black (Senegambia), of dry heat.
Fourth race, olive-yellow (Indians), of dry heat.[5]

the list means to indicate not merely a genealogy of anthropological descent but simultaneously that of evaluative "descent."[6] Racial kinds are for Kant qualitative as well as physiological—a single taxonomy suffices to map both distinctions. Kant does not treat us to a singularly ontological argument justifying racial difference and then, in a subsequent move, overlay comparative worth upon those differences. To exhibit behavioral patterns of comparative worth correlative to physical features is rather just *what it means to be raced*. The list is thus ordinal as well as cardinal—in telling us that there are "four" races it simultaneously indicates their "natural" positions with respect to the human template as "unraced." No additional mechanism is required outside of this declarative to situate races evaluatively; there are no sequential "steps" as in the standard model: no unmarked object that precedes evaluation, no separate judgment of worth, and no "attachment" of value to a discrete yet neutral representation. Value appears here not as external and secondary to racial difference—as a procedure recognizably distinct from and posterior to it—but as the expressive significance of that difference. Races are what they "are" in being thus ethically differentiated.

The question raised is whether race can function as an "ethical object" prior to and outside of value such that it can act as the novel recipient of value's attentions or whether, if suffused by value in its basic configuration, it is contaminated by the very thing that would study and assess it from *without*. The "test," it seems, could not be whether value has infiltrated race in all of its appearances but whether value is nothing other than that differentiating force by which *race* is understood to enact its effects. The affirmation of this premise would signal the impossibility of an "ethics of race" for the reason that "race" would designate thereby an articulation of the ethical. Race could not then be "presented" to ethics as a stranger or inconnu; neither could it stand "before" ethics as what temporally precedes it, for that would mean enjoining ethics to deliver a verdict upon itself—that is, upon a sign that mobilizes in the name of value.

This book maintains not only the impasse of "ethical" analyses *of* race for these reasons but also elucidates the intricate logic and implications of the relation that ensures, likewise, that each and every analysis of race is "ethical," which is to say, always and necessarily that of value. What is meant by "ethics" and "race" will of course be under consideration throughout, but it can be shared in advance that by the close of this study neither term will have ceded to the other nor to any third term that would attempt to secure and temper their effects (e.g., truth, system, description, history, language, etc.). What will be shown instead is that, despite their appearance as antithetical, ethics and race execute similar and corresponding functions as what designate and justify coordinated and relational appearances of differential value. It will be asserted, moreover, that this value is not preceded by an earlier mode of difference—most notably, a purely descriptive difference to which value then can be said to apply, attach, or otherwise adhere. Value, on the contrary, will disclose itself not as this or that *kind* of difference but as that by which anything could show up *as such*—that is, by which any entity exists as "itself." As constitutional and conditional for the appearance of representation and meaning, value (and by extension, race) will at once refer to (1) a historic and material coordination of signifiers or marks through which embodied ethical subjectivity becomes recognizable, and (2) the idiom that sustains simultaneously the causal logic of responsible subjectivity *and* the logic of transferable responsibility and thus inheritable worth.

Such claims may seem implausible as a consequence of a study like this: how could an analysis of "race"—a concept so unrepentantly narrow, historically leaden, and *unjust*—generate insight not only into the structuring of value to which "history" and "justice" are themselves indebted but also to the very possibility of representation? Indeed assertions like these threaten a host of what we have come to believe about the proper place of ethical and racial difference: that a subject's qualities should be determined solely on its deeds and not its embodied features; that deeds are knowable as *pre*-ethical phenomena prior to their evaluative assessment; that ethical worth is uninheritable such that all subjects enter the world as ethically innocent and hence unmarked; and that the subject in its ethical expression detaches from all affiliative lineages of embodied worth.[7] All of these convictions attest, in effect, to the inessentiality of evaluation and racialization—that as subsequent to epistemological determinations of "what is" they in no way enable the representations to which they "attach." Instead these applied ancillary layers are taken to envelop original phenomenal content in a manner that readily obscures and corrupts our ability to grasp that original existent in its primordial value-neutral and unraced state.

It is not merely, however, that ethical and racial determinations are understood to obscure original percepts but are thought to do so by means of a particular force of distortion. Of values, Nietzsche writes that "almost every sense impression [in] our world is *colored* by them"; Frantz Fanon relatedly describes race as a "dye" [*colorant*] that "fixes" the development of embodied self-consciousness.[8] In both depictions ethics and race face incrimination as what discolor or *stain* percepts, a staining that eclipses, distorts, hides, and falsifies otherwise unfettered and directly intuited phenomena. To encounter and contemplate a being or phenomenon as it originally accedes to conscious awareness—as unmarked and uncolored—one becomes thereby obliged to strip from that existent all ethical and racial associations: to perform an interpretive exercise of stain removal.

The guiding question of this book is whether value denotes an inherently secondary, applied feature that succeeds—and thus attaches to or imprints itself upon—already existing representations. Does value by its very definition exhibit the structure of the stain as what "colors" both the world and its inhabitants and thus, simultaneously, tarnishes, distorts, and hides those initial existents as they originally arise to consciousness as value-neutral? Is value truly a valence that we *place* upon phenomena, as an evaluative interpretation conducted separately from and subsequent to the perceptual awareness of phenomena? (How would we then measure this break? This temporal lag between the "unmarked" representation *not yet* stained by value and its evaluative marking? Or the equivalent distance between the "initial" recognition of the subject in its unmarked and unmediated state of disaffiliation and that in which it becomes perceptually yoked into criminal ties of racial association?) If, alternatively, the perceptual world is unavailable to us in the way we have so long dreamt—unmarked, uncolored, unstained—value would not signify a stain one attempts to remove to get at a more authentic and original impression underneath. It would stand, rather, for the differential marking any phenomenon—as *this* and not *that* entity—must presuppose for its appearance, insofar as relations of difference by which existents may arise as distinctly "what they are" would be necessarily relations of *value*.

And if this is so? What then would have to be said about the nature of value? One might begin to think, as Frederick Douglass suggests in the opening epigraph, that the very "character" of something—the qualities of any representation or being—has not only a "shape" but a "hue" or resonance of value that has no intrinsic content or "color" but rather acquires that content—that is, becomes available to perception—in and through its actualized relations to other "characters." One might then start to wonder whether value as a nonsensory, nonempirical condition for the possibility of differentiated representation could be mistaken for an a priori form of intuition like space and time.

Any such conclusion would have to be a mistake. For how could someone like Frederick Douglass—he or any other figure so deeply and historically *stained*—attune us to greater philosophical *transparency*?

Two Alibis

That ethics and race both exhibit the dynamic of the stain neither exempts nor immunizes them from the effects of the other. On the contrary, their greatest danger lies, we are told, in their interaction. Each is said to stain the other so severely as to produce misperceptions and distortions that render the other unrecognizable. Contemporary theory, accordingly, gives us two versions of ethics and race in which each is derided and mourned, respectively, as the attachment that stains and that which is stained. The protestation that race is perverted by ethics is perhaps the less conspicuous of the two complaints so will be addressed first. A discussion of the complementary claim positing the staining of ethics by race follows.

The Ethical Staining of Race

In *Visible Identities*, Linda Alcoff offers that the "visibility" of race enables the exploitation of differences of physical embodiment such as "skin tone, hair texture, [and the] shape of facial features."[9] Although "almost laughably insignificant" in their own right, she explains, these differences nevertheless provide the physiological indices for racial classifications. Such constellations of physiological features, Alcoff emphasizes, are not themselves inexorable referents of race but what have become historically intuited "visual manifestations" and "markers" of racial difference. Each bodily mark by which race is signified and materialized is accordingly a "sign" that "invites interpretation to discern what is behind it, beyond it, or what it signifies."[10] As with any semiological system, these marks of race acquire meaning through their relation to other physiological marks, those both apparent as well as "hidden" on and through the body. Race, like gender, is itself never seen or conceptualized as such; one apprehends only materialized instances of it, instances that are not themselves unified representational figures (e.g., the body as such) but a coalescence of signs that testify, sometimes assuredly, sometimes vaguely, to the synthetic of race.

Visibility, Alcoff continues, is nevertheless only one of three components of racial difference: "The concept of race and racial difference emerged as that which is visible, classifiable, and morally salient."[11] Each element, moreover, bears varying culpability for the discriminatory effects of race. That we *acknowledge* visible corporeal differences, Alcoff contends, is not insidious in itself—neither are classifications based on those differences, she proposes, even when those categories are "arbitrary" as in the case of race. Danger arises, Alcoff asserts, only when the intrinsically value-neutral differences between features become disparately valorized. Accordingly, it is the third element, "moral salience," that for Alcoff converts embodied distinctions into symbolic marks of differential worth. By "moral salience" Alcoff does not mean any simple valorization of racial signifiers as either "good" or "bad" but their more complex linking to dispositional and behavioral tendencies—seemingly descriptive assertions, that is, of the performative qualities of subjects: "What is pernicious about race classifications . . . is the host of attributes purportedly correlating to physical racial features."[12] Classifications of race untouched by ethics have little force on their own; it is their fostered associations with disparately valued traits—industriousness, impertinence, craftiness, equanimity, etc.—that generate the harmful versions of racial categories familiarly deployed over the past several centuries.

If, Alcoff continues, "moral salience" bears a responsibility for the detrimental force of racial categories that neither "visibility" nor "classification" possess alone or together, the temptation to argue that "the whole process of *seeing* race should come to an end" need not be indulged, as the injuries of race are not due, ultimately, to "seeing" visible bodily differences but to their disparate evaluative resonance.[13] A solution like "color-blindness" thus far exceeds the scope of the problem, as "sight does not lead in a direct line to race"; moreover, Alcoff adds, the ability to register and acknowledge visible differences remains important for "human communication."[14] Rather than deny the existence of different bodily signifiers like skin color, she recommends that we work to make these differential marks "less salient [and] less memorable" than we imagine them to be.[15]

Alcoff's proposal turns on the premise of the divisibility of embodied classification from evaluative attributes—on whether, that is, "race" can stand for different collectivities of physiological traits absent evaluative traits. If coarse physiological difference precedes ethical difference then race is not, on this view, an inherently bankrupt conceit but that which becomes so only when value parasitically attaches itself to "genuine" material distinctions, such that "differences of kind become transformed into differences of degree."[16] That a "transformation" from nonqualitative to qualitative difference *could* take place is conditional, however, on the representational feasibility of nonevaluative "differences of kind": those severed conceptually and temporally from "degreed" valences that institute false relations and hierarchies. It is a hypothesis that configures two separate and sequential operations of "difference"— one in which representations come into relation through an ethically neutral, exclusively "descriptive" economy; the second and subsequent in which those signifiers become haphazardly replotted as a function of the spurious and supplementary axis of value. While Alcoff affirms the epistemological and temporal priority of the first mode of difference as "real" she fears the second will always contaminate it: "Visual differences are 'real' differences . . . [b]ut there is no perception of the visible that is not already imbued with value."[17]

Alcoff's worry here is worth restating as a general hypothesis—*that there is no perception without evaluation*—the truth of which would undermine not only conventional objections to embodied differences like race but also, as will be seen later, risks subverting the metaphysical and temporal ordering by which ethics has become theoretically subordinate to ontological and epistemological inquiry. For now, however, we need understand only how *evaluative perception* is taken to interrupt the ability to "see" the "reality" of racial difference, where "reality" designates a preethical state in which shared visible characteristics do not yet operate as evaluatively symbolic marks. If, as Alcoff fears, there is no perception without evaluation, access to this economy of pure perceptual relations of "kind," and any "communicative" possibility within it, would seem foreclosed from the start.

That ethics "imbues" or stains the visible so deeply and pervasively makes unpromising for Alcoff the "liberal" dream of eliminating the "artificial overlay" of value.[18] Despite this, she suggests that shimmers of the real accede to perception when one forgoes superficial glances for close inspection, leading to a recommendation for racial remediation by which "we ... simply need to learn to see better," an urging of the reader to parse what elsewhere is despaired of as potentially inseparable.[19] Ethics as a secondary and *false* symbolic economy that stains (as "artificial overlay") the *true* material differences of race would seem to presuppose, then, at least three axioms on the relation of perception and evaluation: 1) that perception be an activity separate from and anterior to that of evaluation; 2) that the activity of perception be authentic in a way that the activity of evaluation is not; and 3) that this secondary and subordinate status of evaluation be discernable even if all perception appears to consciousness as already "imbued" or stained by value.

Such axioms render "evaluative perception" incoherent and contradictory by casting value as inhibiting proper seeing. At the same time, however, this incoherence is what funds entreaties to change our representational relation to racial difference, for instance, Alcoff's prescriptive that we "simply ... learn to see better". For how can "seeing better" generate more value-neutral, ideal perceptions if that ideality is constituted precisely by ethics—namely, by relations of qualitative difference by which "better" as irreducibly a concept of value could itself have meaning? How, that is, can a greater distance from value be achieved via value itself? Ethical difference can do the damage it does to perception, we are told, because it exists both outside and inside true, representational difference. As secondary and "artificial" it remains external to "real" difference, as what might be easily rubbed off or peeled away. Yet as "insidious" it seeps inside and distorts real distinctions from within insofar as perception already implies, as Alain Locke notes, a differentiation by which one can see *well*: "[T]he importance attributed to the discovery of fact, and the eulogistic sense in which 'reality' is opposed to 'appearance' or 'illusion' are, in fact, values.

This comes out especially in doctrines about the 'degrees of reality,' which are plainly of value."[20] By this duplicitous art is ethics said to stain race as a natural difference of kind.

In developing her analysis, Alcoff credits a similar effort by Cornel West to dissect the amalgam of embodiment, classification, and value in his *Prophecy Deliverance!* Both studies aim for a "structural" analysis of race, where "structural," in part, indicates a theory of race that does not seek the origin or persistence of racial categories in the psychological, political, or economic machinations of a dominant group. Following Foucauldian critiques of traditional and historical materialism, both accounts express skepticism that the problems of racial subjugation are fundamentally the consequence of maleficent actors, instead emphasizing, as West explains, formative "powers [that] are subjectless."[21] The motivating question thus shifts from "who is responsible for race?" to that of how race becomes a predominant category of recognizable subjectivity. The limits of psychologism and materialism are thus emphasized not to indicate that theory has gotten to the bottom of a psychology or economics of race but to affirm that no theory of race will "bottom out" in pathology or class consciousness. Absent such methodological dictates, the theory of race, as the discussion of West will show, subsequently opens onto a series of possible moves that eventually presume, exploit, and affectionately betray these Foucauldian frameworks and similar post-Nietzschean structural and poststructural approaches as what can neither sublimate into biopower, globalization, or post-identity theory nor can be expunged from them. In other words, this structural engagement ultimately positions the attempt to domesticate race as a "true" yet "trivial" discourse of physiological difference as what obligates the subordination of value to interpretation (or of value to "existence," in Locke's words) and thus the purging of ethics from identity.

In his chapter "Genealogy of Modern Racism," West announces his aim to "focus on . . . the way in which the very structure of modern discourse *at its inception* produced forms of rationality, scientificity, and objectivity as well as aesthetic and cultural ideas which require the constitution of the idea of white supremacy."[22] The claim thus launches an indictment of modern conceptual thought as inexorably "secreting" racial inequality. As endemic to the logic and form of modern knowledge, race cannot be dismissed, West insists, as epiphenomenal to and thus easily excised from the "breakthroughs" and "revolutions" in newly conceived regimens of truth. Race, West contends, is no less exemplary of the "controlling metaphors, notions, and categories of modern discourse" than any other conceptual product of that enterprise.[23]

The accusation, however, presents a substantive problem for West: if "white supremacy" is *structurally intrinsic* to modern discourses of knowledge it must perform some function *within* those relations—that is, it must contribute something indispensable to those conditions of knowledge rather than arise as their mere byproduct. The "impossibility of black equality" thus cannot be the *result* of modernist "notions and categories" but, on the contrary, must conductively *effect* such conditioned knowledges. West's inclusive discussion of vanguard figures of this revolution (Descartes, Vesalius, El Greco, Racine, Haydn, and Shakespeare among others on a list surprisingly long for a "subjectless" history), whom he views as taking the lead in formulating and disseminating these new metaphors, gives little indication of how that impossibility is constitutionally prefigured for the sake of scientific objectivity. Why, for instance, must racial inequality have existed for these figures to become representative of new forms of reasoning? How, moreover, can race as intrinsic to modern systems of knowledge also be what that system "secretes," making it simultaneously an element and residuum of that system?

That race functions structurally means, on West's own terms, that it functions other than *for* some purposive end, for example, for the sake of an intentional goal of some group condemnable for having *used* race for this or that purpose. On the contrary, that race have no instrumental functionality "for" some group—its lack of "transitive" functionality—is essential for race having a *structural* function. To render race instrumental, as what serves a particular strategic objective, would configure race as a concept the meaning of which would be found in its origin and correlative telos. Yet as West argues, "[t]here is an accidental character to the discursive emergence of modern racism" that suggests precisely a function without instrumentality, or, alternatively, that which effects without intention.[24]

West thus initially presents race as what effects without instrumentality—as accident without intention—as would be expected of a structural account of race that engenders modern apparatuses of knowledge "at their inception." Despite this foregrounding, his subsequent explanation estranges race—and, with it, value—as an external force wielded by academic charlatans that corrupts rather than enables modern logics—specifically, the early discourses of scientific discovery. Recapping this perversion, West divides modern epistemology into two movements: the development of the empirical sciences and the revival of neoclassical aesthetic and cultural ideals. The former modes of knowledge—those of observation, measurement, and comparison—West posits as metaphysically prior to aesthetic and cultural knowledges; as secondary discourses, he charges, the latter reactively invaded and tainted the former with evaluative racial hierarchies: "the classical revival [in modernism] is important because it infuses Greek ocular metaphors and classical ideals of beauty, proportion, and moderation into the beginnings of modern discourse." Accordingly, the innovations of the scientific revolution that developed universal procedures for the verified representation of objects of the world subsequently became "captive" to a "normative gaze" that "impose[d] some degree of order . . . on a broad field of visible characteristics."[25]

This normative gaze, West theorizes, did not belong to philosophers and scientists but was "consciously projected and promoted by many influential Enlightenment writers, artists, and scholars" celebrating a "recovery of classical antiquity" in their own work. As a result, within the human sciences, *"classical ideals of beauty, proportion, and moderation regulated the classifying and ranking of groups of human bodies."*[26] West thus theorizes two separate, sequential, and ethically opposed processes as configuring the divisions of human classification: the scientific method—as *good* difference—first disclosed bodies whose authentically distinct material features unfurled under the scrutiny of rigorous, methodological observation; subsequently, race and value—as *bad* difference—skewed, through the "conscious projection and promotion" of aesthetic concepts, the nonhierarchical and preethical differences disclosed by these nascent human sciences. For West, race (as a grouping function) and ethics (as an evaluative function) alternately installed the form of modern knowledge *and* corrupted its primary and revolutionary outcome, the scientific method.

How might we unravel the logic of this unnatural birth of natural science? Racial difference, on West's picture, is both constitutive of or at least concomitant with Enlightenment thinking yet also outside of and foreign to that thought as what "infuses," "captures," and "imposes" itself upon it. To hold that this difference invades and perverts genuine scientific observations implies that such observations—free of ocular metaphors and anachronistic ideals—could exist as purely differentiated representations into which prejudicial classifications and hierarchies could be "consciously projected." Accordingly, West's explanation of modern knowledge as a function of race similarly relies on the metaphor of the stain, whereby incipient, autochthonous perceptual experience is deranged and distorted by the imposition of asystematic elements of race and value. While racial difference for West organizes and ranks the physiological characteristics of human bodies, it can do so only as an external, surplus force that "infuses"—introduces and applies as if from the outside—value to initially unmarked and unvalued percepts. By these means West comes to preserve the "breakthrough paradigm" of modernity itself as what is, at its heart, uninflected by race and value.[27]

Although West, like Alcoff, perceives race as a purely classificatory concept, he more readily views that ordering capacity as an external manipulation of our scientifically guided observable representations, and thus as itself a staining of progressive knowledge production. Nevertheless, he shares Alcoff's fundamental premise that ethical difference falsifies racial difference as the more derivative and nefarious stain responsible for the "normative gaze" that transmutes racial orderings into hierarchical rankings. West ultimately posits, then, not one stain but two, outlining the relation of the one (race) to the other (value) in his response to Winthrop Jordan's hypothesis that Linnaeus classified races but did not evaluate them. First, Jordan's statement:

> It was one thing to classify all living creation and altogether another to arrange it in a single great hierarchy. . . . In the many editions of the *Systema Naturae* he [Linnaeus] duly categorized the various kinds of men, yet never in a hierarchic manner.[28]

West's response:

> Yet it is quite apparent that Linnaeus implicitly evaluated the observable characteristics of the racial classes of people, especially those pertaining to character and disposition . . . Linnaeus' use of evaluative terms revealed, at the least, an implicit hierarchy by means of personal preference.[29]

West perceives the quandary as whether Linnaeus reveals any evaluative bias in his description of racial classes. But is not the *structural* question—that to which West manifestly attends throughout the entire chapter—whether, indeed, it is "one thing" to enact classifications and something "altogether another"—no doubt a *second* thing—to place them in evaluative relation? Does not the primacy of "nature," "truth," "authenticity," and "individuality" that racialized value is charged with slandering hinge precisely on whether those distinctions precede evaluative difference, not only theoretically but also at the earliest stage of perception? If West denies this to be the case— that there is no classification without evaluative difference, as such logics are "endemic to the very structure of modern discourse"—then Linnaeus enacts evaluative difference insofar as he naturalizes *any* classification, not because his "personal preference" leaks into and taints them.[30] If, instead, West construes value in the thoroughly modern and *un*-Foucauldian sense of "personal preference," wherein value denotes an intrusion by a radically insular and self-conscious will, then the standard model of ethics prevails as what appends a valence to discursive knowledge and thus what marks it, literally and figuratively, after the "fact." The same predicament would hold where West imputes as a culprit a "historically resurgent aesthetics" rather than "personal preference," as both situate ethics as the force that illegitimately breaks into modern science from the outside, where that "outside" includes simultaneously a) the disciplinary outside of literary and humanistic arts, b) the temporal outside of ancient Greece, and c) the psychological outside of the ethical subject's idiosyncratic will. It should not, on reflection, be surprising that for West race eventually had to be broken off and insulated from value, for this is the condition upon which "racial supremacy" has even a theoretical chance of becoming "racial equality." That is, what semantically and politically prevents "racial supremacy" from becoming "racial equality" is not "race," which remains constant in both, but rather the solitary and rogue variable of value.

Accordingly, the damage to objective natural history that at first appears directly attributable to race turns out to be the consequence of the discoloring force of value, which animates race into a mechanism of qualitative comparison. Exorcised in West's critical reading, then, is less race as classificatory difference than race as evaluative difference, a move premised on the divisibility of that difference *from* value. Such a move, however, requires the abandonment of structural analysis in favor of a causal attribution in which specific agents are invoked as defamatory. In West's study, this causality is exemplified in two portraits: one of Linnaeus as a genuine pioneer of modern science whose inattentiveness allowed what was *unscientific* to permeate his objective findings, and the other of J. J. Winckelmann, a nonscientist and dilettante of art history ("[he] saw almost no original Greek art") who nonetheless "laid down rules—in art and aesthetics" that established precise physical standards of beauty.[31] Of the two transgressions, we are led to believe that Winckelmann's was greater: while Linnaeus, through a careless lapse, inadvertently released a "personal preference" into a universal system, Winckelmann "consciously" foisted a comprehensive and antiquated aesthetic code upon a burgeoning and transformative scientific methodology. Certainly no scientist, he was at most, we are told, an amateur art historian "murdered in middle life" (a fact the inclusion of which cannot but generate a gruesome morality tale). West thereby constructs a precarious story in which race, animated by the menace of value, structurally enables modern modes of reasoning, yet as parasitic to that system, filters in and out of it as contagion and excrement.

Little more need be said to demonstrate the logic by which race is said to be "stained" by ethics. But one might also remark how, in these examinations, philosophy ultimately protects and preserves the idea of pure scientific knowledge by attributing its perversions to nonscientific factors (dilettantism, poor "seeing," unconscious projections, etc.) that compromise it *from the outside*. This protection, one could argue, has proven a recurring theme in analyses of race. Here, in 1915, is Alain Locke's contribution:

> Abstract thinking about the terms of race is a matter of comparatively recent development. Most authorities agree that de Gobineau ... was the man who inaugurated [race theory as such.] Monsieur de Gobineau's attitude was that of an amateur in the social sciences and his whole aim seems to have been to draw a line of demarcation between what he called the "superior" and what he called the "inferior" races. The origin of most of that broad classification ... so strangely insinuated itself into anthropological science.[32]

Locke's narrative of the origin of racial hierarchy contains all the features of the stain: the externality of evaluative difference, systemic knowledge that preexists value, and the primal scene of the "insinuation" of value into knowledge. It includes as well the vindicating elements for science's acquittal from any role in the origin of racial hierarchy: amateurism, gross subjective intentionality ("his whole aim"), and an almost magical penetration of the walls of disciplinary rigor ("so strangely insinuated itself"). What betrays race is thus what betrays science as that singular knowledge in which race can exist in its natural, neutral, and hermetic state, the corruption coming from elsewhere as sloppy, venial interventions that actively if surreptitiously paste "mythic" meanings and values onto merely "factual" distinctions. Or so these depositions aver.

The Racial Staining of Ethics

The means by which race is said to stain ethics, though no less important, will take less time to convey, helped by the fact that the accusations launched against ethics above will be the same made against race: that it is an external and secondary attachment that infiltrates and distorts a primary, authentic difference. Nonetheless, the two accusations effect radically different consequences in theoretical discourse. The conviction that ethics stains race has remained a troubling puzzle of empiricism and value to this day. No similar ambivalence, however, muddies the converse claim that race stains ethics, which is understood as a pervasive truism that affirms the irrelevance of race for the study of value.

This supposed irrelevance may not be obvious given the steady scholarly condemnation of racial inequality. The introduction to the edited collection *Racism and Philosophy* remarks that "Racism is not just a topic for ethics and political philosophy," implying that ethics has been the de facto home to studies on race, as opposed to, say, the areas of philosophy of mind or language.[33] Discussions of racism (and racial "resistance") do indeed circulate occasionally within the philosophical marketplace; these interventions include a spectrum of topics including affirmative action, reparations, multiculturalism, institutional discriminations, and the explicit prejudices of canonical theorists of modern thought.[34] Nonetheless, such work can only tendentiously be called "ethical" in any sense other than applied moral theory, insofar as the study of "racism" is not one that places ethics and race in conversation; on the contrary, it is a project whose aim is to ferret out, expose, and expunge what is already given as a destructive and distorting force of logic and power. "Race" in these accounts speaks to what must be rejected as immaterial to evaluative knowledge, not merely as that which has intrinsic negative worth but, as shown below, as what is viewed as fundamentally and historically antithetical to the modern definition of ethics.

The political objectives of antiracism are not here at issue—or not directly, in any case. What *is* at issue, rather, is the presumption that when one speaks of ethics and race that one *must* be speaking about *racism*, as if this were the only site at which ethics and race intersect. If, indeed, the only discourse of ethics and race were "racism" then it would be a discourse that could say nothing other than what had been determined in advance—that is, if the only possible outcome of this encounter were the imperative to identify and eliminate *racism*, then, as the existing philosophy so aptly demonstrates, how would the "ethics of race" be other than a political call to action?

The slippage from race to racism (reflected in that from "ethics" to "political philosophy") thus tracks the configuration of race as external to the theoretical study of ethics, or rather, within the metaphor of the stain, as what *should be* external to ethics but which, due to the tenacity of its blighting force (for which *racism* is the surrogate expression), infects and corrupts Western instantiations of moral systems. As a result, no discursive space exists for the analysis of ethics and race; there is only the strategizing of the most advantageous means of excluding race from representational difference. The incisive critique by Charles Mills of Rawlsian theory offers one instance of this dynamic. Mills points out that the history of political liberalism for which John Rawls's theory now canonically reigns has been for centuries a "racial liberalism" that methodically "restricted full personhood to whites (or, more accurately, white men) and relegated nonwhites to an inferior category . . . "[35] The expectation, then, is that Rawls's *A Theory of Justice*, as a doctrine that attends from the start to the actual empirical conditions of persons, would engage substantively with the entrenched and egregious racial disparities already in effect.[36] Yet as Mills shows, contemporary political theorists have followed Rawls's lead in avoiding the subject of race to concentrate on the details of "ideal theory"—that is, the presumptive features of a perfectly just society. The irony, then, is that the political theory of justice—the very advantage of which is its on-the-ground readiness to rectify nonabstract social injustices—quickly takes refuge in the fantasy of a nonracial ideal.

For all that Mills has given Rawlsians to think about regarding race, he himself appears committed to the basic premises of this "conception of justice that nullifies the accidents of natural endowments and the contingencies of social circumstance"—those such as race—"that seem arbitrary from a moral point of view."[37] Mills's point, however, is that social justice is not effected by henceforth ignoring all such endowments but by first correcting for past and present injustices resulting from unequal distributions of goods based on "accidental endowments." For Mills, then, there is nothing intrinsic to the *theory* of liberal equality that prevents its nonracial *practical* expression; in other words, he holds that the achievement of social justice is rightly premised on the degree to which racial difference disappears from evaluative determinations: "Thus, the rethinking, purging, and deracializing of racial liberalism should be a priority for us . . ."[38] The insistence that Rawlsians attend to race stems not from a belief in its relevance for moral theory but, quite the opposite, that it cannot but be *irrelevant* for evaluative determinations. That race be "purged" as the blot upon liberalism is thus one of the first and *political* tasks of justice, a justice therefore presumed as already or ideally "deracialized," and thus in relation to which race figures always as an external and corruptive threat. As Michael Monohan observes, such a position renders the notion of racial justice "oxymoronic;" because justice "is construed in a way that treats morally *arbitrary* particularities like race as beyond its universal and disinterested purview, [it] is relevant to matters of race only insofar as it proscribes the use of race in our moral and political deliberations."[39] Justice, we are told, begins with the systematic deployment of stain removal.

Outside occasional citational references, the claim of "racism" makes no appearance in the subsequent arguments of this book. This alone should suffice to indicate a project distinct from what now counts for literature on ethics and race. For to introduce "racism" as the self-evident object of ethics is to concede to ethical theory in advance a capacity it has never demonstrated, specifically, the ability to render judgments unmediated by embodied representations like race. If it is indeed the case that race has wormed its way into modern forms of thought so as to blemish every assessment of ethical subjectivity down to its most pedestrian of activities, denying recognition thereby to the individual for the genuine qualities it exhibits—whether those qualities be varnished by racial favor or disfavor—then by all means, let us scrub away until the last vestiges of racial cognition have faded from consciousness. First, though, ethics will need to show that it can dispense with race in its determinations of value. This means it must expose race as inherently secondary to and distinct from evaluative judgment; it must reveal race as a force capable solely of distortion and obscuration of true worth and not what is constitutively necessary for such judgment. If, on the contrary, there exists any validity to racial embodiment as a *structural* feature of ethical interpretation in the manner West initially suggests then the allegation that race incontrovertibly actualizes in ethics as "racism" will itself require substantive revision.

The tacit conversion of race into racism illustrates one means by which race has been configured as a stain upon value and thus inherently corruptive to ethical discourse. What is required, however, to establish that race can have no fruitful congress with ethics—that all products of this miscegeny are either impotent or discreditable—is the radical independence of ethical judgment from all embodied signifiers of racial difference. The irrelevance of race for ethics depends upon the ability of ethics to ascertain comparative values of events and actions apart from any semiotics of race. The bar for this proof is quite low, all things considered: ethics need demonstrate only that the emergence of value itself, that by which ethics makes its "mark upon" the representational world, be the effect of a process wholly other than that by which race effects *its* mark. The marks of ethics and of race, that is, need to be what circulate within nonintersecting systems of meaning. The possibility of judgments immune to race depends upon this formal incommensurability. Indeed, it is only on this premise—that despite their permeability, neither can serve as the solvent or solute for the other—that ethics could be accused of "staining" race and vice versa. Thus the exculpation of ethics hangs on the racial mark not summoning a mark of value or value invoking the mark of race.

Holding the line between the two would seem easy given the growing view of race over the last century as an impediment to ideal theories of ethics. One could fairly claim in our era the default exclusion of race from assessments of individual deeds, social histories, and lineages: that in general determinations of evaluation, race has no standing. This reflects perhaps the most common expression of this principle for what we think of as the routine judgments of everyday life. On this view, the comparative ethical worth of a subject or group must remain a function strictly of enacted deeds divorced from the perceived race of the performer(s) of those deeds. Accordingly, until the moment of a performed action, that subject or group would remain, by this principle, evaluatively *uninterpretable* and *illegible*. A corollary would dictate the elimination of race as a factor in the evaluation of the deed itself, such that the value of the deed would remain fixed irrespective of race of the performer.

This ordinance that excludes race in ethical determinations attests to a greater orthodoxy contravening the ethical relevance of an umbrella of physiological features like gender, disability, age, and size. It is an orthodoxy, Agnes Heller describes, born of a modern conceptual understanding of these features as the result of "cosmic contingency"—that it is by sheer accident or luck that anyone possesses such characteristics.[40] Heller thus maps the larger discourse of contemporary value from which emerge principles like Rawls's exclusion of embodied features from ethics as "accidents of natural endowment and the contingencies of social circumstance . . . that seem arbitrary from a moral point of view." As a "modern" belief, she notes, the radical separation of embodied features and value replaced a premodern view in which those traits signified inheritable blessings or curses that embedded ethical subjectivity in ancestral genealogies. In the modern era, however, "[c]osmic contingency cuts the umbilical cord between the life of a single person and the person's roots in declaring the connection meaningless."[41] To be born in one country rather than another, in poverty or wealth, with a certain tincture of skin, eyes, and hair rather than another, signifies nothing about the subject's qualities but only the vagaries of chance. The differentiating characteristics of modern bodies, Heller concludes, provide no evidence for anything that might be considered ethical knowledge of someone; also disavowed as "meaningless," thereby, is any embodied mark imagined to signify one's location within affiliative genealogies like nationality, race, and ethnicity. For Heller this contingency obliges us to suspend evaluative interpretations of others until a storehouse of experience is built through our interaction with them.

Outside of this shared "lived history" we must commit to an ignorance of or "withholding [of] the judgement of a person's moral character."[42] Not one of our empirical features, nor any fact about our situated selves, can evidence our truly individual qualities. As Heller remarks, "birth is an accident; it has no meaning."[43]

Heller's notion of "cosmic contingency" is also expressible through the proposition that qualities ascribed to a subject (affable, callous, quirky, etc.) must be assessments the *reasons* for which are *not* credited to inheritable and accidental endowments. If, as Heller contends, modernity has "cut the cord" between, on the one hand, inheritable and embodied signifiers, and, on the other, whom one truly "is," then those signifiers will remain illegible for what we understand as ethical subjectivity. Such traits will have no explanatory value for our subjective dispositions or behavior; they will have no explanatory value for the *kind* of person one is. Quite the opposite, any assessment justified by those traits will constitute by definition a non-ethical judgment: as Williams writes, one is "removed from ethical theory . . . [when] 'he's black' or 'she's a woman' is his reason [for justifying behavior]."[44] As race and gender have no bearing on one's ethical subjectivity, on this view, they cannot serve as reasons for *why* someone might do something and thus as reasons for why one might associate certain types of behaviors with certain bodies. Race is thus "removed from" ethics as a feature discordant with the actual qualities by which a person might be evaluated.

That for Williams race and gender do not count as reasons for evaluative judgments does not mean for him that all embodied natures are so excluded: "'Humanism,' he writes, "is not a prejudice. To see the world from a human point of view is not an absurd thing for human beings to do."[45] For Williams, then, the marks of embodiment and the marks of value are not, in fact, accidental or "cosmically contingent" when they converge at the level of the "human." On the contrary, "humanity," he thinks, rightly indicates more than a taxonomical classification, signaling as well "the concerns of our local ethical life—that is to say, of our [human] life."[46] For Williams, ontology and ethics correspond neatly at the site of "humanity," an embodied ethical category that discloses "the importance of human beings to human beings."[47] Classifying something as human, then, *does* in fact allow us to prejudge the values that govern that being such that, in this case, we receive it not as ethically "foreign," as Heller would have it, but as already ethically resonant. Indeed, much contemporary theory that understands itself as "ethical" would seem to base this self-description on the fact that "human" stands, analogous to Kant's depiction of the races, as at once an ontological and ethical designation. Were this not the case, the terms "human," "humane" and "humanistic" would have no intrinsic prescriptive purchase in these tracts.

Why, then, does the concept "human" legitimately signify ethically embodied being—*acceptably* violating the modern separation of embodied features and value—but race (and gender, etc.) does not? Williams defends this inconsistency by distinguishing two types of prejudice: the first—a species prejudice—refers to an evaluative perception conditioned by shared corporeal features by which human consciousness intuits its common "concerns" or values. The other—a factional prejudice—defines a narrow-minded set of beliefs falsely associated with corporeal similarities that, as unthought values, indicate not intuitive authenticity but lack of self-reflection—that is, a restricted perspective the analytic domain of which is not ethics but abnormal psychology. Williams thus rescues "humanistic" prejudice from being "falsely modeled on racism and sexism, which really are prejudices" by positing—at the level of the human only—what ethics has expressly denied: the corporeal mediation of evaluative perception.[48]

Ethical modernity, then, presents a curious set of proposals about the structural externality of race to value, whereby 1) evaluative determinations about who we are may not be based on embodied features like race unless such features conform to those of the "human" race, in which case ethical prejudgments are not only acceptable but inevitable; 2) the only categories for which ethical judgments obtain are those of the individual and the species; those of any other coordinating category that lie between them—race, gender, age, family name, etc.—are illegitimate and as such invasive to and destructive of genuine ethical judgments; 3) to evaluate the world from the perspective of a "human" subject affirms our subordination to "human" values but to do the same as a raced subject exemplifies, in contrast, an absence of self-reflection that, as nonphilosophical, occurs *outside* ethical evaluation proper; 4) as descendants of humanity we inherit ethical "concerns" reflective of a human "form of life" yet as descendants of racial (or familial, national, etc.) genealogies we inherit no such "local" values except as prejudices that obscure our genuine, individual (and simultaneously human) values.

To summarize, two parallel stories continue to be told in which ethics and race alternately violate the other, corrupting and polluting what would otherwise be, it is said, generally functional systems—namely, scientific (racial) classification and ethical evaluation. The perceptual cues of race, the first story asserts, would have at most minor significance had value not insinuated itself to produce extremes of differential worth; likewise, the second story relates, our judgments of others would reflect greater fairness and accuracy if irrelevant features like race and other embodied traits did not impose themselves as legitimate objects of valuation. Although these interpretations suggest a fierce antagonism of ethics and race, the nearly identical forms of their transgressive maneuvers indicate a close alliance of what is thought to actualize through the guise of the stain. As we shall see, their dual characterization as forces that stain and are stained derives less from some special relation between the two than from their formalized subordination to perceptual representation. In other words, it is because ethics and race are conceived of as subordinate additions to prior existents (i.e., that value is *applied* to phenomena and that race is *applied* to embodied beings) that they cannot but manifest as "stains"—secondary ascriptions to antecedent, unblemished representations. The primary theory under consideration, then, is that which posits prior existents as tainted, obscured, and distorted by a subsequent and external force that "applies" or "attaches" itself such that original existents become inaccessible to representation.

Criminal Intents

Stain Removal is as much about ethics as it is race, if not more so. One might gather this well enough from the title of the book, but such a reminder is nonetheless demanded in order to forcefully configure, from the start, the expectations and receptivity of the potential reader. For something strange and magical happens when the word "race" enters the conceptual arena such that it governs the other thematics at play, gravitationally yoking them into its symbolic orbit. Consequently texts that include race as a substantive topic of interest—particularly in philosophy and critical theory—somehow lose thereby their influence as interventions into other, purportedly more "general" disciplinary debates. Moreover, "raced" texts become "already read" in certain ways; we think we know, or have a pretty good idea, of what such work argues—indeed, the assumption goes, there are only certain things any nonempirical book about race *could* possibly say. It is now assumed, for instance, that every theoretical take on race must make some claim about its "reality." This typically occasions an obligatory caveat that *of course "race" is not a biological reality*, followed by a comparative hypothesis as to where it lies on a spectrum of the fictional. It is an odd imperative, as suggested above, in that it commands a pledge to the unmediated "reality" of the biological sciences, as if biology were not itself dependent upon the "fictional" through, for instance, hypotheses and speculation, evolutionary accounts, myths about the "nature" of humankind, and other narrative conditions.[49] (As noted above, the category "human" may have no purely biological meaning independent of what are understood as the values or "ethical life" of humanity.[50]) A consequence of this imperative is the assumption that analyses of race are fundamentally *prescriptive and political*—specifically, that the overriding objective of such works is not a reconstitution of knowledge but directed social change. Hence discussions of race are believed to have one narrow aim—the end of race as the end of racial prejudice, a.k.a. *freedom from race*, and with it all the social equality and individual autonomy it entails. Accordingly, one might expect a study of ethics and race to similarly absorb itself in "taking on" racial prejudice, a prejudice that, paradoxically, presumes that any theoretical inquiry involving race could only be a call to action whose guiding objective is the unveiling of "hidden racism" *and how to end it*—that implied subtitle ghost-written into every critical reading of race.

The reader is hereby notified—where "notified" signifies simultaneously "reassured" and "warned"—of the criminal intentions of this book: that it will satisfy neither of these expectations. It will not concede the inferiority of "myth" to "reality," as if debunking myths is the task that falls to scholars not fortunate enough to be culling empirical "realities" in well-funded labs. It does not pretend to reveal a dangerous "fiction" that holds a multitude of us in subjugated bondage—or not the bondage conventionally supposed, in any case. On the contrary, it argues that myths about why bodies resonate different values, expressed in our age by the concept "race," are what make notions like "individual moral responsibility" conceivable. It asserts, in other words, that the idea of ethical accountability as restricted to traits *wittingly* developed rather than "accidentally endowed"—as Rawls, Heller, and Williams counsel—could come into modern existence *only* in tandem with a countervailing notion like race in which inheritable and accidental endowments are the active conduits of comparative ethical worth. The book thus makes the argument, opened by West, that while the manner in which "race" manifests is specific to modernity, its *structural* function is not. Accordingly chapters 3 and 4 address how the need to explain—mythically—the transfer of value through inheritable and embodied characteristics long predates as well as anticipates the historical entrance of race.

Moreover, this book makes no explicit prescriptive recommendations. It does not conclude, or even assume, that we should "save ourselves" from race or from valuations of the body or any other philosophically criminal activities. This absence of prescriptive claims would seem strange should one believe this to constitute the entirety of ethics—that the purpose of ethical theory is to determine 'how we should live,' 'what is good and bad,' and 'why we should be good.' It is a common enough assumption, even in ethical subfields of philosophy. Yet "ethics" at its most fundamental designates the study of the origin and nature of *value*. Hence the *first* questions of ethics do not aim to discern 'absolute goods' or 'how we should treat others' (setting aside the debate as to whether such questions follow later or never at all). Rather they investigate, in short, the conditions for the emergence and existence of value. How, ethics asks, does value come into being? What capacity allows for the consciousness of representations as valued? What relation obtains between representational phenomena and value—is it that of "attachment" or "imposition," or might value in some way constitute the emergence of that perception from the start (as West says, "at the inception")? How do embodied subjects resonate complex and contingent assemblages of value? How are they conscripted into affiliative, transferable relations of value—that is, "histories" and "lineages" of responsibility like race? How does one account for the circulation and transfer of value through language, objects, and bodies?

Any prescriptive utterance about what 'should be done' about race of necessity presumes certain answers to the above questions, implicitly if not expressly. Again, however, we are by no means assured that ethics possesses an independent systematicity outside of and prior to the notion of race—more specifically, to the *function* that race has served since modernity. The book's purpose in attending to race, then, is to bring to light the general structural function it enacts for the sake of ethical philosophy—that is, for the sake of producing causal logics without which ethical judgment could not take place. Race is not the only means through which to glean this general function; a semiotics of value conducted through family names, gender, size, age, or other such affiliating features would disclose a similar arrangement of relations. Thus the use of a number of readings in African diasporic thought in the first few chapters is not a prolegomena to any statement about the particulars of Africana experience or its salvation, as if that history were so insular that it is *all* it could ever be about. What is at issue in this book is not any singular racial community but the structural function of race that, in modernity, enables ethical subjectivity and judgments rather than buries the innocent, authentic subject under a crust of distorting and restrictive evaluations. At a further remove, race here serves as itself merely one of numerous idioms by which one might trace a more subtle narrative obverse to that of "accidental" and "cosmic" material contingencies in which physical characteristics have continued to conscript subjects into affiliative ethical lineages.

Ethics, as the study of the origin and structure of value, is where the themes of this book converge; thus the manner and mission of the book's contemplation of race departs in crucial ways from those of social and political theories of race. While the latter can provide occasional insight and confirmation of the assertions made herein, the intellectual history to which those investigations are answerable (designated by names like Hobbes, Rousseau, DuBois, Arendt, Anzaldúa, et al.) charts a different course (with points of convergence, for example, Hegel) than does that of ethics. Accordingly, it is requested that this study be understood throughout as a project of ethics, and thus one engaged with motivating concerns that call upon, in turn, an alternative intellectual heritage. Such is the challenge and reward of this research—that it has few if any comparable studies with which to engage and thereby orient itself. As a result, it occasionally loses its way, lingers where it should sprint, glosses what it should detail, and, to the possible chagrin of Kantians and Nietzscheans everywhere, promises more than it can deliver. For all of this, the reader's forgiveness is begged. The consolation, it is hoped, is that the scope of the work compensates for its contextual indebtedness to an occasionally monologic style.

A brief summary of the book's overall trajectory provides the reader a better sense of how ethics traces distinctive lines of inquiry with respect to race:

The first chapter reconsiders the premise of modern ethical theory that a subject's deeds and not its bodily traits count as proper objects of evaluation. Race would seem a primary violator of this principle if it illegitimately influences how the deed—and thus its performer—is evaluated. A tandem reading of Kantian morality and anthropology gives the first indication, however, that the definition of any deed—that is, the determination of "what" is done—has no identity outside of already executed, evaluative judgments about the performer. The second chapter expands on the idea of embodied values as determinative of the nature of deeds by taking into account affiliative relations across which value may be said to transfer. If the performer is constituted by its location within ethical inheritances like race such that any enacted deed belongs at once to the subject *and* its affiliative relations, how might subjectivity be reconfigured to reflect this?

From here the book must take its leave from ethical and racial modernity to examine ancient and premodern logics that justified the inheritable transfer of embodied value, for in this way one apprehends the *structural* dilemmas internal to how ethical knowledge originates, in particular those that the modern idea of race evolves to address (and why, accordingly, race can neither be thought as entirely arbitrary nor as invented/constructed).

Chapters 3 and 4 thus examine ancient Greek and early Christian theories of the origin of value, and, more specifically, how knowledge of the
natural order of the world discloses itself to consciousness through ethical
difference. Critically, these accounts of how value (and thus ethical knowledge) enters the world attribute that emergence to a precipitating criminal
action, one said to justify both the causal chain of personal responsibility
as well as the inheritability of value in the form of "blessings" and "curses."
Through these accounts or "myths," one more clearly grasps how race
enacts this same function for the sake of reconciling subjective practices as
at once unique and ethically prefigured.

Although the idea of a precipitating crime that generates inheritable ethical lineages sounds, as Heller notes, distinctly premodern to us, chapter 5
proposes, through a reading of Sartre's and Althusser's narratives of subject
formation, that "modern" bodies have remained sites of ethical inheritance
in ways we hardly recognize but which are no less configured through the
projection of original criminal action. Lastly, in addition to summarizing the
implications of rendering ethics and race through the metaphor of the stain,
the conclusion examines dreams of ethical and racial futures other than those
of unmarked or ethically insignificant bodies—specifically, those in which
cursed markings become blessings and vice versa. Such dreams of ethical
inheritances whose fortunes rise and fall suggest how thinking subjectivity
and representation as prior to and outside of evaluation has produced its own
historical set of nightmares.

I

Ethics and Race

"Aylmer," resumed Georgiana, solemnly, "I know not what may be the cost to both of us to rid me of this fatal birthmark. Perhaps its removal may cause cureless deformity; or it may be the stain goes as deep as life itself."

NATHANIEL HAWTHORNE, *The Birthmark*

IN THE MOST recited of Martin Luther King, Jr.'s rhetorical exhortations, he pleads for the release of ethical subjectivity from the tyranny of the racial body. His dream, that his children "one day . . . not be judged by the color of their skin but by the content of their character" offers a prescriptive fantasy of disembodied ethical knowledge.[1] In this future, an individual's genuine qualities are apprehended *despite* the body rather than through it. The dream thus envisions percepts of racialized bodies as irrelevant to evaluative interpretations of that performing body's deeds. Such a future, however, is peculiarly tied to the (false) idea that race *does* disclose ethical worth, for if the *true* "content of character" remains for individuals a "not-yet" realized dream it is because, we believe, an illegitimate and perverse dream or fantasy has displaced it. Both existences are thereby mythic—the "genuine" dream of perceptual racial difference that signifies independently from value and the "actual" delusion we now valiantly strive to escape by which race inflects ethical subjectivity.

One of the primary objectives of this book is to examine the logic, as well as history, of the idea that the body marked by race and other material signifiers *could and does* attest to ethical qualities of the subject. Few ideas could sound less popular and wildly anachronistic: modern Western ethics—for all the knocks it has weathered from cross-cultural, post-Nietzschean, and neo-Aristotelian theories—has retained unswervingly this elementary conviction. If not ultimately persuasive in its finer points of argumentation it can at least boast this achievement—that none of its detractors and critics has quarreled with its extraction of the body from ethical interpretation. On the contrary, they too insist that material signifiers reflective of affiliations of national heritage, gender, and race are not legitimate variables in determinations of ethical subjectivity. (One could argue that Nietzsche's critique of morality has been wittingly employed against modern theories of value *only* up to that point at which it arches into notions of value expressed on and through the body—for example, those uncomfortable passages about "breeding," "race," "Jews," and "Aryans," as well as eyes, noses, and stomachs.) Such scholarly unanimity has effected this premise into what is today a general and widespread truism, a commonsense belief that catches in its tumbler those who posit the individual as presocial and autonomous as well as those who advance the ethical subject as a socially situated yet "singular" being. On seemingly all logically admissible accounts, the idea that racially and otherwise marked bodies could speak the true worth of subjects lacks any reasonable justification, its rhetoric consigned to the language of fantasy and ethical dystopia.

If a reading of the raced body is not to be believed—if it provides only false representations of the genuine qualities of a person—then one must remain vigilantly suspicious of how these bodies signify. Whether one endeavors to shut one's eyes and ears to those markings in a display of "color-blindness" that aspires to illiteracy, or whether one struggles to glimpse the authentic ethical subject lodged beneath those distortive images, it would seem that all now imagine themselves engaged in some strategy of disillusion. Who even still listens to the ramblings of racial-speak? Who still dreams this false dream of the ethical legibility of the raced body, the *bad* dream the persistence of which inhibits the manifestation of the true and *good* dream of fundamental corporeal neutrality shared by everyone else?

This passionate consensus on the raced body as the improper object of ethical evaluation raises the question of how the sordid association of bodily signifiers and value could have ever held sway: why dream such a fictitious relation between subjectivity and value at all? In what conceptual framework could corporeal difference signify disparate worth? How would one explain the development of associations between bodies and value: as a cunning strategy of political domination? As an effect of an asymmetric power of the ocular? One might conceive it as evidence of an extended and ugly chapter of national and ethnic allegiances—those said to be giving way to transnational and cosmopolitan configurations of the subject. Or it may express an antiquated theological mode of reasoning that this secular age has made obsolete through its progressively scientific methodologies. From the perspective of metaphysics or metaethics, one might believe the answer irrelevant to the larger philosophical lesson of the radical independence of representational objects from value. If we cannot explain why this relation persisted for—as we will see—two millennia prior to its modernist rejection, we are unlikely not only to transcend it but, more vitally, to know *what* it is, exactly, that we are trying to move beyond. If, in other words, it is in dreams that our ethical future beckons, it is similarly to fantasies past and present that the marked body remains ethically beholden and stubbornly chained.

The *good* dream of ethically neutral embodiment, a dream for all communal individuals, comes to us through Martin Luther King, Jr. as the idiosyncratic reverie of a sovereign individual (i.e., the King). The dream is indeed *his* dream, but not therefore *for him*, being also a dream for and of his descendants, his children, as well as his children's children—on down the line in perpetuity until its mortal prophecy is fulfilled. This lineage King bestows to more than biological progeny; the "children" of civil rights nationally and internationally, in addition to those who carry the egalitarian torch of modernity, figure no less as those whose ethical liberation from the racialized body is foretold by his ordination. To be a child of King is to inherit an ethical subjectivity struggling to cleanse itself of the stain of race: it is to descend within a philosophical genealogy keen to advance racial emancipation through constant rearticulation of that subjectivity as constitutionally unmarked by the impurity of corporeal valuations.

King does not, we can note, describe a dream he *had* but one that recurs indefinitely into the future. He thus speaks "of" and "within" the dream at the same time; like Descartes, he plays both narrator and subject of his meditation.[2] Yet unlike the *Meditations*, dreaming here will not distort the subject's relation to the rational; on the contrary, the illusion that Descartes forsakes as deceptive provides for King the indispensible mechanism and site of true knowledge of the contiguity of value and being. If wakefulness for Descartes constitutes the ongoing condition necessary for rational self-consciousness and the correlative ground of subjective realism—the representational capacity for clear and distinct percepts—"dreaming" is for King the similar condition within which self-consciousness perceives clearly and distinctly an ethical reality that is *not yet* real—that is, it is in his dream that King discovers the *true* yet nonactualized relation between value and bodies. It is moreover through this dreaming that King apprehends as "deceptive" the evaluative assessments actually accorded subjects as mediated through the racial body.

In this respect, King's dream of pure ethical subjectivity espies a "kingdom of ends" from a vista not far distant from where Kant gazes. For

Kant and King alike, moral autonomy charts the path (back) to a homeland named "freedom" where liberation awaits those who recognize themselves and others as ethically sovereign. Such freedom, Kant enjoins, awaits the one "not subject to the will of any other" but, as the law-giving individual, the one who "belongs to [the kingdom] *as sovereign*."[3] Each morally autonomous being becomes a King in this kingdom, or rather, each King reigns over its own kingdom as, in effect, a sovereign with only itself as a subject; though structurally identical to all other kings, each sovereign being remains "free" from any "relation of these beings to one another."[4] According to the dream of moral sovereignty, then, ethical self-unity is inhibited when valuations accrued through coefficients like race affix themselves to the subject, as such corporeal affiliations attest to governance by external forces rather than self-governance. Hence liberation from such "relations of beings to one another" is conditional for the formation of individuals whose worth (in will and deed), as Kant remarks, stands outside of those relations.[5]

That ethical autonomy requires the rejection of relational value suggests nonrelationality—the erasure of inheritable "familial" and genealogical indices in particular—as a necessary condition of freedom. Specifically, then, race precludes this sovereign freedom by grounding subjectivity within illegitimate relations of value. If so, what for we Kings obscures the genuine "content" of our ethical subjectivity is not the body per se but the qualities correlative to certain shared corporeal markings that override or tarnish the true characteristics of the individual. In consequence, sovereign ethical subjectivity, to protect the borders of its kingdom, must break from those affiliative relations of physiognomy, size, hue, etc., predicated on an imagined commonality of qualitative traits that, as heteronomously or extrinsically determining, undermine sovereign ethical self-definition. Once untainted by these relations, ethical subjects transcend networks of corporeal identities like race to achieve sovereign freedom as the full commensurability between subject, deed, and worth. Proper valuation thus requires a subject isolated from these criminal networks of bodily associations irrelevant and untruthful to the authentic qualities of a unique being or singularity.

This means, in effect, that the ethical sovereignty that King ordains for his "children" obligates their extraction from precisely those genealogical affordances—characteristics of the subject inferable from perceptual signifiers—by which they could register as anyone's familial descendant. His dream, that is, fantasizes a dynasty in which, ethically, he becomes nothing to his children—those who, for the sake of being judged only on their finely limned content, must refuse any and all inheritances, bearings, names, and blessings bestowed by this King. All "birthmarks" are to be forsworn and rendered illegible.

A series of problems, however, would seem to follow: how might one cognize a material subject whose features did not refer to any genealogy of meaning, network of relations, or way of being? How does one configure a subject who is not *dis*figured by the stains of associative embodied relations? Another way to ask this is to wonder, as does the character Georgiana in the Hawthorne epigraph above, whether the process of stain removal can do anything but exchange one "cureless deformity" for another—that is, whether the self enters the perceptual field through marks whose differential identity is secured through associative qualities and thus, concurrently, differential worth. One might then ponder what King could have possibly pictured in that dream: how his children could even be representational objects for the imagination outside of these affordances, or of what that phenomenal content could possible consist. Does he not, in this respect, dream a dream? That is to say, does he not dream that such ethically self-identical beings *could be* phenomenal objects? That the true ethical subject, as an aggregate mass of its genuine characteristics, *could* appear before our eyes in its unmediated totality?

Perhaps. Then again, perhaps the contemporary mind, stained with the residue of thinking such criminal lineages, cannot bring such untainted figures into representation; perhaps only the removal of these stains will permit the imagination to commence drafting the scope of such worlded beings. But it is also possible that such ethereal natures never quite appear to consciousness because they belong exclusively to the dream of the dream—that, restricted to this genre of fantasy that evokes rather than describes, such mythic ontologies serve only to draw ethics *away from* rather than *to* the primary objects and relations of its disciplinary inquiry. Should this be the case, the dream of ethical sovereignty would mislead not in its conjuring of an impossible ideal but in its implicit disavowal of its own structural conditions.

Consider, to begin, that all dreams maintain the possibility and risk of the nightmare—especially, as in this case, when the dream is recurring. That is to say, within every honored sovereign prophecy, threatening the chimerical gloss of self-identical ethical subjectivity, runs the concurrent horror of the ineradicable stain. This nightmare is not that of the *unethical*—of the fear as common as it is mistaken that a society could be without "values"—nor is it fear that we will ultimately fail to extract ethical subjects from the criminal relations that evaluatively mark their bodies. The nightmare consists, rather, in the active possibility of evaluative perception—and thus the indicative, associative body—as a necessary condition *for* ethical subjectivity, whereby the subject exists as valuable only within those affiliative and marked corporeal relations. What threatens is the idea that ethical subjectivity has identifiable worth only in the context of the "cureless deformities" in which its body partakes, not prior to it as an array of qualities subsequently stained in their expression. Dissolved herein are those traditional components of moral striving essential to the theatrics of ethical contemplation past and present: the evaluatively unmarked individual, noninheritable value, the corporeally uninflected deed, moral innocence, ahistoric responsibility, and other vernacular scaffolds of the "good." The nightmare of the permanence of the "stain" of ethics and race, then, is that value, rather than "attaching" to phenomenal subjects and deeds instead constitutes them in their appearance such that a structure like "race" does not signify that which corrupts ethical subjectivity but names a syntactic and idiomatic function by which evaluatively differentiated subjects come into recognizable existence.

But this is still to come: in this first chapter, in the remainder of the book, in future theoretical studies of value. From these will emanate a fundamentally different story about ethics and race, one that does not assert "race" as an important and legitimate *object* of philosophical study but itself something *philosophical*. These pages will spin a tale or fable—this may be admitted up front, without hesitation or qualification—in which race does not corrupt the delicate philosophical operation that decodes the origin of value as well as the conditions of its identification and dissemination. Instead race here will refer to a historical instantiation of an irreducible, necessary, and mythic logic that fashions a synthetic arrangement of subjectivity, materiality, and value. It will divulge itself as the indispensable relation that mints the ethical subject as the effect of genealogically inheritable bodily markings as well as the productive and differentiated operator of comparative qualities. Race thereby functions as a *clip*—in the sense of what unifies through separation— to bring into being the recognizable ethical subject through genealogical relations that remain always and necessarily evaluative and transitive.

And what if this story of the resilient perpetuity of the bodily stain or mark, and thus of the *structural* impossibility of a kingly ethical sovereignty and isolatable moral content, strikes the ear as uncannily familiar? What is to be done if the reader catches errant glimpses of the self in this portrait of ethics and race that admits no interpretive disaffiliation? What price will be paid for interpreting these night terrors as disguised yet inadmissible wish fulfillments?

There is no reason to be afraid. Is not the nightmare, too, only a dream?

Race as Structural

As offered in the introduction, the productive features of race as an evaluative force become clear only through a structural reading of it—that is, as signifying a modern configuration that constitutes embodied subjectivities through differential relations of value. This is not the only or even predominant way of understanding race as structural. Theorists like Cornel West and Linda Alcoff, as discussed earlier, propose a structural function of race in order to disclose its integral role for knowledge production. In affirming race as constitutive of objects of knowledge, these accounts depart from more common theoretical and cultural analyses of race that shy away from structural readings to emphasize race as historically particular, transient, and unstable. While West and Alcoff challenge the implication that race cannot be both structural and historical, rejecting the idea that only essential differences can ultimately govern concepts, the notion of structure they employ ultimately ratifies this tension by imagining racial structuring as epiphenomenal to other, more metaphysical operations. For West, race denotes a value system that "*infuses* Greek ocular metaphors and classical ideals of beauty, proportion, and moderation *into the beginnings of modern discourse* . . ." and thus what invades and corrupts more legitimate structural relations of scientific difference.[6] Alcoff likewise asserts that "racialization structures the visual sphere and the imaginary self," yet because it has no "biological" grounding it thereby has no claim as a "naturalistic" difference as do gender and "family."[7] More specifically, while race is for her animated through false hierarchies of worth, and thus essentially evaluative, she views other embodied distinctions such as gender as preethical, "descriptive" facts of difference. The knowledge structured by gender, while not therefore objective insofar as "pernicious prescriptive effects" invade and stain these foundational relations as well, can nonetheless, she continues, generate basic, nonevaluative distinctions among subjects. For West and Alcoff, then, race refers to a secondary system of evaluative difference superseded by a more primary, material, and objective order of difference through which emerge nonevaluative subjective identities and genuine qualitative traits. Accordingly, while race may, as West claims, condition the idioms and metaphors that make certain discursive knowledges possible, it is itself, like value, taken to be dependent upon nonmetaphoric ontological distinctions of pure, preethical description. In sum, for West and Alcoff, certain genres of embodied subjectivity precede ethical as well as raced subjectivity: autochthonous lines of difference like gender and other materially legitimate categories are presumed to trace boundaries in advance of any introduction of value; these genuinely formative and nonevaluative differences are similarly understood as what race, as a (spurious) system that metaphorizes material features but is not itself material, appends itself to and misrepresents.

Consider, as an additional instance, Omi and Winant's influential *Racial Formations in the United States*, which provides a similarly tiered conception of the structural relevance of race: "[T]he concept of race continues to play a fundamental role in structuring and representing the social world. The task for theory is to explain this situation. . . . Thus we should think of race as an element of social structure rather than as an irregularity within it; we should see race as a dimension of human representation rather than an illusion."[8] Race for Omi and Winant is here not only an "element of social structure" but also that which "structures" "human representation" of the social world, and as such would appear to operate, as West avers, "at the inception" of knowledge and meaning, inflecting the ordered appearance of the world before us.

Elsewhere, however, Omi and Winant qualify that race structures not our phenomenal reception of the world but only discursive exchanges about it, defining it as a secondary and "ideological" representation of primary agonisms: *"race is a concept which signifies and symbolizes social conflicts and interests by referring to different types of human bodies."*[9] In this weaker sense of "structure," race randomly assigns genuine pre-discursive interests (such as class) to bodily differences that it invests symbolically. In this revised definition race produces no authentic interests or desires as do the labor conditions of materially situated individuals but instead distorts that primary intuited or experiential self-knowledge. The resulting claim is that racial difference obscures real "social conflicts" predicated on these primary knowledges. Thus, they charge, the knowledge race structures is "at best imprecise, and at worst completely arbitrary."[10]

As a productive social force, race generates, it would seem, only linguistic obfuscations of the real. Clouding the genuine "conflicts" and interests borne of legitimate class differences, race instead fosters "political" struggles over "social meanings" that obscure the fight over real social disparities.[11] For Omi and Winant, then, the "social world" that race "structures and represents" is neither material reality nor illusion but the discursive realm of ideological debate. More precisely, there would seem for them two "realities:" an "unstable" and "decentered" discursive reality mediated by race that is supervenient on a comparatively stable and unified ontological reality rooted in material difference.

Is race as mere "social" reality thereby epiphenomenal to the material reality that configures consciousness? Such a view would thereby deny, as Lewis Gordon observes, that "an impact of social reality . . . is ontological; it transforms concepts—knowledge claims—into lived concepts, forms of being, forms of life."[12] If race structures "social" representation then it also, as Gordon suggests, structures what we take to be ontological reality, a reality that cannot be proven or disproven through reference to the "truth" of lived experience, for that experience is itself a reflection of those ontological premises. As a result, race cannot be said, at the same time, to structure social consciousness *and* to do so well or poorly, precisely or imprecisely, through contrast to nonsymbolic difference. The discursive, ideological "struggle" over the meaning of material difference of which race is thought constitutive is precisely an ontological contention about the nature and identity of the phenomena on which that meaning is presumably parasitic.

Like West and Alcoff, Omi and Winant hold that there are true lines that divide us but that they are not "racial lines" but rather those like class, family, and gender.[13] If, however, race refers to a complex of signifiers preceded and contradicted by systems of difference both more natural and value-neutral, can race really be said to "structure" knowledge at all? Would one not have to conclude, as Jean-Paul Sartre does regarding anti-Semitism, that race does not produce knowledge or even opinion but, quite the opposite, "devaluate[s] words and reasons?"[14] Would race not similarly be antithetical to the "responsible" use of words and discourse? Put otherwise, were such structural readings of race Foucauldian in that manner with which West and Alcoff align their own readings, or Althusserian in the vein that Omi and Winant mirror, would they issue "real" hierarchies of knowledge? Or would they not, instead, historicize race along with gender, class, and other various biologisms as comparatively dominant and subjugated knowledges whose claims to authenticity, value neutrality, nature, and objectivity seek the effects of discursive power?[15] In asserting that race informs knowledge production, these analyses make the crucial point that race is a creative rather than purely destructive force; by deeming those creations fabrications that distort and stain objective knowledges with symbolic values, however, they accuse race of producing "anti-knowledge"—that is, as Foucault writes, knowledge "disqualified as inadequate to [its] task . . . located low down on the hierarchy, beneath the required level of cognition or scientificity."[16] Stating that race enables only false or anti-knowledge thereby circumvents its study as productive of evaluative difference, an avoidance that will long keep race in play however much it is "disqualified" by its lack of scientific validity.

Reading race structurally means, accordingly, facing the evaluative impasse that prevents one from distinguishing absolutely and emphatically "representation" from "illusion," as Omi and Winant attempt—as if representation could be tethered to any reality not itself a representation. In other words, the distinction between "representation" and "illusion"—that which purportedly splits preethical, descriptive interpretation from evaluative, manipulated fabrication—is at bottom a distinction between two different chains of representations, one "good," one "bad," and thus *already* a value judgment. The desire for this prophetic knowledge of "good" from "bad" representation recalls for us the Kingly dream in which the sovereign, disembodied ethical subject can shake itself awake from the living nightmare of a racially stained body. As we will see below, however, the determination of an object of knowledge—specifically, of what can appear as a differentiated and valid performance eligible for evaluative interpretation—necessarily partakes of evaluative and racial semiotics of meaning.

It was suggested above that the symbolic "struggle" over the meaning of material differences is itself a contention about the nature and identity of ontological phenomena. This is to propose that symbolic or "social meanings," as ethics and race are perceived, inform our reception of phenomena such that none but an abstract separation of "material" from "symbolic" difference is possible. Two corollaries present themselves as plausible consequences: the first is that no isolatable, circumscribed subjectivity or universally coded "human" identity exists as interpretively prior to symbolic structures like race, meaning that subjectivity does not begin as an ethical blank space but as already marked by criminal associations. The second and related is that ethics structures phenomenal representations such that no purely descriptive interpretation of beings, things, and events is available absent differential marks of value; this suggests that what something "is" has meaning only within already existing economies of value. The demonstration and analysis of these two corollaries through readings of Immanuel Kant and Frantz Fanon comprise the remainder of the chapter, as a way of showing how a structural analysis of race might be conducted that does not rely on appeals to more authentic, natural, or original differences that race then purportedly stains and distorts. It means as well as to place pressure on "ethical" discussions of race that feel obliged to recite the primacy of truth over value, the material over the symbolic/mythic, and gender and class over race as organically nonevaluative concepts. In short, it aims to underscore that the good dream is not good because it is true and the bad dream bad because it is false; that this *be* the case is, rather, itself the dream of the good.

Breaking In

In his *Metaphysics of Morals*, Kant articulates a basic postulate of moral philosophy to explain why children do not inherit the immorality of their parents: "For every man is born free," he certifies, "since he has not yet committed a crime [*weil er noch nicht verbrochen hat*]."[17] Condensed herein is the conventional notion of an original "freedom" common to all upon entering the world, a freedom coexistent with an equally primordial ethical condition, that of the *precriminal*. This condition, existing prior to the possibility of transgression or violation, is what could be called *moral innocence* or *purity*. With respect to criminality, then, moral innocence or purity indicates the condition of a clean record or history, that possession of a status completely free of inscription and hence legibility. Accordingly, the newborn has no criminal history because, to be sure, it has no history; nothing as yet signifies its active subjectivity. Its (permanent) criminal record is a blank sheet— uninscribed and unmarked, and, therefore, necessarily unstained.

It is the guarantee that one has not committed a crime [*verbrechen*], has not violated or broken [*brechen*] the law, Kant says, that vouches for this prehistorical freedom. As such, freedom here is contingent upon a preethical innocence. Moreover, the absence of criminality rests upon the impossibility of having committed any action whatsoever. There can be no crime if there has been no action; to do something criminal, the subject must enact a deed on its own behalf. Hence the possibility of crime is opened up by, and only by, an act freely committed and attributable to the subject. Not only must the subject act freely in order to commit a crime, but it is through this initial act that subjectivity is itself expressed. Free action, Kant implies, brings the historical, ethical subject into being. And yet, as free, that initiating action becomes an object of moral judgment, acquiring a comparative moral valence that retrospectively attests to the worth of the subject. And what, then, if this first action that produces the subject as ethical violates moral duty? Would it not be, in this case, that the subject has entered the world *through* crime— as a criminal? If we cannot simply "be" in the world without having acted, and, further, if every action retains a value indicative of our moral worth, are we therefore not marked from the start by that action? And if, finally, that authorizing action is indeed criminal, would not the incipient mark it inscribes upon our moral record be a stain?

If so, our first genuinely free action could be our last. Having committed a crime, even through an inaugural deed that underwrites our subjectivity, we risk already a correction that could strip from us immediately our self-determination. Indeed the stipulations of redress for our crime, Kant informs us, may require that our freedom be relinquished to the hands of a jailer or master. Punishment, he explains, refers to a circumstance in which the criminal is "kept alive, [yet] is made a mere tool of another's choice (either of the state or of another citizen)."[18] Upon entrance into the world, one risks becoming instantly a "tool" of the government or of another being, to wit, a prisoner or a slave, to be used without regard to one's own will. But is not this peril of entering a state of servitude at one's birth precisely what Kant says cannot happen? Everyone may be "born free;" however, if the expression of that freedom exposes one to its simultaneous forfeiture, how could that freedom ever be experienced as innocent?

Note that in Kant's earlier statement the original freedom granted at birth and the initial action that threatens the forfeiture of that freedom come as two moments separated by what is "not yet": "For every man is born free, since he has *not yet* [*noch nicht*] committed a crime." Natal freedom precedes all else, yielding a state "not yet" compromised by a transgressive act; herein lie the seeds of full potentiality "not yet" given expression. But what then does the "not yet" signify? An omen, perhaps, foreshadowing the inevitability of immorality: "You have *not yet* committed a crime, but soon will." Or perhaps this status of deferral maintains, in the blur through which the newborn arrives, the abstraction of the original and morally pure being as necessarily prior to the one in which evaluative judgments inhere, even if the self conceptualized as anterior to the "not yet" remains unavailable to experience and thus unrecoupable. The value of preserving this distinction and succession of two moments here—the arrival of the preethical, free being which then, by dint of its autonomy, performs some action that incurs a particular value—is that the worth ascribed to individuals can be said, in the last instance, to be based on their freely chosen actions. Thus the "not yet" serves as the virtual threshold between the subject's inaugural innocence as potentiality and its criminal possibility as corporeal.

But such innocence appears less viable when recalling the subject as located not merely at the start of its own history but also at the terminal point of another. As the descendant of a nation, culture, and race, the newborn figures as the most recent corporeal instantiation of an ongoing cycle of production rather than as one whose entry signals pure origin—its appearance always marks simultaneously the end of the family line. And such lineages are possible only insofar as descendants are understood to inherit something that has come before them, some way of being that is passed down the line. But if this process of inheritance allows for the transference of qualities across generations, should one be surprised to learn that value transfers across generational bodies as well? And that, despite his assertion that the innocent, value-neutral being precedes all action and therefore all evaluation, Kant himself seems to acknowledge such ethical inheritances several sections later in the *Metaphysics*? The child born out of wedlock, Kant says, justifiably can be put to death for having obtained its existence through transgression. Having "*stolen into the commonwealth . . .*," he reasons, "the commonwealth can ignore its existence (since it rightly should not have *come to exist* in this way), and can therefore also ignore its annihilation [at the hands of its shamed mother]."[19]

The illegitimate child commits a crime of trespassing and as retribution incurs the penalty of death. Critically, this crime takes place not *after* the birth of the newborn as its "first deed," that moment when the "not yet" of moral innocence gives way to ethically marked subjectivity; rather, it is the "coming to exist" as an embodied presence which itself constitutes the violation. This material entrance into history and society amounts to an invasion, a case of "breaking and entering." Yet how can one criminally break into the space of innocence, one held to precede the enactment of all violation and thus of value? In advance of any action attributable to the illegitimate child, and thus presumably any authoritative knowledge about its creditable moral worth, how does it bear already the mark of immorality?

If it is the case that we are not born free, then, it is not because we have committed a crime in the traditional sense, through a willed action, conscious or unconscious, but because, as Kant's example indicates, our bodies as sites of inherited value already resonate ethically; value defines and delineates them from the start. The child is no less a bastard for not having "caused" the illegitimate circumstances that brought it into being, for as the product of those circumstances its body serves as a relay point for the marks of its parents, community, class, etc. (as is true for those "legitimately" bred children as well). Value inflects the subject's entry into representation insofar as there are good ways (having been "given" birth to) and bad ways ("stealing" into life) of "coming into being." And if by chance it is through the latter—if the subject comes by its birth criminally—that commencing negative valence automatically compromises the pure, inaugural freedom said to make this entrance possible.

Those who desire to judge individuals solely on the merits of their actions would have humans enter the world as ethically unmarked, only to slowly carve a moral reputation over time that remains strictly commensurate with their behaviors. Yet in the purported originating moment of being, as Kant unwittingly discloses, the freedom that first authorizes action and thus historical, ethical subjectivity unconditionally opens up the threat of death or a servitude in which one is sentenced to acting out only the commands of the other. Freedom here is won and lost in the same instant; or, rather, it is far from clear that the "not yet" meant to separate these two moments secures an agency sufficiently meaningful to prevent their collapse. Value, it would appear, is not what the subject brings upon itself through social interaction, like a scarlet letter sewn to the soul; rather, *value brings the subject itself into being*. If the subject is *always* an "ethical subject" it is not because it is always "good" but because it always resonates evaluatively.

Destabilized here is the claim that the subject secures evaluations solely as a direct consequence of its actions; as Kant's discussion of the illegitimate child illustrates, the subject bears responsibility as well for actions done by others, in particular, for those whose names configure the subject within a shared identity. Newly embodied beings, as conduits of genealogical values, would reflect then no blank, unmarked moral record or disposition but one stained from its inception. One could, to be sure, regard this example of Kant's as itself illegitimate, and, furthermore, as easy to excise from his broader moral theory without serious repercussion. But what if this unsightly blemish is not superficial or accidental? What if it extends into the very marrow of his understanding of the relationship between value and human nature?

Born White

That one can "freely" be born into a kind of ethical "bondage" is a familiar yet undertheorized dynamic. Kant provides a somewhat detailed discussion in the *Metaphysics* on matters of forced servitude, mostly regarding the contractual particularities of these relations, yet here the critical issue concerns the viability of criminal inheritance. On this matter, Kant says more than once that one can become the slave of another solely through a crime that the subject itself has committed; consequently, the offspring of slaves cannot themselves be held in bondage, in that they have committed no crime.[20] He disputes explicitly, in fact, the idea that bondage, and thus criminality, can pass through ancestral lines: "Even if [an individual] has become a *personal* subject by his crime, his subjection cannot be *inherited*, because he has incurred it only by his own guilt."[21]

And yet, all of this conscientious examination of servitude and slavery strikingly omits any substantive contemplation of African chattel slavery— the most notorious instance of inherited bondage at the time.[22] Kant's anthropological writings leave no doubt as to his attunement to the historical existence of such bondage, an awareness further confirmed by an oblique reference to enslaved "Negroes" in the *Metaphysics*.[23] Thus the absence of any objection to the African slave trade as a patent violation of his overt repudiation of criminal inheritances powerfully exceptionalizes genealogies of race as those that suspend by nature this otherwise apodictic truth. To be sure, a ready approach to this exception would be to situate it as an historical prejudice that, when simply ignored, restores the inviolability of this rational duty. Such a strategy would bracket Kant's philosophical treatment of race as an unfortunate if brazen contradiction of his claim against inheritable worth, excising it from his larger critical project with no further need for reparative intervention. Yet it is not obvious that these exceptions Kant makes for inheritable value reflect a commitment to prejudices of his day rather than a parallel accounting of how material beings come to bear differential worth. Put otherwise, the theoretical aperture of race as an ethical inheritance—akin to that of the illegitimate child—may explicate a more general and systematic rationale for how subjectivity may be stained at its inception.

Robert Bernasconi is correct that "one is left with the impression that the enslavement of Africans had Kant's attention when he was writing on anthropology, but not when he was writing on ethics," and yet it is an impression we would do well to question.[24] For in many respects, "whiteness" in Kant's anthropological writings plays the same role as does "freedom" in the passages on servitude in the *Metaphysics*. Like freedom, racial whiteness accompanies the birth of "man" as the expression of an initial purity that risks becoming compromised, constrained, and "darkened" over time. Such whiteness, he submits, constitutes the existing "stem genus" from which all other races descend.[25] From this primary and original hue "the color of humans goes through all the shades of yellow, brown, and dark brown until it becomes black in the hot parts of the earth."[26] The epidermal pigmentations indicative of these "races" thus produce a *dis*coloration of original whiteness. Hence, in referring to Africans, Kant characterizes darkness of skin as a "stain"—an inking that defaces and tarnishes what begins as immaculate.[27]

Moreover, Kant's notion of whiteness as original and pure is, like that of freedom, ultimately undone in its supposed generation of its opposite, in this instance "blackness" rather than crime. Blackness, Kant persists, degrades whiteness as a degenerate version of it; it is whiteness stained. As what exists only in relation to that which it blemishes, the stain as ontologically secondary remains parasitically attached to and dependent upon that which it disfigures. Consequently, as with criminality, Kant holds that something must *happen* for the whiteness of skin, that spotless sheet, to become marked and blackened; blackness must arise, he hypothesizes, as an effect—specifically, as a reaction to environmental, nonhereditary conditions. Kant thus attributes the production of African physical features and "temperament" to the climate, food, and soil in Africa, alternatively to a "hot, moist climate" and a "superabundance of iron particles" that "cause the blackness that shines through the superficial skin."[28] Racial difference herein belongs not to the original essence of being but is accidental with respect to geography, having developed and diversified in concert with the dissemination of humans around the globe.[29] Thus racial features appear "according to circumstances which the creature may get into and in which it must maintain itself."[30] As contingent, however, any racial modifications one "gets into" one can also, theoretically, "get out of" by altering the environmental venue: "on another soil and in the presence of other food . . . [such difference] disappears in but a few generations."[31] If blackness is a stain upon the original and primary whiteness of being, under the conditions Kant lays out for how such a blemish arises, it seems reasonable to imagine a nullifying process of stain removal in which those conditions are halted and reversed—a means by which such a mark upon skin and temperament could be "bleached" out.

Unless, of course, the stain is permanent. As Kant well knows, Africans transplanted (or, rather, subjected) to European or colonial environments do not produce white offspring; correspondingly, generations of whites living in Africa fail to become "black." Kant is thus forced to concede that the features he elsewhere claims could only be secondary and therefore not a "generative force that would be capable of again producing itself without this cause" (i.e., "necessarily inherited") can sometimes *become* self-generating and inheritable.[32] Racial features and characteristics fostered through environmental conditions, Kant admits, through "a great number of generations . . . become part of the species and hereditary."[33] Indeed the necessary inheritance of racial "peculiarities" becomes the factor that distinguishes racial difference from the more irregular differences of "stock" or "variety."[34]

Such racial features for Kant do not originate, it is important to note, from the environment itself, but exist *from the beginning* as "predispositions" in the nature of humankind.[35] Which predispositions ultimately express themselves depend circumstantially for him on the topographical and climatological peculiarities of the region inhabited. After some indeterminable length of residency, he contends, the stain of race becomes "fixed" or set in a manner that emancipates it from its dependence on the features of that particular environment. At this stage, the predispositions "complete" their development; no longer will a migratory shift or change of climate alter or "extinguish" them.[36] Conversely, according to Kant, this completion destroys one's ability to function efficiently outside one's generative environment.[37] From this moment on, the once heteronomously engendered and reversible qualities of the "distinctive mark" of racial genealogy become both "self-transmitted" and "inevitable."[38]

Even at this stage, wherein blackness is capable of reproducing itself without regard to environment, Kant nevertheless insists that whiteness still drives and underlies this transfer, arguing that the phylogenic history of each black newborn plays out this process of degeneration on the screen of skin itself: "The Negroes are born white apart from their genitals and a ring around the navel, which are black. During the first months of life the black color spreads out from these parts over the whole body."[39] Blackness erupts as two stains or birthmarks on an otherwise undefiled epidermal canvas, and at exactly those loci that "heredity" would dictate: the navel, as the site that, figuratively and literally, ties the body to its ancestral past through which that mark is passed down, and the genitals, as the organs symbolically responsible for the birth of future generations who will continue to bear this inscription. It is, critically, at these two embodied, historical transfer points that whiteness has been blotted out permanently.

Kant thus posits an origin of racial subjectivity structurally identical to the original principle of ethical subjectivity that "every man is born free"—namely, that every man is born *white*, an alignment that effects whiteness as the embodied, empirical manifestation of freedom in its original and pure state as well as the material and identifiable expression of premoral innocence.[40] Whiteness and freedom relate here as complementary, first-order qualities of rational humanity that subtend universal personhood. But this association in which whiteness is no less original and primary than freedom inverts the firmly held presupposition of genuine ethical subjectivity as pre-racial. The juxtaposition of Kant's anthropological and moral theories positions whiteness as what *precedes* value as the unmarked, innocent being in all of its not-yet actualized potentially, a being that in *not yet* committing a crime remains outside ethical signification. Thus the logically reconstituted and equivalent propositions would state alternatively that "Every man is born white, for he has not yet committed a crime" and that "Every man is born white, for he has not yet turned black," both appositives of the explicit premise on freedom contained in the *Metaphysics*. And the only evidence contrary to these propositions is those stubborn stains—ethical and racial—that mark certain subjects from the very beginning (e.g., the illegitimate child breaking into the world as well as the "Negro" baby with darkened navel and genitals). Such stains might yet disappear, fading into the philosophical silence that surrounds them. Yet the threat they pose to modern ethical thought, should such exceptions prove not exceptional at all, is the unsettling hypothesis that one comes into being via its bearing of material and ethical stains.

To be sure, this condition would similarly disclose those bodies marked by whiteness as no less coded through the tint of criminality; exposed in Kant's discussion on race is the contradiction of whiteness that discloses it as both more and less than a neutral, universal structure. Like freedom, it represents the pure, unmarked origin of all humans, but as a distinct race must also be said to have developed under particular environmental conditions. If whiteness describes the natural and primordial state of humankind it cannot be a "race," that which Kant defines as a "deviation" and degeneration from an original; instead, whiteness would have to be that which race defaces or stains.[41] In order for this purity to remain undefiled, however, whiteness would need to retain an immunity to all environmental influences, one that, given Kant's theory of anthropological development, would preserve whiteness as a potentiality of dispositions that never actualizes into embodied, earthly subjects. So how can it be that white people exist without location or body? How can whiteness itself not also be a distinctive and differentiating mark?

Kant's answer, in effect, is that whiteness, while technically a race, distinguishes itself as the most proximate to an original, unraced humanity. Thus the "stem genus" of whiteness from which all other races descend is itself grounded in a "natural genus" or stem rendered as the "single natural cause" of all humans, irrespective of difference. All races, he reasons, thus deviate from this "original stem-formation;" hence, "Negroes and Whites are not different species of humans [but are] different *races*."[42] Whiteness, therefore, as a race, reveals itself *also* as a degeneration or flawed, secondary reproduction of an unmarked original. In that respect, whiteness figures as no less a stain than blackness—and for that matter, no less permanent. Could one remove the thin gloss of whiteness, Kant implies, one would behold underneath the natural human prototype, that genuinely uninscribed and innocent form of being that had "not yet" received its inheritable due. But, Kant laments, this radically pristine infrastructure has gone lost forever: "To be sure we cannot hope any more to come upon the unaltered original human form anywhere in the world."[43]

In the face of this "extinction" of the original and pure genus, however, Kant insists that "we must seek among those extant [deviations] the one which we can best compare to the stem-genus," that is, the race that succeeds as the purest of the impure as veiled by the most diaphanous of opacities: "[T]hat portion of the earth between the 31st and 52nd parallels in the Old World ... [is] where man too must have departed the least from his original formation. ... Here, to be sure, we find white inhabitants ..."[44] Whiteness is a stain, but, fortuitously, as a "first variant" deviation, is not nearly the stain that is blackness.[45] It can be said, in effect, that whiteness *is* blackness to the extent that it deviates from the natural genus. What makes it a beneficent or "happy" st(r)ain—a positive mark—is that through it the "original formation" ostensibly remains visible.

Histories of Responsibility

The black mark of the body signals a criminal irruption into history—an ethically stained entrance to the world—that configures racial subjectivity within genealogies of value. The particular ethical and racial stains that constitute black subjectivity corporealize the DuBoisean problem of fractured consciousness in effecting, as Frantz Fanon writes, "difficulties in the development of [one's] bodily schema."[46] For Fanon, such development requires the practice of self-determined "movements" through which, in Hegelian fashion, one negates and transforms the world around one. Such exercises result in a "slow composition of [the] self as a body in the middle of a spatial and temporal world."[47] The only context in which this "definitive structuring of the self" can take place, he explains, is one of "certain uncertainty."[48] Effective development of one's "bodily schema" depends thereby upon experiencing the future as an open field of possible "movements" that one could make, a contextualized freedom crucial for being able to identify the actions of a body as one's "own."[49] Fanon comes to believe, however, that his social codification as black impedes this process by which the subject achieves being-for-self. Specifically, he contends, race thwarts his ability to impose himself on the world, allowing the world to instead "imposes itself" on him, making him not "a man among other men" as he desires but one more "object in the midst of other objects."[50] In contrast to the "atmosphere of certain uncertainty" that guarantees the self-determined movement characteristic of a normative development of embodied consciousness, racial objectification arrests the self, inhibiting its development and skewing its relation to its own body by determining it from the outside. Fanon thus criticizes race for the very heteronomy that Kant deems necessary for the actualization of material consciousness. Kant, that is, understands race to name the externally driven maturation of natural predispositions in accordance with the teleology of diversity sought by nature. What for him inhibits this successful trajectory is precisely the "certain uncertainty" of multiple, shifting environments, such that the full expression of one's dispositions occurs only when one stays rooted in a single, racially designated region.[51]

Fanon, in contrast, interprets race to stand for the very interruption of the natural stages of development that prevents actualization of the subject, leaving it a mere thing among things in the world. Fanon's conception of "environment" here goes beyond regional topographies and proximate objects to include, critically, other beings with whom the subject interacts and depends upon for recognition of bodily integrity. It is thus the external environment comprised of racialized others that impedes proper self-formation of the subject by denying it freedom as *movement*. Immobilized by "the glances of the other," by "the white man's eyes," development seizes up. This stoppage occurs, Fanon writes, "in the sense in which a chemical solution is fixed by a dye [*colorant*]."[52] The stain of race disrupts physiological and cognitive development, displacing what should be a dawning self-awareness and bodily integrity with an externally enforced interpretation: "the corporeal schema crumbled, its place taken by a racial epidermal schema."[53]

The "racial epidermal schema" signifies a "crumbling" or "explosion" of the proper relation to the corporeal; here the body disintegrates into stained, disunified fragments, preventing cohesive self-identification. Fanon does not initially recognize these pieces as "himself" but comes to do so only because others respond to him *as* these fragments—returning him to himself not as he desires but as "sprawled out, distorted, recolored [*retame*], clad in mourning . . ."[54] His reconstitution demands an assembly based not upon a blueprint or code buried within his being but in staking relations with the "legends, stories, history, and above all *historicity*" through which his embodied practices appear meaningful.[55] In the normal development of the corporeal schema, according to Fanon, the self achieves embodied consciousness through actions it comes to recognize as having resulted from its own freedom. The self is thereby delimited through a responsibility that sets off its own body from those of others, corresponding fully with that freedom; the racial epidermal schema, by contrast, prevents the body from achieving full differentiation from other objects; doubled, it both does and does not belong to the subject.

Teresa de Lauretis reads the racial epidermal schema as an "excess"—an echo of percepts construed in the context of a race-conscious society (its legends, stories, histories): "The epidermal schema, culturally constructed by racist discourses, is superimposed onto the corporeal, phenomenal schema that is the source of bodily sensations and comes to displace it altogether."[56] Qualifying Stuart Hall's claim that Fanon's alienation derives from a substitution of racial discourse for biology, de Lauretis emphasizes that this schema is "not merely discursive" but plays out through the "irreducible material ground" of the body, a reading that underscores the critique of racial representation as subordinate to material representation discussed above.[57] While Fanon indeed conceptualizes this racial schema as an "excess," it is less clear whether the displaced corporeal schema he nostalgizes is in fact an unmarked subjectivity violently supplanted by an inferior and permanently tainted (fixed) "double" (i.e., the racial epidermal schema). If Fanon, like Kant, thinks of race as a stain, as something "superimposed" onto the "clean," original corporeal schema, as de Lauretis suggests, does he conceive of that unraced corporeal schema as ethically innocent as well? A neutral entity, born free? If so, Fanon's criticisms of the racial epidermal schema as secondary and deviant would signify at bottom an objection to the body as ethically resonant. Race for him would be invalid not because it has no "biological" truth or because it produces difference per se, but because it constitutes difference through hierarchies of comparative worth, in coarse fashion, prior to and without respect for individual actions of the subject.

Those who think cleansing the self of ethical and racial stains easy should not lose sight of Fanon's correlative insight that the racial epidermal schema, in being pieced together through "fragments" indelibly marked by discourses of race, results in a body that is both self-identical and ecstatic—that is, again, one that does and does not belong to the subject. To the extent that Fanon's body is not his own, neither are his actions; more precisely, they are his own *insofar as* they are those of a "black male" and thus *belong* to black males as what black men *do*, remaining indissociable from the actions of others who share that inheritance. Fanon's racialized body does not correspond with its "own" actions, for it performs as well in the name of other racialized bodies past and present: "I was responsible at the same time for my body, for my race, for my ancestors."[58] His body acts in the context of other bodies living and dead, and of a history of judgments, "legends," and "stories" accorded to them. He cannot reject this body as fully other, for to perform an act of refusal requires the very body he wishes to refuse. That "his" action is also the action of black men, diffused from the start, means that to act at all is to act in the name of race and gender such that, in turn, one bears responsibility for all actions committed in those names.

But what could "responsibility" mean in this sense? How can one be accountable for actions understood as committed by others? This responsibility would have to signify other than a generalized stewardship—that is, responsibility as an entrusted oversight of the actions and welfare of another being, for instance, as those with pets are "responsible" for their animals. This latter definition conceived of as moral guardianship maintains a fairly uncomplicated idea of a cohesive bodily schema even when it struggles over the assignment of blame. Fanon's use of "responsibility," in contrast, subverts even this caretaking relation, as it does not fully distinguish his own body from those of others as the source of action. Accordingly, included in the repertoire of "Fanon's" actions are those committed years, even centuries, before his birth. Such actions belong to his "race," to his "ancestors," and, insofar as he achieves his embodied subjectivity through this designation and lineage, to himself as well. By dint of a *history of responsibility*, then, he inherits precisely what Kant says can never be inherited: an already marked record—stained, in this case, by racial criminality.

Fanon—chagrined, convicted—rattles off the perverse list of judgments the West has levied against him:

> The torturer is the black man, Satan is black … when one is dirty one is black—whether one is thinking of physical dirtiness or of moral dirtiness. In Europe, whether concretely or symbolically, the black man stands for the bad side of character … In every civilized and civilizing country, the Negro is the symbol of sin. The archetype of the lowest values is represented by the Negro.[59]

Such judgments sustained by black males in this modern collusion of criminality and "dark features" are well-known in their disheartening ubiquity; peculiarly absent, however, is any particular crime with which black men are here charged. For all their adjectival criminality, which is what Fanon's list rehearses (sinful, dirty, low), they appear not to have committed any *specific* offense that would warrant these evaluations. Rather such charges against them surface as marks upon their moral record in the absence of any precipitating transgression. One might reason that this absence simply establishes the original innocence of black people; yet this claim of innocence—the insistence of a clean, unmarked record—is itself not innocent but doubles as the assertion of whiteness as the most transparent and fundamental mark, the inheritance of which postures as Western history.

Apart from this, one should not forget that blacks are certainly and abundantly charged with crimes. Insofar as their criminality does not rest upon any precipitating action, however, blacks do not owe their suspiciousness to any identifiable transgression; it is, instead, what is bequeathed to them through a legacy of race—a birthright—that long predates and establishes their particular and historical resonance as ethical subjects.

Evaluative Representation of Action

Could it be that modern subjects bear, from the beginning, the entire history of responsibility of their racial ancestry as an array of valences expressed through their bodies? If so, the consequences for philosophy would be more serious than a retooling of theories of attribution—a challenge more "ontological" than a dilemma of equality and bias in moral evaluation, that which currently stands as the only tenable meaning of a study of ethics and race. It may be, formidably, that those inheritances of responsibility read through the body shape our interpretation of its practices. This would mean, for instance, that no action by Fanon—the "what" of his performance—could be named outside the context of values that he embodies; such values would condition, rather, the very nature of the acts "he" commits. Inflected from the beginning by a criminal record that originates well prior to his birth, Fanon's actions—again, never strictly his own—would have no ethically unmarked essence prior to that which manifests the indelible stain of a "racial epidermal schema." An embodied subject steeped in value from the start, Fanon can do only a criminal's deeds, which means not that everything he does is a crime but that the determination of what he is doing or has done acquires its identity within the evaluative context of his criminal subjectivity.

A potent example can be drawn from Fanon's renowned account of being fixed by the assaultive cries of a white child who insistently and repeatedly invokes Fanon's body as threatening and malevolent.[60] What deed can Fanon perform to dispel this interpellation, to establish his innocence and goodwill? He laughs, he smiles, but these efforts to convey his innocuousness only confirm the child's impression that Fanon wishes to harm him; the child reads Fanon's forced expression of amusement as a gleeful savoring of this scene of terror. Fanon, in response, ceases laughing, a fact that now serves to assure the boy (or is it others nearby?) that Fanon has become angry, that he could strike the boy at any moment, his silence a portentous calm before the storm. The encounter concludes with a mirror-effect of deeds that illustrates how actions achieve their definition through evaluation:

> . . . [T]iens, un nègre, il fait froid, le nègre tremble, le nègre tremble parce qu'il a froid, le petit garçon tremble parce qu'il a peur du nègre, le nègre tremble de froid, ce froid qui vous tord les os, le beau petit garçon tremble parce qu'il croit que le nègre tremble de rage, le petit garçon blanc se jette dans les bras de sa mère: maman, le nègre va me manger.[61]

> . . . [L]ook, a Negro, it's cold, the Negro is shivering, the Negro is shivering because he is cold, the little boy is trembling because he is afraid of the Negro, the Negro is shivering with cold, that cold that goes through your bones, the handsome little boy is trembling because he thinks that the Negro is quivering with rage, the little white boy throws himself into his mother's arms: Mama, the Negro's going to eat me up.[62]

Consider the tension between the original French and the English translation. The French "tremble" describes the action of both Fanon and the boy in the original, suggesting that they indeed perform the same deed, that each body responds in kind to the other. Yet the equivalence implied by the repetition of the term is contradicted by the radically different meanings conveyed with reference to each subject. Given the "same" bodily movements, the "same" physical (even *involuntary*) convulsions, what Fanon and the boy are "doing" is simultaneously *not* equivalent. Instead, the word "tremble" in this passage is deployed against itself, an incongruity voiced by the translation's use of different terms to identify the action of Fanon (shivering), of the boy (trembling), and, finally, of the boy's interpretation of Fanon's action (quivering). The boy's understanding of what it is Fanon is doing, the salience or *truth* of Fanon's action for him—seething, boiling, shaking with rage—arises in the context of the interpretation of Fanon's embodied ethical identity. Moreover, there is not discoverable under or prior to these race- and gender-inflected determinations any "true" original action—despite the ability to employ a single verb (e.g., *trembler*)—insofar as the evaluative, unraced authority capable of affirming this equivalence is one, as Kant says, "we cannot hope any more to come upon."[63]

This asymmetric nonidentity of action suggests not the distortion of a proper phenomenological encounter but the structural rendering of irreducibly distinct performative subjectivities. In other words, the stark power of the scene comes not from Fanon's deed being *mis*recognized but from the impossibility of recognizing any of his deeds outside of a racial history of responsibility. Indeed Fanon identifies as part of that impossibility the claims by others that their judgments of him are racially uninflected: "When people like me, they tell me it is in spite of my color. When they dislike me, they point out that it is not because of my color. Either way, I am locked into the infernal circle."[64] These disavowals, more than mere denials, chart a "refus[al] to recognize the reality of a traumatic [evaluative?] perception."[65] For psychoanalysis, that refused percept speaks to an unacknowledged absence (as in castration), though it may be, in the case of Fanon and others, equally predicated on a hypothetical overabundance (as illustrated by Kant's focus on "iron particles"). What remains analogous, however, is the apophatic negation of a disempowerment that simultaneously affirms it. Fanon despairs that he can have no authentic Hegelian or Sartrean encounter with a stranger insofar as his recognition as black means that he is never truly foreign or other but in some sense *already known*. Fanon thus depicts for us the *structural* impossibility of theoretically primal encounters that posit the origin of intersubjective ethics as the confrontation of universal and anonymous beings whose deeds unfold as those "not yet" evaluated. It is this imagined interval of the "not yet" in such encounters—that period of ethical latency when judgment is rightfully "suspended," as Agnes Heller claims—that preserves the modernist belief in representation without evaluation.[66] Contrary, however, to this standard view of representational objects as preceding their evaluation, Fanon's insights gesture to a quite different arrangement by which the very determination of *what action is occurring*, of the supposedly value-neutral factuality of *what is happening*, presumes an ethically resonant body, and thus partakes of the histories of responsibility that bring that body into being.

Perhaps, then, one is *not* born free, should freedom depend upon a moral innocence or clean record that future actions would either preserve or forsake. If, instead, one "comes into being" as already ethically marked, through, for instance, histories of responsibilities such as race, the identification of any action attributable to those value-resonant bodies would consequently partake of rather than precede those evaluations. It is easy to think of this predetermination as a mode of heteronomy and thus, as Fanon often seems to, the constriction of pure freedom, and, beyond that, a prejudice against the crafting of one's own subjective qualities. Yet if the ethical stain inherited through historical relations extends the field of actions beyond and prior to those of the circumscribed body, then it may be that it is only through crime that the subject can experience freedom at all.

Pure Fantasies

The relation of ethics and race as structural deviances owes itself to their common breach of the innocent and unmarked origin of being, signaling the emergence of the corporeal stain. If, as is commonly asserted, that stain appears *upon* a preexisting "unaltered original human form," its concealment would not denote a wholesale destruction; the original form, despite its marking through inheritable physical features and evaluated deeds, would maintain its intrinsic composition as what has only been *covered* and darkened rather than eradicated. In other words, such a stain would purportedly do no damage to the original form itself by eliminating or transforming its essential properties. This tiered model of subject and value suggests that beneath Kant's "happy" white people and behind the Fanonian black body "fixed" by the imperial gaze rustles this natural condition: unharmed, but buried deep under a thick patina generated by interpersonal and environmental exposure. Here the original form maintains its ideality throughout the material and cultural existence of the subject, a disembodied consciousness that resurfaces in portrayals of ethical performance central to popular Western moral discourses: the Rawlsian participant behind the "veil of ignorance," the Habermasian enunciator in the ideal speech situation and the unironic, public persona of Rortian solidarity—each a version of the spectral *pre*-racial and *pre*-ethical figure of original human subjectivity. Such a view of race and ethics as expressions of a superimposed deviance upon an earlier, more authentic state continuously holds out the utopian possibility of a return to this original status. The retention of the value-neutral prototype as still immaculate and unharmed by the pollutions of racial and criminal suspicion believed merely to repress or conceal this pure potentiality opens the door for it to be "found" anew with each affected return to a "stripped-down" ethics of life. This fantasy of rediscovery, heralded by King and all those before and after who dream of rescuing the innocent subject unrecognizable under the avalanched and fossilized layers of misattributed and impersonal value, is nothing other than the possibility of stain removal.

But it is difficult to fathom such a first-order existence, one seemingly undercut in the very moment of its expression. What exactly would one be hoping to reclaim here? "Thus the descendents of the first human couple," Kant clarifies, "for whom the *complete* original predispositions is still undivided for all future deviate forms, were (potentially) fitted for all climates."[67] The parenthetical is of critical importance: what does it mean to be an entity of sheer potentiality? What would a physically and hence ethically unmarked being have been like given that, for Kant, physical, moral, and intellectual features of subjectivity can actualize only in a practical, material environment: the line of the nose, the vicissitudes of temper, reflective understanding—all predicated on corporeal instantiation in the world. That subjects of pure potentiality could "occupy" the world in any sense would seem fanciful—how, without features, could a body, much less a rational being, appear or be recognized? One would wonder as well why this state of pure potentiality would be an ideal worthy of reoccupation or mimicry. Why would it not follow that white people, as those who have "departed the least from [the] original formation," are *less* intellectually and morally capable insofar as their humanistic predispositions have only partially actualized? Why not seek to become *more* "racial," which is to say, to stimulate one's predispositions toward further development?

The twofold function of race here is contradictory: in its one role, it defaces the subject, perverting and polluting its original perfection and innocence. In the other, that "defacing" turns out to be what makes the subject *visible* in the broadest sense—it is what *gives it a face*.[68] If one views race as something *done to* the subject it is only because race is simultaneously the name for the differentiated ethical and cognitive embodiments by which the subject could *do something*. Value enacts a similarly dual function. Like race, it is said to stain an original and neutral state, shading it with judgments consequent upon a deed in advance of which there is no possible object of evaluation. Yet as Fanon's encounter with the white child suggests, it is the evaluatively resonant body—that which originates not as ethically unmarked but as the latest instantiation of a history of responsibility—that provides the field within which a meaningful deed can occur. What Fanon is "in fact" doing—allaying fear, suppressing rage—has no content as a preethical "objective" deed but only as an action the identity of which already and necessarily reflects in its essence the criminal associations of the body.

The evaluative quality of race is neither foreign nor exceptional to it. Race stands precisely for a historical structure of signs by which embodied subjects become recognizable through evaluatively differentiated features.[69] Race thus takes the blame for this constitution of material subjects and deeds as necessarily distinguished through markers of value *despite and because of* modern philosophy having deemed such relations impossible. Hence the ethical can no more drop out of analyses of race than can race from ethics.

Marked Subjects

" 'There is but one danger—that this horrible stigma shall be left upon my cheek!' cried Georgiana. 'Remove it, remove it, whatever be the cost, or we shall both go mad!' "[70] In Hawthorne's short story, the "crimson stain upon the snow" of newlywed Georgiana's skin indeed drives her husband Aylmer to the breaking point.[71] A "philosopher-scientist," Aylmer becomes obsessed with finding a potion to eradicate the "visible mark of earthly imperfection" marring the pure beauty of his beloved.[72] "I am convinced," he boasts, "of the perfect practicability of its removal."[73] For him the stain represents "the fatal flaw of humanity which Nature, in one shape or another, stamps ineffaceably on all her productions"—yet it is unclear whether the flaw is in fact *on* humanity or *is* humanity itself—that is, whether humanity could exist other than through such markings.[74] In the end, the blemish that Georgiana laments was "laid upon me before I came into the world" is treated by Aylmer with a "universal solvent by which the golden principle might be elicited from all things vile and base."[75] As the stain recedes, Aylmer reels at the consequence: "Its presence had been awful; its departure was more awful still."[76] Georgiana slips into death with the "parting breath of the now perfect woman," one returned at last to the purity of her original, unmarked form.[77]

In its laudable desire to eliminate the stigma "lain upon" modern bodies, does ethical theory not find its personification in the character of Aylmer? Does not a similarly tenacious laboring toward complete stain removal similarly risk losing the very thing it seeks to preserve in its ideal form? One way to reassess this commitment would be to ask what it would mean to think the stain not as foreign to ethical subjectivity—and thus as what desecrates and occludes it—but as the means of its material expression. The stain, on this interpretation, would exist from the beginning as those marks through which a subject comes into being as an already recognizable *someone* by virtue of its inheritable location within several associative genealogies of value. Instead of pathologizing the ethically resonant body through repeated applications of toxic "universal solvents," the active ingredient of which is some purported "golden rule" of morality or humanity, one might instead reflect upon how those resonances come to be, how they shift and mutate over time and between spaces, and the conditions under which their intensities increase and decrease.

The fundamental issues raised by the structural study of race are those that provoke a reconceptualization of ethics as something other than what "attaches" to bodies and deeds subsequent to their conscious representation. They further prompt a revision of the presuppositions grounding our conventional understandings of the relations between value, truth, and embodied subjectivity. How, specifically, value as constitutive of the subject and its actions resituates the common view of the responsible ethical subject as necessarily autonomous and individuated comprises the focus of the next chapter.

2

The Everlasting Stain

> *Damaging charges against the Negro's social character are usually based upon the following facts and assumptions:*
>
> 1. *That the Negro shows an overwhelming criminal record as compared with the white race.*
> 2. *That the percentage of crime has increased under freedom and education.*
> 3. *That the Negro of the North shows a much higher criminal average than his more benighted brother in the South.*
> 4. *That the colored man is especially addicted to crime of an execrable and nameless character.*
>
> KELLY MILLER, *Race Adjustment*

THE PREVIOUS CHAPTER proposed that we understand value and race not as external qualities affixed or attached to a preexisting subject but as structural relations of difference through which the embodied subject becomes recognizable. Such a recommendation runs counter to the current of contemporary disputes about race as well as long-standing quandaries in ethics yet does not, as it were, come down on any particular side of these debates, aiming instead to reenvision the discussions themselves. Because this structural reading of ethics and race does not depend on a determination of the real from the fictional it does not require the production of an epistemological hierarchy (e.g., of science as what grounds the cultural or the material as what grounds the political) for the purpose of analyzing race. It therefore can also dispense with an explanation, in the vein of post-Marxism, of how race is both external to and distortive of "real" material relations yet simultaneously "structural" for the self-understanding of subjects. Furthermore, as it does not view ontology as prior to value, it does not posit a definition of race as that upon which one could then take an evaluative position—as if race could become available to us in a purely contemplative manner, offering itself up for our detached judgment. Finally, because it does not equate ethics to *morality*—where the latter designates the development of a system of pre-scriptive obligations—but views ethics instead as the study of the formation, circulation, and expression of value, the argument does not arrange itself as a set of factual premises about ethics and race that intersect and collate into readily actionable practices that the conscientious reader might implement.

Advancing ethics and race as other than external attachments thus inca-pacitates some of the classic paradigms—as well as dilemmas of—modern subject formation. It also, however, instates a few troublesome dynamics of its own, the foremost being that of how racialization configures ethical worth as what belongs *both* to the subject and to others of the same race. Several potential objections, such as those provided in Kelly Miller's epigraph above, might be made to contest the connection between race and the nature and meaning of action. All draw, however, from a structural contradiction that extends beyond race, complicating the evaluative significance of any shared qualitative characteristic: Is not the extent to which race (or any other set of features) determines the nature and value of deeds precisely that for which the subject bears no authorship and thus no responsibility? In other words, if what is determined by race is by definition what is not self-determined, how can it ethically reflect the subject at all? If different races signify varying criminal dispositions, how do raced individuals remain responsible, as Fanon observed, for that criminality? The challenge is to conceptualize evaluative deeds as both an effect of race as well as those the subject effects and for which it thus remains culpable. Speaking broadly, the explanation requires a theori-zation of our conscription into genealogies of responsibility—as national citi-zenries, demographic generations, sexual communities, etc.—without which there is no subjectivity but that for which the subject may be interpellated as the producing force.

The objective of this chapter is not to refute these dynamics as irratio-nal and contradictory but to present the alternative logics of their seemingly paradoxical components. It means to show, specifically, the difficulty of maintaining the model of individual ethical responsibility when contemplat-ing histories of race. Ordinarily, scholars might understand this difficulty as attesting to the illegitimacy of race as a constitutive force of value, and thus evidence that value is neither inheritable nor signified through bodily difference. Such a view is expressly espoused by the primary authors dis-cussed in the first half of this chapter, Kelly Miller and Alain Locke, both of whom, along with others like W.E.B. DuBois, rehearse the premises, by then paradigmatic, of modern moral systems within which transitive and corporeally signified racial responsibility is deemed incoherent. Miller and Locke endeavor to refute the idea that criminal tendencies can be imputed to any race—that there exists, in the phrase of DuBois, a "racial morality." Towards this end they do not undertake a study of value but instead look to scientific forms of evidence, aiming to separate the "facts" of race from attributions of criminality. Much like race theories today, their analyses seek to restrict legitimate claims about shared racial qualities to pure empirical assertions. As we will see, however, the production of these arguments repeatedly summons the "racial morality" that it overtly tries to exclude. Specifically, this racial morality comes to function as the context within which those "facts" can appear as such; it provides, as will be shown, the "explanation" and condition of "necessity" that call such facts into being. Through these texts, then, a finer picture emerges as to why the topic of race cannot be adequately addressed by empirical methods that presume to lay open any genuine truths it may conceal, and thus why modern sciences lack any privileged purchase on the notion of race.

From here, the chapter continues the discussion on inheritable, bodily worth by addressing the ethical subject as both autonomously responsible for its performed deeds as well as determined through racial histories of responsibility. Contemplating this quandary involves rethinking the condition implicit in Martin Luther King, Jr.'s appeal for ethical judgments uninflected by embodied signifiers of difference, itself a concise rendering of modern moral systems, that ethical autonomy be apprehensible in its manifestation of a deed independent of all determining forces. This condition presumes that autonomy falls to a subject in a manner distinct from how the subject "falls into" its historical way of being, and in this suggests a structural schism between autonomous and determined expressions of ethical subjectivity. In contrast, it will be argued, via a return to Kant and Fanon, that autonomy as "self-discipline" has no meaning outside of determining forces such as those of evaluative bodily context. Autonomy in this respect operates as that through which heteronomous forces are themselves mediated and represented as such. This logic functions, it will be argued, as a "clip" in the sense of what executes at one stroke differentiated ethical subjectivity as well as the subject as irreducibly the effect of genealogies of value. The question of why we should investigate genealogies of value as enacting the transfer of criminality in a contemporary era in which such reasoning is routinely dismissed as "myths" and "fictions" of a premodern and unscientific age will be addressed in the final sections of the chapter.

Shared Tendencies

Having made explicit the unstated premises of black criminality, Kelly Miller endeavors in his book *Race Adjustment* (1908) to locate corroborating empirical evidence for this association. A mathematics scholar, he plumbs a well of data that includes census results, prison populations, and marriage and church attendance rates, sifting through them to isolate and identify the incontrovertible pattern of concrete violations that would justify these generalized and racially inheritable features of character. He ultimately detects, however, "nowhere any traceable causal connection between crime and race" that would authorize the four principles of racial criminality above.[1] No predictive relation between bodies and illicit behavior surfaces from the data, and thus, on empirical grounds, Miller rejects the opening quadruplet of accusations. In contrast to previous modes of counterevidence against racial criminality that advanced profiles of morally stellar people of color, Miller's statistical tables and comparisons reflect a shift in racial logic in which the burden of proof rests on those who make the charge of ethical deviance.[2] Asserting that such claims hinge on the demonstration of hard data, Miller puts the onus on accusers to produce independently verifiable evidence of the criminal propensity of the race, the lack of which will, he expects, exonerate those bodies from anticipatory evaluative judgments.

What does it mean, though, for such allegations to stand or fall on a quantitative record of transgressions? The demonstration of an "overwhelming criminal record," as the first charge attests, would appear based on the registration of certifiable and nameable violations. In this though one might quickly note, as Miller does, pitfalls in the gathering of such data—that those of color are more likely to be tried than whites for perceived transgressions, that they are more likely to receive convictions for those offenses, etc.—all of which place under suspicion the accuracy of the criminal record itself. At the same time, however, such criticisms of methodological precision reinforce the idea that quantitative accounting, correctly pursued, would indeed confirm or acquit races of accusation of criminal tendencies. Specifically, it presumes the existence of facts about (racial) criminality that validate or invalidate ethical worth, and, consequently, the idea that criminal propensity is properly predicated on such facts.

The language of ethics and race that Miller commonly and casually employs in his letters and articles in *Race Adjustment*, however, indicates at best a shaky commitment to quantitative facts as authorizing the assignment of qualitative features. While calling for empirical proof of denunciatory racial characteristics imputed by others, Miller himself routinely posits such traits as a way of *explaining* the "factual" deeds said to bring those traits about: "It should not give surprise that the black man has given his allegiance to the policies of the North rather than the South, especially when we remember that the African is very largely a creature of affection and is controlled mainly by emotion."[3] Later, reflecting on why more black people did not migrate from the South to the North, Miller reflects that the "Negro has an attachment for locality that almost amounts to instinct. He is not of a nomadic nature, and lacks the restlessness and daring spirit of the pioneer."[4] Surprisingly, we learn that what black people "do" is unlikely ever to be surprising. Here, qualitative tendencies function precisely as what anticipate and configure the determination of "what has been done" such that the "character" of an action itself is never truly "out of character," wherein "what is" taken to happen is formulated in this evaluative context. Miller thus provides the counterargument to his own assertion: what black people "did," he writes, is to give their "allegiance" to Northern policies; but to "give allegiance"—to pledge or aver unreservedly, unconditionally, not from the head but the heart—is an interpretation that emerges within the understanding of black people as "creatures of affection." What are taken as the facts on which ethical traits are thought to depend—again, the neutral objects of modern ethical theory—are themselves determinable, as *this* rather than *that* action, as a "giving of allegiance" rather than a "granting of consent" or "acquiescence to" (or as a concurrence between "policies" advocated by blacks as well as the "North"), only through an evaluative logic in which those traits must be already presumed.[5] In both cases, what for Miller constitutes a *reasonable* account of what black people have done is that which is in keeping with their perceived ethical nature. This evaluative nature is not simply the conclusion of such facts but simultaneously a condition for what can appear as a logical explanation and thus *as* factual.

That his statements on the ethical dispositions of African descendants so closely echo those in Kant's anthropological work does not so much reflect a personal or interpretive failing of Miller as it supports the central contention that evaluation is not foreign to race and vice versa. It reaffirms, that is, that the concept of race is not available for statements about actual racial instantiations outside of a discourse of evaluative qualities. This might explain why someone like W.E.B. Dubois, commonly invoked as Booker T. Washington's ideological rival, posits claims similar to those of the starchy Victorian about the "irresponsibility and criminal tendencies" of post-Emancipation African Americans. [6] Nevertheless, while DuBois and Miller both engage the language of "racial morality" they acknowledge, as Fanon later will, its contradiction of fundamental premises of modern ethical thought. Miller, for his part, appears torn between an insistence on the isolable, autonomous performer of deeds responsible only for practices properly attributable to that subject alone and to the ethical subject conscripted into a history of transitive responsibility, by which any member of the race becomes culpable as the initiating force of all actions attributed to same-raced bodies. He remarks that crime "has no color; the criminal no race. . . . It is folly to punish a race for the wrongdoings of an individual" while elsewhere affirming ethical transitivity across race in asserting that "[t]he individual is the proof of the race, the first unfoldment of its potency and promise."[7] DuBois exhibits the same ambivalence, certifying that "To speak of a single racial morality . . . is not to speak intelligently" even as he "speaks" of the African American "tendency . . . to become surly in temper, or pessimistic or hypocritical."[8]

To restate, the criminal tendencies of a race are not self-evidently the expression of the truth-function of empiricism but partake of an evaluative field within which evidence can appear as such. This is not because data can support multiple causal claims (e.g., that the abundant "criminal record" of certain races may equally testify to systematic discrimination as to "criminal tendencies") but because, as discussed in the previous chapter, the phenomenal identification of any crime—that which could serve as a unit of data—arises within the evaluative context of the performing body. Accordingly, no table of data can thoroughly establish or wholly discredit the "tendencies" of a race (or of any other configured group, whether those tendencies are subsequently defined as cultural, reactive, strategic, etc.) insofar as what it means to invoke a racial representation is to coalesce a complex interrelation of qualities signified through collective embodied features. Simultaneously, one's "criminal record" can be neither compiled nor exhausted through recitation of "actual" crimes alone. Consider here the spectral nature of the "nameless" crime in the fourth and final complaint, that *the colored man is especially addicted to crime of an execrable and nameless character.* What statistics could Miller collect to refute this assertion? Those of every violation from index crimes to moral turpitudes not subject to legal prosecution? The innumerability of offenses one would be obliged to pry from "negro character" in this instance would confound any hope of a refutation *through* quantification—no acquitting table of data could meet the standard for demonstrative proof that the charge of a "nameless" crime imposes. This is because the "unnamed crime" signifies here not a vacancy or placeholding reserved for a particular crime that *could* be named but instead designates criminality as *productive of* actual, identifiable crimes. The criminality Miller attempts to disprove is not a conclusion drawn accurately or erroneously through a study of traces that may or may not be shown to exist; it operates, rather, as the evaluative context within which distinctly embodied subjectivities come into recognizable being.

To his final book, Miller gives a title that encapsulates the strange resilience of this enclosure of criminality. In the opening of "The Everlasting Stain" (1923), Miller wonders whether blacks "stand doomed to eternal infamy from the foundation of the world unto the end of time."[9] Distinct from his earlier owing of declarations of black delinquency to factual ignorance, black criminality is now explored as an "everlasting stain," drawing Miller's focus away from hard exculpatory data toward meditative ruminations on how an entire race of people can be marked at once and so deeply, conductors of a judgment that offers no process of expiation or absolution. "Doomed" and damned to carry the mark of criminality—without trial, without jury, without even memory of any perpetration of a precipitating violation—blackness symbolically certifies an ongoing punitive status even though such subjects remain, Miller remarks, "wholly guiltless of the stain for which [they are] stigmatized."[10]

This criminality signified by blackness (a blackness itself figured as part of the punishment) testifies, Miller suggests, in the most explicit and corporeal manner to ethics as indiscernible through analyses of the state, sovereignty, law, or justice. As precisely what do not map onto or manifest as politics, he deduces, these relations of criminality belong to a different logic of ordination: "By some sort of divine favor it is claimed that [white people] are predestined to rule over their darker brethren for all time to come."[11] Race as an everlasting stain, corporeal and ethical, denotes here neither superficial identity nor cultural solidarity—it is not, hereby, a "thing" at all but what designates and authorizes the differential and hierarchical emergence of ethical subjectivities. As a "stain" race is a secondary, distorting, and unwelcome additive to subjectivity; as "everlasting," however, race becomes a stain whose origin and future demise fade into indiscernibility to the point where the stain is nothing but *what has always been and will be*. Miller reasons that "There can be no satisfactory solution of the race problem while this notion prevails."[12]

Why, though, *would* this notion prevail into the 20th (and 21st) century? How could discourses of race as conduits for inheritable and transferable criminality even survive the rush of the empirical social sciences and the hegemony of modern theories of moral self-determination, much less threaten to dominate them? We have considered already, and will again below, how criminality does not simply describe a general condition born of distinct, recordable crimes but is presupposed for the sake of designating crimes as such. We can also, however, see more clearly now how race as evaluative has evaded elucidation by standard ethical accounts. Within such a model the racial stain can signify only as a shallow and distorting blemish destructive to rather than productive of ethical being. As "nonphilosophical," the stain would evidence only a fallacy or lapse of logic rather than a logic that persists and prevails, as Cornel West suggests, as belonging to the *inception* of modern thought, and thus as what, from that origin, is "everlasting."

Miller's disavowal of "traceable connections" between crime and race has continued as a litany for contemporary theorists who, in league with the dream of the morally sovereign individual, dutifully attempt to rub out the stains symbolic of illegitimate relations of value that have yet to fade on their own. These cleansing rituals, however, betray and abandon the very crisis that should give it pause—force it to draw up and reflect upon its inability even to delimit the contours of the racial normative that so animated European discourses in which arose the hegemony of autonomous subjectivity yet which, according to philosophy's own autobiographical retelling, in no way influenced or marked that formation.

How, then, might we begin to unravel this logic by which races function as symbolic and material conduits for the inheritability and transference of value?

Scars and Traces

The path begins at a confusing roundabout: by what means does a stain establish itself in perpetuity? What constitutes a nameless crime, and how is it committed? While Miller had the insight to elucidate the criminalization of black subjectivity through the trope of an "everlasting stain," it was philosopher Alain Locke whose work offered some of the earliest attempts to survey its asymmetric topography. A colleague of Miller's at Howard University, Locke wrote an introduction to *The Everlasting Stain* that attempts to give coherence to the transitions in Miller's thought. Locke remarks that Miller "seemed to shift from position to position" over the span of his writings, moving from an initial "moral" stage through those that were scientific, anthropological, and economic, returning "oddly enough" to that of moral theory in his final work.[13] Locke concludes that while Miller frequently shifted his take on the problem of race his solution remained steadfastly "a singular and almost unpopular insistence on the solvent of reason."[14] Could there be,

Locke continues, any other possible "solvent" for removing the everlasting stain of race "except [that] two and two are four?"[15] A subtle jab, perhaps, at what Locke saw as the mathematician's battered yet sublime faith in the curative power of positivistic responses, one that may have disclosed as well his own doubts that empirical science could undertake the history of dark bodies in a way that so arithmetically reasoned away their concurrent ethical stain.

Unlike Miller and early DuBois, Locke sought the divorcing of value and race not in comparative observational and evidentiary data but through epistemological self-regulation. He therefore does not plead the moral innocence of blacks but instead raises philosophical objections to the "facts" of black criminality, rejecting as a contravention of the limits of knowledge the extraction of moral and social worth from scientific distinctions among races. At the turn of the 20th century, correlations of racial and moral characteristics were fairly common in anthropology as well as philosophy, disciplines whose debates questioned not the existence of this relation but its nature and scope. In 1908, for instance, Josiah Royce urged philosophy not to bog down like anthropology in trying to ascertain the precise ranking of races and instead attend to "how these physical varieties of the human stock[,] . . . these shades of color, these types of hair, these forms of skull, or these contours of body, are related to the mental powers and to the moral characteristics of the men in question . . . "[16] Royce did not doubt the intellectual and ethical inferiority of certain races but wanted to understand, as had Kant over a century earlier, how much of that "degradation" remained climate-driven (and thus potentially alterable) and how much had converted into fixed, inheritable features: "It is easy to show that an Australian [aboriginal] is just now far below our mental level. But how far is his degradation due to the inherited and unchangeable characters of his race, and how far to his long struggle with the dreary desert?"[17]

Locke, whose aim to study with Royce at Harvard was precluded by the latter's death, delivered in 1915 a lecture entitled "The Theoretical and Scientific Conceptions of Race" that responds to this presumption of racial classifications as indicative of ethical proclivities and comparative worth. In the paper Locke criticizes such interpretations as beyond the scope of what empirical reasoning can justifiably infer: "[A]nthropology is only supposed to be a descriptive science [and therefore] could establish no such standard as [a] *normative* standard between superior and inferior races."[18] Though acceptable for "registering biological history," he continues, racial differences "when carried further and made the basis for normative principles of mankind . . . become the most iniquitous of the scientific conclusions of [our] age. . . . "[19]

For Locke, anthropological studies of the corporeal features of racial inheritance generate at most a "biological register"—that is, a *genealogical record* that is not simultaneously a *criminal record*. Their purpose lies solely in annotating the value-neutral history of the physical characteristics of raced bodies. Early anthropologists who ignored these limits, he chides, "misused" race by allowing "anthropological factors [to be] erected into social distinctions."[20] Locke thus articulates what will become the default prohibition against associating "race as social inheritance [with] race as biological inheritance," protesting that the two "are in no way so interdependent that one can argue from one to the other."[21]

On Locke's "separatist" account, then, this naturalistic fallacy between "biological" and "social" inheritance holds that the normative qualities of a people—where "normative" signifies those practices and beliefs designated as typical as well as evaluatively ideal for a group—are not incontrovertibly transferred across generations as are shared physical features, and thus maintain no presumptive or predictable relation to the latter. The inheritable, embodied markings of a group, he asserts, channel no shared tendencies or dispositions; raced bodies conductive of the ontological in no way conduct the ethical.

Despite such adamant declarations, when Locke tries to explain how unequal normative statuses reproduce themselves across several generations, he discovers himself unable to talk about this inheritance without drawing upon the "anthropological" inheritance he insists remains "incommensurable" with it. In order to chart shifts in the ethical performance and status of blacks, he returns abruptly to their materiality as the site and marker of these values. Stating that normative inferiority has an "historical explanation [that should be] traced to historical causes," he then comments that this inheritability of inferiority strikes black bodies such that they "[go] through history *with the birthmark of history upon them*. We see them going through with *the scars and traces* of almost every contact and influence to which they have been subject."[22] Though earlier disconnecting the aspersion of ethical inferiority from racial materiality, Locke here suggests that historical worth carves itself on the raced body through "scars" and "traces," where materiality provides the site and marker of this value. The skin that sustains these abrasions becomes the document upon which accorded vices and infirmities etch themselves.

Locke perceives modern racial theory as treading a thin line. Early "modern" scientists, he proposes, argued for unswerving correlations between inheritable physical histories and socially normative histories unsupported by empirical data. "Modern" anthropologists reacted by arguing that physical differences "have no meanings other than for purposes of descriptive classification."[23] Though Locke lauds this latter counterdiscourse for rejecting the facile tie between bodies and value, he cautions that the antithetical denial of the existence of any such relation—a denial he himself espouses at his most condemnatory—contradicts the core tenet of the (human) sciences by which race theory "must have correlation with our practical ideas of human society. It must reinforce what is currently believed about human society."[24] History—even physical or biological history—"must incorporate the factor of human belief, because history is not merely a record of facts but, as well, a record of beliefs. . . . "[25] On this other, more "integrated" view, Locke states that "it must be admitted impossible," then, for theories of race ever to dispense with normative, social, and evaluative interpretation.[26] Not only, he writes, is a "pure science of race" as an objective and ethically neutral knowledge impossible, it is also, in the end, neither "desirable" nor "necessary," since, he adds, "we have very little use for a merely abstract science of race."[27]

How, then, are sociological studies of value to suitably embed the decreasingly "pure" science of race? Although Locke disputes objective racial hierarchies he views the analysis of normative ways of being as also a science that, conducted properly, "can account for the superiorities, the real, the admitted, and the unchallenged superiorities at certain periods, of certain ethnic groups and civilization types." He continues by affirming the importance of determining "what [are] relatively higher, and what are relatively lower states of culture," stating that we "need to know what is better [and] perhaps what is the best [of] civilized types."[28] For Locke, the anthropological history of race *and* the normative history of race are equally "scientific"; normative racial hierarchies do not corrupt descriptive inquiry but rightfully deploy anthropological categories of race for the sake of evaluative comparison. The disparate ethical status of races for Locke comes to be neither illusory nor "anti-science"; what *is* complicated and contested for him—and rife with dangerous traps for the theorist—is the delineation of the proper relation between the material and ethical, a relation for which abstract separation is essential and practical separation impossible.

The Semiotics of Race

A seminal pivot for race theory, Locke's intervention signals the close of those strategies seeking to combat accusations of inheritable racial criminality by adducing portraits of upstanding individuals or comparative statistics of actual crimes by racial populations. Though engaging the same motivating questions, Locke's separatist approach does not refute charges specific to any race; rather, it posits a structural parallel between physical and normative inheritances across which no content may pass. This position thus anticipates contemporary theories that imagine "race" as hierarchical only when differential value displaces anthropological and biological objectivity—obscuring those exclusively descriptive accounts of difference. Locke provides the model for such theories of race that acknowledge, if begrudgingly, the assemblages of inheritable material features that might track classifications of human types but also absolve science of any sordid collusion with ethics by simultaneously dismissing the social significance of that physical history—the "value" of the "factual" body. Yet his integrative statements in the same discussion provide an alternative, concurrent discourse that concedes some exchange between the body and value even as it preserves the body as the primary and foundational object of knowledge.

In diagramming how such a theory reconciles the separatist and integrative threads we can more clearly identify how and where value is said to enter descriptive accounts—those stained sites of exchange that, as with the navel and genitals of raced bodies in Kantian anthropology, suffer the ingress and egress of value, and thus denote where the body and criminality become both indivisible and incommensurable. Rehearsing his major claims, we see Locke stating 1) that physical racial history and normative racial history are fully separate and incommensurable, the former being the sole province of anthropology/biology and the latter of sociology; 2) that normative racial history is inscribed upon physical racial history such that one can "see" and interpret that history given an instantiation of a physically raced body; 3) that sciences of necessity include as a structural component a normative history ("human belief") that is inexorably understood in conjunction with physical difference; 4) that because of (3) a purely neutral and descriptive science of race is impossible.

According to these principles, our physical, biological selves constitute a generally stable and historically resistant foundation upon which are etched inheritable cultural and sociological histories of the race. That such "scars and traces" inscribe themselves *upon* the body for Locke points, as with Kant, to the operative framework of an unmarked, socially and ethically unwritten figure—the original stem formation (Kant) or the inessential yet purely biological being (Locke)—that stabilizes the subject as a "truth" that remains ultimately impervious to the stain of dynamic history that depends upon and distorts it. Significant here is that neither of these evaluatively unmarked entities though posited as the philosophical ground and substratum for value as a secondary and discursive racial history, is ever available in that pure form to representational discourse. They are, in this context, rather, "figurative": metaphorical devices that invoke and stand in for the inaccessible and untainted authentic subjectivity always and forever *disfigured* by the "pull of what men currently think human society is"—that is to say, by the dreams, fantasies, nightmares, and delusions of our evaluative ideals of what we *should be*, aka, in this era of scientism, *what we naturally are*.[29]

If one cannot produce or speak of a pure physical history of a people, how can one avow its existence? In the previous chapter it was suggested that Kant's "original stem formation" be understood not as a species of unraced, embodied beings who spawned deviant racial progeny before disappearing without historical trace but rather as a structural concept abstracted and retroactively installed through the theory of racial difference. On this reading, "shared humanity" did not precede or underlie racial difference but signified, rather, its covalent effect. We might then reconceive the theory of a pure anthropological or biological history as similarly a structural abstraction retroactively installed as the fixed site of an originally unmarked subjectivity whose corporeality is subsequently inked by an evaluative history. In this way, "biology" or "evolutionary history" would not disclose "real" differences onto which are projected (false) evaluative differences but would be grasped as itself a mode of evaluative marking, a means of distinguishing "trivial" physiological inheritances (skin color, etc.) from "important" ones (genitals, etc.).[30] Moreover, as Locke adds, because "almost every contact" leaves its mark, that epidermal document—the "bodily schema" that Fanon protests—would forfeit in its immersion into the flow of cultural and symbolic meanings any "original" unblemished, undesignated surfaces, becoming overwritten patterns of scar tissue.

From this perspective, the "physical" subject would not preexist its entry into a semiotics of race, the historical system of signification within which bodily "scars" and "traces"—the amalgam of physical features and traits designating racial membership—acquire their relative meanings. Rather, those "birthmarks of history" would introduce the subject into a symbolic order by which it becomes "readable" to itself and others within hierarchical histories of responsibility. Accordingly, one could not hold, as does the standard model of ethics, that racial inscriptions pervert the idiosyncrasies of the unique individual by forcing it into fixed relations with others but would instead grasp this effecting of the subject through its conscription into genealogical legacies of value as producing an evaluative context—those "criminal tendencies"—through which any meaningful, idiosyncratic deed could appear as such. (Note that here "idiosyncratic" aligns with the "idiomatic" as what is irreducible to its component parts and thus what is never exhausted by that context.) As this normative context remains, according to Locke, "dynamic," the epidermal scars and traces of racial history have no "fixed" associations; as such, their resonances are not instinctively available to the raced subject itself, who therefore is also obliged to decipher them in order to "know itself."

The structure of race ensures that it cannot be spoken except as a discourse of value. Locke sometimes admits as much: "when the modern man talks about race, he is not talking about the anthropological or biological at all. [He is really talking about the historical record of success or failure of] an ethnic group."[31] Continuing, he contends that because these groups "have neither purity of blood nor purity of type" that, "from the point of view of anthropology, [they] are ethnic fictions." But is there any nonevaluative way to see "from the point of view" of anthropology given that a "pure science of race" is impossible? Why would one even think that evaluative histories that do not *begin* with or secure the consent of anthropology or biology risk the designation "fictional?" Such a belief is analogous to the idea that a sheaf of blank paper is the original and real "book" that graphic marks subsequently stain, insofar as no natural and causal link exists between the physical pages and what is inscribed on them. Yet the book, assuredly, does not possess its true identity in its materiality before being appropriated into and for the sake of some narrative from which it always maintains a crucial independence. Rather, the "book" or "race" becomes what it is as material in its discursivity; moreover, as Locke acknowledges, when people talk about race they are most likely speaking, as when talking about a book, not about an exclusively physical instantiation but of *meanings*. By failing to grant primacy of that meaning to the paper stock we are not thereby putting "fiction" in place of "fact"; equivalently, then, one does not "go beyond" and violate the limit of the racial "real" in speaking of historical, evaluative, and inheritable racial meanings.

As the embodied transits point through which histories of responsibility conduct themselves, the birthmarks of race cannot locate the subject within a physiological lineage without thereby writing its ethical lineage; the differentiation of subjects has no purely descriptive, nonevaluative mode of representation. Locke, stymied by what he views as an obstinate intrusion of ethics into race, wrestles with how something that "amounts practically to social inheritance [nevertheless] parades itself as biological or anthropological inheritance."[32] How, he wonders, does an ethical stain imposed and enforced from the outside (socially) purport to arise and reproduce itself from the inside (physiologically)? Having reflected upon this disorienting synchrony of value and embodiment, he subsequently provides a succinct premise of the confounding kinship of ethics and race: "[t]o the extent, therefore, that any man has race, he has inherited either a favorable or unfavorable social heredity, which unfortunately is ... ascribed to factors which have not produced [it,] factors which will in no way determine either the period of those inequalities or their eradication."[33]

If what this book attempts to explicate were condensable to a single yet multitiered enquiry, not unlike Nietzsche's *Genealogy of Morals*, it would be this passage of Locke's. Already the first chapter has taken up the conditionality of the first premise of Locke's statement—the "extent to which any man has race"—holding that it is to the extent one *is* marked through bodily difference (e.g., raced) that one exhibits "humanity." This and the succeeding chapters attend directly to the seemingly incoherent phenomenon of ethical inheritances that propagate, as Locke affirms, "favor" as well as "disfavor." Such inheritances are foremost not concrete social advantages or disadvantages but rather structures of comparative valuations in light of which subjects and their actions become ethically legible. These evaluative qualities that attend to raced subjects, Locke warns, are "ascribed to factors which have not produced [them]"—they neither, that is, reflect the intrinsic values of such subjects nor the proper causal accounting of their accumulated criminal and evidentiary acts. But what, then, are the "factors" generating such inheritances? By what logic does a genealogy *become* favorable or unfavorable such that an ancestral line operates as a conduit of criminal identity—fabricating, as it were, a faultline?

Autonomy and Dissonance

Let us address first the seeming incoherence of the idea of ethical inheritance. To inherit one's station in life, so to speak, would seem to proscribe ethical autonomy. If comparative ethical status is inherited, and, furthermore, if that status configures the evaluative contexts of bodies in accordance with which performed actions arise, then the subject's deeds would not be "freely" enacted in the sense that they would not be the exclusive expression of interior forces of the subject but would include as well those "external" forces of its inheritances. There would seem, at least, no clear way to disaggregate those forces so as to isolate the ones for which the subject would be answerable as sole author. This suggests that rejection of the ethically unmarked and free being thereby negates as well any ground for autonomy and freedom.

Because autonomy, freedom, and determination are topics too large and complex to address substantively here, the objective in this section is accordingly modest—namely, to point out that, even in modern moral systems, no simple dichotomy is to be had between autonomy and heteronomy, suggesting an opening for how race might be conceived as enabling rather than restricting ethical subjectivity. Second, it means to offer a concept of the "clip" by which that enactment may occur, specifically, when autonomy and heteronomy are both understood as "disciplined" expressions—that is, as regulative formations of the self. A significant worry for ethicists and theorists of race, as we have seen, is that race is not merely secondary and inessential, as value is also thought to be, but that it swallows up our ethical identity as individuals; under race, actions are thought distorted through perceived criminal tendencies, and thus disciplined in their nature and value by forces purportedly foreign to our will. Such a concern presumes that truly autonomous expressions are those that lack determinative influence. It suggests, in other words, that the condition for the enactment of autonomy is its hermetic "purity," as what exists only as uncontaminated and untainted by any power not originating from the subject's conscious intentionality.

According to Kant's view of the will, however, subjective determination is not inherently prohibitive of autonomy. Heteronomy, Kant contends, determines us as material beings whose actions must of necessity conform to laws of nature. Such laws constitute us as effects of causal chains of "external" origins, where "external" refers as well to bodily forces other than the will such as affect, desire, and instinct.[34] Our subjection to these laws, he holds, yield what might be called instrumental responses to stimuli, indicating behaviors that may be purposive though not strictly willed. This category would include performances we nonetheless think of as the most overt expressions of personal freedom and individuality, for instance, spontaneous actions, expressions of heartfelt desires, and idiosyncratic gestures and utterances. Such practices, though conventionally imagined as exemplifying a sovereign and unhampered personality, are nevertheless attributable, Kant avers, to determinative instincts, desires, and inclinations, whether of social or physiological origin.[35] Autonomy, by contrast, encompasses for Kant those enactments of the subject that interrupt the causal sequence of heteronomous determination; ethical subjectivity, in this respect, is evidenced not by deeply felt and guileless "authentic" deeds but by a disciplined adherence to self-grounding conditions and principles—in other words, to rational decision-making.

In giving the rational law to itself, the subject enacts its autonomy through acceptance of a disciplining of the will no less comprehensive than that of natural law. Autonomy thus emerges not in the absence of disciplining forces but through a self-discipline that effects those conditions by which an action could possibly count as belonging to the subject.

Freedom for Kant is not defined by the absence of limits and conditions; no state exists in which impetuous and unconstrained actions are reflective of autonomy: if not conditioned by rationality, such deeds manifest impulses that, adhering to laws of nature, cannot count as self-determined. For Kant, the subject is thus disciplined no less by autonomy than by heteronomy. But what, then, would mark autonomy from heteronomy? As Onora O'Neill explains, heteronomous action for Kant has meaning only on a presumption of autonomy—laws of nature are themselves comprehensible as such only through that "self-discipline."[36] In other words, the self-consciousness required for "recognizing" that one is subject to external laws, O'Neill observes, of necessity mediates those laws. This capacity does not signal thereby the presence of an unconditioned power, O'Neill notes, but rather an equally disciplined autonomy, one through which heteronomous forces are themselves recognized and represented as such.

If determinism, then, is not what must be escaped for the sake of freedom or ethical autonomy, objections to the everlasting stain could not be launched on the exclusive grounds that such stains install the subject as an effect of history that thereby extinguishes its capacity for autonomy. At the same time, insofar as the *grasping* of ethical subjectivity within this determining chain presumes autonomy, the assertion that the actions of the subject acquire meaning only within genealogies of embodied value is not a claim of naturalism or biologism. Accordingly, ethical subjectivity can neither be explained nor exhausted by, for instance, evolutionary or neuropsychological arguments that race genetically predisposes or compels certain traits or practices. This would be the case not only for race but for any ethical inheritance, the *apprehension* of which would recursively prohibit its purely heteronomic possibility. (Consider, for example, that the grasping of one's behavior or trait as "instinctual" thereby negates that very possibility to the extent that "instinct" signifies precisely those causal relations of stimulus-response that cannot be thematized.[37]) Rather than what defies the ethical as immutable destiny, biology is properly understood as a historically powerful species of it, whereby the actualization of material being and actions does not precede but extends out of value. Race would thus install ethical subjectivity through a disciplining mechanism that, even if biological and heteronomous, would not foreclose autonomy but enable its expressions. This would require that race render ethical subjectivity inheritable while, strangely, occasioning thereby the autonomy it is imagined to destroy. How, though, as the previous chapter concluded, can the stain source and site freedom?

This revised notion of autonomy that does not oppose or struggle against determinism is to be conceived instead as a condition for representing it. Such autonomy cannot be therefore the simple rupture or incommensurability between cause and effect—a dense pivoting by means of which a programmatic reaction is overwritten via intentionality—but, more formidably, would constitute the rift by which are produced distinguishably discrete events—that is, the singularities of "cause" and "effect" themselves. Ethical subjectivity, it could be said, *clips* this causal flow, in the common and paradoxical definitions of the term as a procedure both of separation ("to clip" as to divide into smaller pieces) and unification ("to clip" as to fasten or join together): a *cleaving* that differentiates and identifies "events" as such through an operation that, in the same move, maintains the relation of these elements, forestalling pure difference or otherness.[38] This clip of autonomy, therefore, would not be that which disrupts an ongoing, organic causal trajectory either from an interior "agency" or "from the outside" but would execute— as a bringing-into-existence and a severing simultaneously—the relation of events perceived to comprise any causal sequence.

The suggestion here is that autonomy, even in the guise of "autonomous" historical change, need not oppose or stand outside determined relations for the sake of a vibrant theory of ethical subjectivity. On this premise what are regularly advanced as motors of that subjectivity—will, agency, intentionality, etc.—would designate similar forces *of* determination rather than those imagined to resist, exceed, or overcome it. From here it would make little sense to contend that the ethical objective of the rational will is to oversee and facilitate from "above" the competing, genuine drives of self and other, as there would exist, following Nietzsche's lead, no authoritative self-governance that similarly escaped the economy of those drives. It is the retention of this "groundhog" theory of ethical subjectivity—in which the subject can pop its head out of the world of value, neutrally survey the ethical terrain, then pop it back in again to knowingly and confidently enact its next move—that has made it virtually impossible to render coherent the evaluative constitution of embodied selves and accordingly the structure and function of race. To finally put pressure on this version of the subject would be to initiate the critique of contemporary ethical discourse (and thus of political and legal discourses) already waiting in the wings of value theory, one that would lower the curtain on those prescriptive theaters in which autonomy serves primarily to arbitrate conflicts among "personal" inclinations (consequentialism, liberal pragmatism, contract theory, discourse ethics, etc.). In these accounts, achievement of the ethical ideal occurs not in the full expression of autonomy but in the moment when autonomy no longer has appetites to inhibit, tolerate, sublimate, or do justice to—that is, at the moment of its obsolescence or effacement.

The metaphor of interiority on which individual worth commonly turns endows the subject with intrinsic, qualitative predicates that may or may not be fully expressed in the practices of that subject's body and that may or may not be reflected accurately in the public interpretation of those practices.[39] On this view, the subject preserves through this indeterminacy an always concealed and authentic reserve insofar as the body's gestures and articulations function as indicators whose relation to that hidden truth is indisputable yet enigmatically uncertain. (Even when poor fortune prevents its worldly fruition, states Kant, "like a jewel, [a good will] would still shine by itself, as something that has its full worth in itself."[40]) The pertinent question for ethics thus becomes in what manner the body in its social context constitutes a proper indicator of that interior content and how the body should be read so as to truthfully disclose these qualities. For the last century, at least since the intervention of Locke, the repeated assertion has been that the raced body speaks only ethical fiction, its signifiers distorting the value and nature of this interior content, making near impossible the ascertainment of the intrinsic worth of racial subjects, especially those burdened with unfavorable stains that bar access to the unspoiled source of their conduct.

Yet if, as suggested here, the signs and stains believed to obscure ethical subjectivity constitute rather than distort it, such qualities would be neither inside nor outside the subject. Accordingly, the body's gestures and articulations would not evidence *symptoms* of evaluative worth but would be discursive components of it. In turn, autonomy would have no meaning outside of an evaluative context. As configured within shifts of genealogical value, reproduced and realigned through its multiple and comparative stains, the ethical worth of the subject would not be "fixed" by its embodied reading but instead would find its various qualitative associations strengthened or enervated as an effect of its accorded relations to others. This configuration is not a demonstration of disempowerment; on the contrary, its location within rather than outside or in excess of historical determination, apprehended and effected by the clipping force of autonomy, confirms the subject's worth as no less than the authenticity of its being. For here, subjectivity is *always* ethical subjectivity, not in virtue of its innately "good" disposition, its performance or nonperformance of worthwhile deeds, or because of anything it owes ontologically to another being or thing (as if ethics were fundamentally an obligation—an "ought" or *sollen*) but by its necessarily evaluative quality as stained and scarred, on which depends its differentiation and thus its particular or "singular" appearance.

Still, if ethical autonomy is indebted to rather than independent of embodied genealogies of responsibility, such as those of race, by what logic can the subject affirm those lineages as its own? It is not sufficient that the subject be the material conduit of values if those values alienate the subject against itself; there must be, in addition, a complimentary dynamic by which that alienation is simultaneously appropriated by the self in its own name. Frantz Fanon laments that his body is "not his own," as he comes to understand that he does not control the full meaning or worth of its actions— angrily denouncing, silently seething, mischievously plotting—the body, he contends, betrays him. But this experience of dissonance, a sense of betrayal, can occur only because of his concurrent acceptance of those alienated actions as "his own"; conversely, a disinvested or discounted body, a detached body, could not produce this same tension. It is, importantly, *his* body that is estranged and foreign, *his* body that is *not his*. Moreover, this estrangement is not itself "strange" or foreign in the sense of what fractures an already unified ethical self from the outside but as what indicates the non-self-identity of his corporeal self-consciousness. It is, then, the clip of autonomy that is not "agency" but a unifying break that permits this apprehension of embodied worth mediated asymmetrically, as Fanon describes, through historical signifiers of race. To conceive autonomy instead as a capacity to step outside of embodied value and then subsequently *direct* that body against this mediation is to set ethical subjectivity against historicity, as what the subject combats for the sake of its freedom. Fanon's analysis of race as structurally incommensurable with the ready opposition between self- and socially-determined worth, however, situates ethical autonomy *within* rather than against determination, not as what preserves ethical singularity in defiance of disciplinary forces of language and heteronomous "power" but as what, in mere conscious apprehension, discloses and facilitates those forces.

To be clear, the idea is not that the subject clips itself *to* this determination— it is not a procedure of binding or attachment of the self to its subjugations, a model that in casting these as opposing (if inverted) forces must therefore invoke an anonymous power to produce this fastening linkage.[41] Instead, the notion of subjectivity offered here proposes ethical autonomy as the breaker for those circuits of determining value without which constitutive relations of force would not be possible; for Fanon it proves the exclusive structure of autonomy, as it is in the self-conscious recognition of this history of responsibility that actions belong to him, despite (and because of) the nonexclusivity of that inheritance. Because Fanon cannot act except in the name of a body evaluatively charged by race and gender (even in the attempted rejection of that body), the responsibility by which practices become "his" lies contiguous with, as he himself remarks, a responsibility for the actions of all black men, past and present.

The Nameless Crime

It might be asked what the subject takes responsibility for on this view. If criminality does not result from the commission of any particular crime, from what does it arise? Moreover, how is it possible to imagine the subject as "responsible" in the same manner and degree as the actual or "original" perpetrator? Let us return to the fourth and perhaps most vexing formula of black criminality that Miller relates, that of black people's purported "addiction to crime of an execrable and nameless character." The postulate has this criminality surfacing not from any legislated infraction but from an unspeakable deed, one knowable merely through a reading of the racial body. The nameless crime, analogous to the Kantian stem formation, suggests a potentiality that, having itself no realized content, nevertheless defines the contours and limits of any criminal expression. As a repository of possibilities, the nameless crime would not be one among a number of possible crimes but rather the imagined classificatory identity by which the nature of any action becomes recognizable *as* criminal. It can be no ordinary transgression—a lawbreaking or malfeasance that reveals an acute flaw or weakness of the subject—but must be instead a precipitating action so corrupt as to contaminate all forthcoming actions, an offense sufficiently grave as to be subjectively constitutive rather than indicative.

Furthermore, to produce the everlasting quality of the stain as an infinitely perpetuated mark—the compulsion without end that an "addiction" promises—the nameless crime must be sufficiently powerful to transmit that corrupting property to the actions of each and every future descendant, and, through some precise art, *only* to those descendants. In other words, this founding deed that produces criminal subjectivity must do so in such a way that the stain of criminality becomes permanent and inheritable. At the same time, that criminality must remain no less the expression of the subject's autonomy; it must "belong" to the subject in the way that Fanon's practices belong to and individuate him despite being practices that acquire their identity as how black men "are." Satisfying the first condition means being transmissible across generations, as a criminality that reproduces itself along a lineage or faultline through a protean set of embodied signifiers. The second requires that this hereditary stain function as the sign, rather than the cause, of criminal intentionality. The stain, that is, cannot express merely a physiological trait that makes the subject a passive vessel of neurological compulsions to which its "will" ultimately submits; on the contrary, the stain must serve as the manifest and legible corroboration of ethical autonomy. The nameless crime, then, is to be understood as *the imaginary, constituting force of relation between the subject as historical materiality and as the autonomous site of evaluative worth.* It is what reconciles the figural dissonance of the subject as the embodied effect of inheritable arrangements of differential value and as the self-determining and responsible producer of value.

In modernity, this reconciliatory function is served primarily by race but is not identical to it; other embodied arrangements of value also perform this structural role (e.g. gender, age, physical size, etc.). Thus while race remains in our time a predominant stain by which this coordination of embodiment and value is accomplished it is by no means the only one. On the same count, race has little truck as a tool designed to justify discriminatory distributions of social capital; rather, it is the name for the modern form by which inheritable value is thought to travel, a model somehow compatible with, as seen with Kant, the development of the autonomous agent of universal morality as sole author of its deeds. It is in the context of this dawning of the subject who begins its existence as evaluatively unmarked, "born free" of communal and familial dispositions and debts, that the embodied inversion of this figure, the racial subject, comes to bear the full responsibility of its genealogy. Race thus serves the vital function of naturalizing and "explaining" what modern ethics will concurrently and consistently disavow, specifically, the always evaluative quality of embodied difference and its attributed practices.

The criminalities clipped or executed by an apparatus of ethical marking such as race derive their confirmation from the event of a nameless crime. The nameless crime, however, is less the causal force of criminality than the event that announces and warrants the representational appearance of the stain. Criminality remains thereby primordial in the sense that it contours the body from the beginning such that no deed, in the traditional sense, can be said to precede or initiate it. Indeed what could demonstrate a generic and inexhaustible criminality but a crime equally borderless and abyssal? The crime, then, remains nameless not because it cannot yet be articulated; it is not, in this respect, an incipient injustice or differend, to use Lyotard's term, resisting the translation of injury into discourse; rather, encompassing the totality of all possible transgressions, the crime is both absolute yet void of definitive content.[42] It demands no staging, implicitly or theoretically, of a sacrificial violence, like that of Abraham's filicide or the patricide of Freud's natal clan, although both narratives represent content-based instantiations of this structure.[43] The nameless crime is unspeakable not as absurdity or taboo but as what is itself without "deed"; in itself it is "nothing" in that no particular "thing" occurs, thereby offering up nothing to contextualize, defend, or refute. Moreover, while discrete offenses occasion punishments of finite scope, the nameless crime, in contrast, bespeaks a continuous offense that has no obvious conclusion, supporting punishments that thereby extend indefinitely into the future.

How, then, might the nameless crime be conceptualized given that it is not an identifiable deed but the structural context for all such transgressions? How does it confirm and configure value without content? Let us consider a comment Kant makes—seemingly in passing, as he traces his own path of reasoning to an anthropological explanation of race—in which he recalls the narrative of a nameless crime as the first of several possible "origins of blackness." This founding myth not only initiates a deductive chain of indeterminate, hereditary value, but also catalyzes in early modernity "blackness" as a stain of body and soul: "Some people imagine that Ham is the father of the Moors and that God made him black as a punishment which now all his descendants have inherited. However, one can provide no proof as to why the color black should be the mark of a curse in a more fitting fashion than the color white."[44]

Quite right. There is, as Miller would concur, "no proof" that the stain of blackness takes the shape of a curse, and yet, Kant does not dispute blackness as a differentiating, inheritable mark that signifies deficiency. In his anthropology, blackness registers the deviance of the delineated and situated being from the translucent universal of the original stem formation; accordingly, if "no proof" exists for him as to *why* blackness signifies criminality it is because blackness itself functions in his natural history *as that evidence or proof.* For Kant, race fundamentally *is* the mark of blackness; in other words, "separate" races do not each sport a *different* mark, for instance, a "white mark" or a "red mark," but varying saturations of a single opacity. Whiteness, therefore, is not the *opposite* of blackness but a *lesser* blackness—that is to say, a state comparatively *unmarked* and accordingly less deviant. This is why Kant alludes to the potential signification of whiteness as a curse, for whiteness is for him also a stain, albeit one that doubles, as we have seen, as pure and primordial. The marks of embodiment, within this guise of race, are always criminal.

So while Kant appears to dismiss the notion of a racial curse, the theory of race he proposes draws more from it than he suspects. Indeed it may be that Kant must explicitly raise, then reject, the story of Ham because his anthropology aims precisely to overwrite this theological narrative with a secular and scientific one, the objective of which remains nevertheless to explain and justify the inheritable embodiment of worth. What Kant explicitly rejects in his ethical theory—the inheritability and bodily constitution of value—thus returns in the anthropology; moreover, it must return here, for this is where the subject exists not as an isolated and disembodied consciousness but as a descendant whose subjectivity is inextricable from and thus unknowable outside of its relations within those lineages. In current discussions of Kant's anthropological writings and race the presenting question is understood as one of intentionality and contamination—that of Kant's culpability for wittingly forging a "racial morality" given the contemporary evidence of the day, and of the extent to which this intervention poisons the remainder of his corpus (and, given its centrality to the discipline, the late modern and contemporary practice of philosophy itself).

Such a framing, however, mistakes race as a nonphilosophical stain that taints neutral theories of representation and difference. It tries to rescue a naturalistic interpretation of human difference from race that, relieved of this false patina, will result in representations not discolored by value. "Difference" is thus remanded to its purported natural meaning as that difference solely of kind. Locke's effort to fortify such a definition, however, examples the limits of this attempted stain removal, arguing against, ultimately the possibility of nonevaluative representations of inheritable difference. The most that anthropological and biological science can produce, his analysis affirms, is the metaphorical "figure" of the unraced human as a derivative abstraction, one retroactively installed in a historical narrative of being. This is because, as he writes, the "scars" and "traces" of social history become the legible expression of the subject within its genealogical identity, an ethical context outside of which no embodied act could be recognized as a performed "deed."

Moreover, the debates about Kant's "philosophical" writing as permeated by "racial thinking" forecloses the possibility of understanding race as formative of the linguistic, social, and physical distinctions it is then accused of distorting. Characterizing race as inessential to philosophy and obstructive of "real" difference accords race no function in the production of reason, in which case it fails to have any structural or constitutive force; it is here said to contour nothing yet color everything. To analyze race as effecting the differential force that could explain its presence at the inception of ethical subjectivity, its symbolic marking of bodies across generations, and its always evaluative configuration requires instead investigation of its function in modern theories of subjectivity, value, and embodiment. The starting point for such an investigation is the consideration of knowledge that has become unauthorized in the transition from the premodern to the modern, knowledge whose explanations of phenomenal relations between bodies and value were rendered invalid within new conditions for meaningful statements. In other words, the structural analysis of race begins with the hypothesis that its appearance (for instance, in Kant's anthropology) reflects a procedure of epistemological replacement or substitution in which the dissolution of a prior discourse explicating the relation of genealogy and value (that of "cursed identity") demands the coalescence of a new explanatory discourse exhibiting a serviceable if fraught compatibility with naturalistic and secular explanations of the world. The language of race would have developed, that is, as a modernist rejection and rehabilitation of earlier philosophical accounts of the transfer of symbolic value and nature of ethical subjectivity.

The study of race thus begins by exploring such premodern, nonracial discourses of embodied, evaluative genealogy or histories of responsibility, considering in particular the constellation of dilemmas they mobilized to interpret and reconcile. What uncertainties and inconsistencies of criminal, inheritable subjectivity did this earlier logic of the curse resolve in such a way as to generate a coherent and unified theory? In what way was this reasoning connected to and enabling of a general theory of knowledge? How does the modern dynamic of race both incorporate and renovate these resolutions and their justifications? Understanding the structural function of race requires that we attend to its philosophical predecessors, those genealogical lines from which it has itself descended—in part, Christian as well as Jewish conceptions of embodied moral consciousness and, prior to that, ancient Greek discourses on the nature and origin of ethical knowledge. The operation of race will not be unlocked, in other words, by asking how and by whom such an evil was unleashed into our era, disorienting our perceptual reflexes; that is a framing that discloses no genuine interest in "race" but only in deracination—a pulling up by the roots for the sake of outright annihilation, reflecting, more than anything, the predominant mode in which race now appears in theory: as a troublesome notion taken up solely so that it can be put to permanent rest, either through extermination or political governance. This is, in sum, what every conventional "ethical study *of* x" implicitly promises: the submission of a dynamic to a regularized and authoritative practice.

The next two chapters, in which the curse as an antecedent structure of race and a dominant logic of ethical knowledge is reviewed, should not be thought peripheral to the primary arguments of this book in their focus on modes of ethical reasoning that precede the formal configuration of race. As with all conceptual paradigms, race too has a history and provenance that precedes its actual naming, a history without which any study of race's theoretical force would be incomplete. A similar shift must occur regarding what are now held as legitimate methods of philosophical argumentation, specifically, those theories that presume a value-neutral, empirically exhaustible subject at the heart of knowledge. This assumption in race studies over the twentieth century has sought to bring dispassionate order to an area of inquiry in which unruly speculation has long seemed to carry the day. This attempt, however, to bring rigor and precision to the study of race by theorizing the descriptive apart from the evaluative and meaning apart from the symbolic has done little to illuminate race as historically emergent rather than engineered or adventitious. The persistent and noble effort to show that little to nothing of race survives its verification by processes of scientific apprehension—in the guise of data, statistics, facts, and other creditable evidentiary marks—has largely succeeded in arguing that race is "fictitious," "mythical," and "social": in a word, we are told, *evaluative*. What it has not succeeded in demonstrating—and has often unwittingly refuted—is that the evaluative and its composite forces of "myth" subsequently attach to and stain those neutral percepts, or that any interpretable mark of identification could signify outside the evaluative. It is with this in mind that the next two chapters turn not only to pre-racial conceptions of bodies and value but also to the logics of ordination, fate, pacts, and other configurations of meaning by which such relations conduct themselves.

The remainder of this chapter will introduce the Hamitic curse and its more contemporary racial iterations, proposing some general considerations regarding the association of ethics and genealogy. Chapters 3 and 4 attend in more detail to the structure of the curse that the story of Ham spectacularly renders but does not elucidate. In chapter 5 we return to more recent theories of ethical knowledge to assess the continuation of the "mythical" logics of inheritable, bodily value in our current discourses of criminal subjectivity. Throughout, race discloses itself not as sound or unsound scientific classifications to which immoral attributes become unjustly attached but as the name for the seemingly inexplicable yet naturalized modern configuration of ethical inheritance.

Premodern Logics

Here, then, is the Biblical passage that Kant actively disassociates from the inheritability of black inferiority:

> Now the sons of Noah who came out of the ark were Shem and Ham and Japheth; and Ham was the father of Canaan. These three [were] the sons of Noah, and from these the whole earth was populated. Then Noah began farming and planted a vineyard. He drank of the wine and became drunk, and uncovered himself inside his tent. Ham, the father of Canaan, saw the nakedness of his father, and told his two brothers outside. But Shem and Japheth took a garment and laid it upon both their shoulders and walked backward and covered the nakedness of their father; and their faces were turned away, so that they did not see their father's nakedness. When Noah awoke from his wine, he knew what his youngest son had done to him. So he said, "Cursed be Canaan; A servant of servants He shall be to his brothers." He also said, "Blessed be the LORD, The God of Shem; And let Canaan be his servant." "May God enlarge Japheth, And let him dwell in the tents of Shem; And let Canaan be his servant." Noah lived three hundred and fifty years after the flood. So all the days of Noah were nine hundred and fifty years, and he died.
>
> [Chapter 10] Now these are [the records of] the generations of Shem, Ham, and Japheth, the sons of Noah; and sons were born to them after the flood . . .[45]

The story of Ham begins with the character Noah planting a vineyard and subsequently discovering the intoxicating properties of fermented grapes. Drunk and disrobed, he passes out uncovered in his tent. The second of his three sons, Ham, unexpectedly stumbles upon this display. What then transpires in the tent remains cryptically unelaborated: the story relates only that Ham, upon exiting the tent, conveys his father's compromised condition to his brothers Shem and Japheth, who then cover their father while averting their eyes from his naked body. Noah awakens, "knows" what Ham "has done to him," and subsequently, and curiously, curses Canaan—one of

Ham's sons—to serve Ham's brothers. Immediately following this directive Noah blesses his two sons Shem and Japheth.

Let it be affirmed, to avoid any misconceptions, that the curse in the biblical narrative does not employ the word "race" or make reference to skin color. It does not, in fact, identify any explicit, embodied characteristic as the symbolic mark of the curse. Thus Kant's racial invocation of this story, and the one with which we most are familiar, partakes of a more circumscribed yet widespread version of the narrative that develops with and through the modern conception of race in the 16th and 17th centuries.[46] In this retelling, those with dark skin, usually designated as the inhabitants of sub-Saharan Africa and their diasporic offspring, figure as the direct descendants of Ham or Canaan, and therefore as contemporary bearers of the original curse. This purported heritage has legitimated subjugating practices against darker-skinned peoples as divinely warranted desert while constituting the deeds of such people as innately wicked and thus in need of vigilant oversight and correction. The eventual, near-worldwide insinuation and hegemony of this racialized version into political, cultural, and religious discourses both folk and intellectual could be said, in fact, to have far eclipsed in familiarity the historically preracial biblical account, due in part to its critical role in naturalizing and thus lending normative force to scholarly and public support for grand episodes of raced-based subjugations such as the modern slave trade and colonialism.[47]

Recent historical and theological scholarship reveals a body of work anxious to clear the record on the biblical tale, particularly with respect to its racial associations. These interventions clarify dutifully that the very idea of "race" and the formation of identities based on skin color postdate the emergence of the first recorded instances of the narrative, and that, genealogically, dark-skinned inhabitants of Africa descended not from Canaan but from Cush, another of Ham's sons, repudiating therefore any association between Canaanites and blackness.[48] Further, they contend that the passage contains several flaws of fact (e.g., the reference to Ham, Noah's second of three sons, as the "youngest"), of consistency (the confusion as to whether Ham or Canaan is cursed), and, most frequently, of causal logic (why the curse affixes to Canaan and not also his brothers as well as how anyone, Canaanites or otherwise, could be punishable for a crime they did not personally commit, especially one occurring millennia prior to their existence).[49] By these and other hermeneutic challenges, recent interpreters of the passage aim emphatically to disqualify what they see as two dangerous untruths: first, that a divine, inheritable curse (and blessings) could ever attend the differentiation of primordial classifications of embodied humanity; and second, that darker-skinned peoples, especially those of African ancestry, are, or ever were, recipients of a curse that would explain or warrant their discriminatory treatment. And while a number attempt, unsuccessfully, to locate the precise historical origin of the racialized version (a search notable mostly for its own unseemly racial posturing), they nonetheless collectively aver that the "curse of Ham" as an explanation for the subjugation of past or present communities is and remains, in a word, "mythic."[50]

This summary contention appears indisputable, and therefore nothing with which one need take issue—not directly, in any case. Yet the question must be raised as to what it means to say that the curse, racialized or not, is "mythic" in the context of its relation to other passages in a theological tome that, however powerful and influential, may not itself satisfy conditions of non-myth. Are the criteria that determine the truth-value of the curse different from those that grant the truth-value of the Old Testament itself? Or is the curse illegitimate as a "false" parable, which is to say, a "mythic" myth or unauthorized overwriting? How, exactly, does the emphatic characterization of the curse as mythic bring about its eradication without a concurrent devaluation of narrative itself?

The same point is made more clearly perhaps by an additional question, one that does not depend upon a premise of biblical authenticity: why, after such extended global dominance of Western secular and scientifically driven epistemologies, does a myth of innate inferiority occasioned by divine judgment *still* require refutation? Most remarkable about the current stream of debunkings of the curse is not their fresh insights or rigor but the fact that such interventions continue unabated a history of refutations that extend as far back as the first known instances of latent racial formations and that rehearse essentially the same contrary evidence against it. Presuming the consolidation of the myth's racialization around the turn of the sixteenth century, one need not go far before encountering a staunch rebuttal to the idea that African features denote the conferral of divine punishment. In 1646, for instance, Sir Thomas Browne includes a detailed refutation of the myth as a "vulgar error" that contemporary arguments mimic almost verbatim:

> For first, if we derive the curse on Cham [Ham], or in general upon his posterity, we shall denigrate a greater part of the earth then was ever so conceived; and not only paint the Æthiopians and reputed sons of Cush, but the people also of Egypt, Arabia, Assyria and Chaldea; for by his race were these Countries also peopled. . . . Secondly, [t]he

curse . . . was not denounced upon Cham, but Canaan his youngest son. . . . [Also,] to have cursed Cham had been to curse all his posterity, whereof only but one was guilty of the fact.[51]

One better grasps how long ago this discrediting occurs when situated within other claims that Browne debunks, for example, that a diamond immersed in goat's blood becomes soft, or that one testicle yields male-producing sperm and the other female-producing sperm. Indeed while Browne harbored no doubts as to the fictitiousness of black skin as the mark of a divine curse he remained cautiously undecided about the existence of unicorns. Even Kant, as mentioned above, interrupts his praise of the white race long enough to provide a cursory rejection of the Hamitic myth as insufficient to explain the iniquity of blacks.

Continuing this pattern, during the eras of the African slave trade and bondage when recitations of the Hamitic curse frequently rebound, abolitionists just as frequently and vehemently dispute the association, such that by the mid-19th century such objections become sufficiently banal for a *New Englander* commentator to coolly remark that "it was hardly worth while" for anyone "to expose this oft-exposed fallacy, except for the purpose of illustrating the fatuity of those who defend slavery from the Bible."[52] Such exasperated sentiments regarding the (by then) shopworn repudiations of a divine curse appear to support the speculation of Werner Sollors that at this historical moment the reign of the Hamitic myth collapses, its narrative authority and value replaced by the rise of empirically based methodologies of anthropology, biology, and similar sciences, discourses with which such a transcendent-based racial reading becomes incommensurable. Sollors thus locates "the end of Ham's usefulness" in the "ascent of nineteenth-century racism, [when] the subjugation of blacks could be anchored in biology rather than in theology."[53] Concurrent with the definitive deposing of the religious by the secular in late modernity, Sollors suggests, justifications for slavery and discrimination increasingly came to favor science over scripture as the primary authoritative source of admissible evidence of racial capacities, stressing, thereby, intellectual and biological inferiority over innate immorality and criminal character.

That excoriations of this mythical curse continue into the present, however, indicates that the narrative, scripturally oriented conception of race never quite yielded to the new order of scientific reasoning. In contrast to Sollors' identification of the 19th century as that in which the scientific understanding of race replaces the mythical, and thus, subsequently, codifies deficits as biological rather than ethical, Alexander Crummell, writing in 1852, sees the former as continuing unabated: "During the long controversy upon the slavery question which has agitated Christendom, no argument has been so much relied upon, and none more frequently adduced [than blacks as inheritors of the biblical curse]. . . . And now, although both slavery and the slave trade are condemned by the general sentiment of the Christian world, yet the same interpretation is still given to this text. . . ."[54] Moreover, at the turn of the twentieth century, where Sollors identifies a hegemony of biologically sourced racial subjugation, Locke announces that the "biological meaning of race has lapsed and the sociological meaning of race is growing in significance,"[55] differentiating thereby the social from physical sciences as that which engages in a semiotics of empirical bodily traces in the context of extant myths or "beliefs" about the origin and meaning of human difference.

The claims of Sollors, Crummell, and Locke, however, can be reconciled with each other as well as with the ongoing refutations of the story of Ham by instituting two critical distinctions. First, as Crummell implies, the function of the curse, however advantageous it may have proven for the expansion and maintenance of chattel slavery, is not reducible to that role; not having been designed for this instrumental purpose (or "designed" at all), its efficacy in the public imaginary would not necessarily wane, therefore, with the extinction of the slave trade. In the same vein, as the subjugation of blacks is not the fundamental objective of the curse any more than it is of modern biology and anthropology, the purported "anchoring of racism" in the latter, as Sollors hypothesizes, would not render obsolete in itself the function of that curse. Second, although the tale of Ham as a narrative of criminal inheritability derives from theological literature, its abiding thematic structure does not originate in either Christian, Jewish, or Muslim exegeses. The dilemma of the genealogy of ethical subjectivity troubled no less, for instance, those of Ancient Greece, who engendered in turn theories that, though less tidy and concentrated than that of the biblical curse, similarly sought to reconcile the contradictions of the origin and development of embodied worth—for example, by the fraught concept of *akrasia*, or, alternatively, through contrary etiologies of virtuous character as indicating one having been "touched by the gods" (i.e., blessed or cursed) or as *techné* (embodied knowledge acquired through self-disciplined practice.)[56] The Hamitic curse, neither exclusive nor structurally indebted to monotheisms, need not suffer therefore a significant contraction of its social force due to the expanse of secularism or the intellectual marginalization of nonscientific mythic narratives. In other words, the continued survival of the curse and the frantic attempts to deactivate it despite the presumed trumping of biological over theological narratives of race attests to the long-standing quandary of embodied value (rather than religious fervor) that occasions its emergence and for which it persists in conjunction with all explanatory sciences.

One should expect, then, the continuation of ardent "demythologizing" writings on racialized versions of the biblical passage on Ham so long as race is imagined as a superficial and dispensable phenomenon that serves no structural function. Such a perception is facilitated by contemporary critics of the curse who imagine their targets as religious fundamentalists who still broadcast a doctrine of divine white racial superiority (Are their numbers so large and influence so great as to explain the persistence of the myth? Are their psyches really the final resting place of racial supremacy?). The more salient effect of such sweeping dismissals of the curse is to deem incomprehensible the logic of bodily markings as signifiers of ethical worth. The curse for them persists as a residual pre-Enlightenment atavism that awaits a succinct and rationalist "solvent" of the kind championed by Kelly Miller or Hawthorne's fictional scientist that would eradicate the everlasting stain. Yet the relentlessness of scholarly "refutations" almost four centuries later of a biblical interpretation whose explicit invocation and promotion is now largely absent leaves this corrective literature bereft of any active dissemination to correct, an absence that renders cryptic the motivation for this most recent cycle of predictable objections.[57] The determination of this literature to disable a set of relations that it believes still virulently pervasive despite its inability to provide any example of its ideological social manifestations suggests a stain so deeply woven into the fabric of existence that it has become indistinguishable from those threads themselves.

Indeed, that even the close of a metaphysics heralded by situated knowledges, hermeneutics of suspicion, and hybrid subjectivities has so far been insufficient to nullify or lift a curse that, on the face of it, is but a vague and clumsy fable, should indicate here something more philosophically elaborate and resilient than a tiresome folk prejudice. Rather than address the curse of race with respect to incontrovertible truth ("Does the curse of Ham really exist?"), historico-political origin ("Who first initiated and propagated this discriminating interpretation?"), or allegorical reference ("What genuine if banal moral truth does this tale mean to convey?"), we might better interpret it in relation to the logic by which it structures value as genealogical and inheritable, yet simultaneously as that for which the subject bears responsibility and for whom that responsibility opens up the possibility of ethical autonomy.

3

The Secret of the Mark

Creon: *I will tell you, then, what I heard from the God. King Phoebus in plain words commanded us to drive out a stain* [miasma] *from our land, a stain grown within the land; drive it out, said the God, not cherish it, till it's past cure.*

Oedipus: *What is the rite of purification? How shall it be done?*

SOPHOCLES, *Oedipus Rex*

HAWTHORNE'S CHARACTER GEORGIANA in *The Birthmark* provides the cautionary voice for the science of stain removal that becomes her husband Aylmer's deadly passion. As the story relates, his scientific triumph comes through a colossal defeat, the obsession with purifying losing him the very thing he wishes to purify. But this staging may do disservice to those waging similar battles against ethical histories of responsibility by underestimating the damage that such inherited stains can effect. A crimson blot upon the cheek like that marring Georgiana's figure, a slight aesthetic irregularity, would be evaluatively insignificant, it could be argued, compared to corporeal marks like racial features that sustain prophesies of criminal behavior. At stake in the latter are generations of peoples and communities who have suffered and continue to suffer extensive injuries as a consequence of such birthmarks. If Hawthorne's point is to encourage toleration and acceptance of stains such as Georgiana's as humanizing inscriptions, what would he make of those inheritable marks that bring about beneficent and condemnable endowments—in particular those that, as Charles Mills argues, signify one as a "subperson?"[1] Would he really advise against interventions to mitigate or eliminate, for instance, punishments that fall upon those who endure the mark of criminality? We might take some lessons from perhaps the most well-known instance of this predicament that of the curse signified by

Oedipus's "birthmark"—his fettered ankle certifying his entry into criminal bondage—that brings about a torrent of calamities upon his city, forcing it into painful submission.[2] And, similar to the Hawthorne story, the only way to eradicate this misfortune is to embark upon the systematic and logical pursuit of knowledge that leads to a discovery of the nature of the stain and, ostensibly, the means thereby for its removal.

The persistent if shortsighted drive of the scientific thrust of modernity represented by Aylmer in Hawthorne's story is anticipated in the Greek tragedy by the resolutely methodic quest of Oedipus for the origin of his city's woes, both investigators tirelessly seeking the causal force of the stain, believing that its elimination will cleanse the body to which they have pledged themselves, whether that of the betrothed or the body politic. In the Sophoclean play, this will to knowledge encounters resistance from Oedipus's mother-wife Jocasta, cast here in the role that Hawthorne's Georgiana later reprises, who begs Oedipus to cease his campaign lest he, like Aylmer, destroy that which he aims to rescue from impurity. (Why is it the figure of woman that urges the preservation of mystery over knowledge? Is not this advocacy for mystery paradoxical, offered as it is on the basis of a prophetic knowledge of the destructive truth that is sought? In both stories, the warnings of women, like those of Cassandra, go unheeded, at the cost of these women's lives.) Oedipus brushes aside Jocasta's entreaties, determined to isolate the perpetrator of the original crime, to bring to revelation the one who set the stain in motion. The solution is concealed in the "secret of [his] birth," but like all the best kept secrets, this one is hidden in plain sight; the curse does not "secret" itself away, under the skin or within the soul, but lies openly exposed on his body, its meaning available to any who know to read it.[3]

Jocasta pleads that Oedipus cease his dogged exorcism of stain removal, proposing that it is "best to live lightly, as one can, unthinkingly."[4] It is a case made strategically against history and memory but also, perhaps, against a certain practice of philosophy itself. Specifically, it disputes the idea that pursuit of knowledge invariably enables *eudaimonia*, especially when that quest ultimately leads back to the self, divulging not an impersonal "self-knowledge"— one that merely makes present the self *as* self—but instead returns the self to itself as *implicated*, as the *perpetrator* of knowledge as well as of its own compromised being. But can one afford such blitheness, such imperviousness to the lure of philosophy, when one's people are in the grip of an assault, such as that on Thebes, and refuse to trace the history of criminal responsibility to its origin? Does the spread of death, miscarriage, and disease that cripples the city—injury that may well, like the stain of race, continue indefinitely into the future—allow for a strategy of spirited, Dionysian detachment?

Perhaps the Oedipal *hamartia*—the flaw of character upon which critical interpretations of the play routinely speculate—is, as Jocasta suggests, the tenacious seeking out of the source of the stain itself rather than a disposition of *hubris* or incestuous and parricidal acts. But the problem faced by those who would discern Oedipus's precipitating misdeed turns itself on a suppositional dilemma—namely, how a "misdeed" could possibly make sense given the determining logic of a curse. More compelling than any exegetical puzzling out of his particular defect, then, is the reliance of claims of this sort upon the resurrection of Oedipus as a willful agent who retains responsibility for actions that, *by the very notion of a curse*, are performatively predetermined by heteronomous forces. On what grounds, then, can Oedipus—who, like Canaan, is the *son*, the inheritor, of the father's punishment, and thus more readily the conduit rather than cause of these misfortunes—be accused of bearing the ethical "flaw" that sets these events in motion? How can the original crime that instigates the irreversible chain of disasters "belong" to Oedipus in any properly ethical sense? Finally, what motivates this resurrection of responsibility, not as what rescues autonomy from heteronomy but rather insinuates it as the clip—the conductive transition—by which ethical subjectivity emerges *within* rather than outside of or against that determination?

An etymological translation of *hamartia*—to "miss the mark"—directs one to look not for a causal deed or vice to which this tragedy is beholden but instead to Oedipus's "missing" of his own bodily mark or signature, the scar denoting his inheritance of a history of responsibility that belies his self-identification as a "stranger to the story [and] stranger to the deed."[5] Indeed Oedipus' early speculations are rebuffed by the old seer Teiresias as "words [that] miss the mark."[6] His dawning recognition of the curse is but recognition of his embeddedness in ethical ancestry, a relatedness that unfolds not through patient and methodic exfoliation of the past but in the accumulation of social testimonies—as Fanon relates, the "legends, stories, [and] histories"—that continually overwrite and overtake each other. In that respect, one would need to reverse the premise of those who take the notion of "character flaw" to designate a defect in an otherwise unmarked and fully virtuous will to indicate instead the stain or scar by which one becomes an integrated "character" in a historical narrative. The "flaw" of Oedipus's fettered ankle, like Georgiana's crimson stain, is not an accidental physical feature that produces the individual as an alienated singularity but a birthmark that brings him into embodied subjectivity and accordingly into the "moral fold." No one, it becomes clear, is a "stranger to the story" of ethical descent—to stand outside of or prior to the mark is to be without history or materiality. This mark that reveals the subject to itself as perpetrator enables a revelation not of the precipitating crime but rather of the fortune or destiny of its bearer, one for which the subject persists in its responsibility. Thus the comprehension and justification of Oedipus's ultimate suffering no more depends upon an accurate discernment of his specific vice than, as will be shown shortly, the legitimacy of Ham's curse depends upon the similar formulation of a corresponding, identifiable crime. In the cacophony of voices hoping to alight upon and finally speak the unspeakable crime, the mark itself is missed.

Thus the Oedipal challenge replays itself in the modern confrontation of the curse of race: on the one hand, crises occasioned by the crushing and exorbitant dues the curse collects, whether in the guise of ancient plagues or racial fevers, compel investigation of the ethical stain. At the same time, the counsel of Jocasta and her reincarnate Georgiana urges resistance to the universalist gesture that would aim at washing away all traces of the stain and thereby seek to convert this reconnaissance of the logic of cursed inheritance into a program of eradication or removal. Without privileging one consideration over the other, a precondition may be advanced that any intervention toward a curse should include, at the least, a fuller grasp of how ethical inheritances conduct themselves through conduits such as community and race, what comprises the procedure of such transfers, and how the physics of their movement might be discerned—how, in short, an inheritance becomes "cursed" or "blessed," and, correlatively, how any punishment could be enacted in perpetuity. To enter this pursuit is to do so with awareness, however incomplete, of the likelihood that the path into the scene of the crime is bound to end in self-incrimination.

A Confederation of Feints

Formally, the biblical passage of the Hamitic curse may be parsed as two entwined narratives: first, that of a transgression and its correction, and second, that of the postdiluvial commencement of human civilization. The narrative of transgression relates Ham's perpetration of a violation, the exact nature of which goes unspecified. That it is serious is not immediately obvious; only the pronouncement of the curse allows one to comprehend the offense as grave; and yet, the curse befalls someone (Canaan) seemingly unrelated to the events that transpire. This morality tale or scene of crime and punishment comprises one thread of the passage. The second entails Noah's issuing of declarations forecasting the fates of his three sons and their families ("Blessed be the LORD, The God of Shem . . . May God enlarge Japheth, And let him dwell in the tents of Shem; And let Canaan be his servant."). Because at this point in Genesis all other humanity has been destroyed, it is from these "families" that the entire world will be repopulated. The race of man begins here anew. Affirming his sons as the sole progenitors of all future humanity, Noah enacts the reemergence of history along three distinct ancestral lines. The passage as a whole thus delivers an "ethical" narrative that merges with, if not generates, a second "genealogical" narrative. Already the modern framework of an ethical anthropology is prefigured, though in more explicit if less proficient terms. These backstage theatrics that precede and initiate the raising of the curtain on the stage of history are those by which the principal "characters" will make their first appearance as *already differentiated* by the comparative worth of their futural line of descendants. The show begins upon this casting of characters that needs only an infraction, trivial or severe, to trigger the formidable diasporic dissemination of humankind.

By some heightened engine has this story—inordinately brief, confusingly inconsistent, and clumsily fabricated—replicated itself, much like a curse, in a bizarre perpetuity extending well beyond any particular theological context into modern and contemporary secular discourses social and scientific. And while fairly skeletal, the passage yet possesses an unusual anatomy, the dissection of which yields a rudimentary architecture for apprehending the articulation of ethically embodied beings. At the risk of reviving this "not-yet" corpse whose eternal death is universally sought and frequently declared, "Let us clench our teeth," as Nietzsche says, and descend into this collection of textual bones, the ossuarium of our decaying myth.[7]

The story of Ham effects a confederation of feints that simulate the appearance of origin. These deceptive reflections do not fabricate a starting point of human history in positing a first presence—a being, a deed, a word. To do so would put the story at risk of being itself the original crime, as the active installation of a primary falsehood. More importantly, the putting forth of the first determinate would be to produce the terms and ground for its opposition and thus undoing. Hence, the passage does not open through *logos* but rather in the ostensible reflection of its effects. The story, that is, summons the commencing event of history as a negative space circumscribed by its consequences both immediate and distal. These effects mean to function, in that sense, as the "developed" or colored image against which the instigating crime appears in relief. Yet these trace elements, the manifest reactions and responses of which the narrative itself consists, are but endlessly mirroring echoes of representations without any precipitating "presence." Via this structural circuitry, neither closed nor infinite, unravels the tale of inheritable ethical ancestry.

The Hamitic passage takes advantage of its essential paratextuality—specifically, as what takes place prior to the recommencement of the proper text of history through the formal ordination (Noah's pronouncement) of communal genealogy. The crime of Ham joins together through a breaking apart the first and second instances of humanity, that which as paratextual exists within and external to the two evolutionary successions—Adam and Eve's expulsion from the garden of Eden, the immediate result of which is Eve's reiterative and reproductive "expulsion" of humanity through the folds of her womb (those who will be destroyed by the flood), and Noah's ordination that metonymically converts his three "individual" sons into distinct genealogical lines. Hence the passage composes an interlude between the postlapsarian and postdiluvial movements of historical generation. In this liminality, neither a fully worlded nor utopian state, occurs the inaugural offense. This transitional scene that takes place in the non-space of history is accordingly built around an inaccessible cavity: the unarticulated (non) event that transpires in Noah's tent. Appropriately, then, the pre-text to the "real" origin of humankind emerges from a nontextualized lacuna, a potent yet evacuated space in the myth itself that reflects its indeterminate formal status in the larger story of Genesis. Thus the crime that explains and justifies the ethical differentiation by which Noah's sons emerge on the historical stage as already individuated, separate "characters" is not what happens *in* this narrative non-space but *as* this non-space itself—that is, as content that is *compositional* rather than evidentiary.

This is the first fake or illusion; the passage contrives to make the reader a backstage witness to the violation of all violations as a concrete happening, insinuating that by doing so it already goes beyond its narrative obligation, showing more than it should by divulging the catalyst that initiates and propels what is "not yet" the corpus of history. Yet the text (in truth, a pre-textual pretext) itself illuminates not this inceptional force but rather another set of curtains—the screening flaps of Noah's tent, a partition behind which the causal abomination is purportedly both committed and "known." The story thus presents as a revelation the thing it cannot reveal, making the reader complicit in a pact of shared knowledge whose content is the sacred preservation of ignorance, the cognizance of a crime apprehended, to invoke James Baldwin, through the evidence of things not seen.[8]

This simulated pre-text solicits readers as joining Noah and his sons in "knowledge" of the crime, the content of which it insinuates as readily supplied by the reader's own intuitive powers. This omission, according to subsequent interpretations, will be vindicated, as discussed later, as either incidental or as critically necessary. For now, one need recognize only that this feint subsidizes that contoured absence as one that *could be* made present, that which would "restore" to the narrative its internal coherence as well as its original ethical meaning. This intimated possibility of a resolution, Werner Sollors suggests, largely drives the exegetical compulsion to prove that the passage suffers a textual lack: "No matter what Noah's curse meant, the feeling among readers was that there *had* to be more to Ham's transgression than was told in Genesis."[9] But why must there be more? What about this story seems to obligate as the first and *ethical* interpretive act the fixing of the named identity of the crime and thus its immediate rewriting? The need to assuage this unsettling "feeling" of textual insufficiency as structuring in advance the "meaning" of the passage indicates that at stake here is not the *particular* moral system that the passage purportedly generates but the desire for value *as* systematic, or more precisely, as a systematic generated from a foundational *and* representational origin. *What* name the crime carries is thus less critical than that it *have* a name by which it can sustain identifiable properties and qualities. That the violation "have a body," as it were, becomes key not simply for comprehending the Hamitic crime but crucially for comprehension of criminality itself. As what gives crime its name—a name that need encompass all potential future misdeeds—this founding offense, like the human stem form of natural anthropology, functions as the prototype of criminal potentiality by which all manifest and thus lesser crimes—"deviances" from the doubly pure and deviant "original" transgression—acquire their comparative worth.

The Deed as Definition

All previous exegetes of the passage have accepted its interpretation to be predicated on the naming of the transgression, if only to categorize its basic nature and relative severity. In this they succumb not only to the compositional feint of the narrative but also to a propagating magic that would draw something out of nothing. The myth succeeds as a concentrated vessel of fantasy for the same reason—a "crime" is snatched thus from Noah's tent that does not issue from the nonspace of criminality but is rather what has been placed there in advance. Accounts of both kinds—those that reproduce the structure of criminality in the crime itself and those that "find" there the enactment of a primal evil or taboo, the prohibition of which founds community—afford an instructive apprenticeship to this metaphysical shell game.

The former explanatory reading of the myth belongs mostly to recent and modest interpretations that hold that Ham erred either by witnessing his father naked or by sharing this information with his brothers—committing therefore a scopophilic or discursive misdeed—or, alternatively, by failing to hide his father's nakedness.[10] The core of each of these misdemeanors is defined as the serious yet utterly conventional offense of "disobedience," a transgressive banality even in its most felonious expressions of patricide and regicide. This crime of "disobedience" houses a wide breadth of infractions from the superficial to the capital to encompass a violation both inexcusable yet inevitable for "humans." This definition asserts merely that disobedience violates an absolute moral authority or rule; it is thus, at heart, an analytic proposition that restates the nature of "criminality" itself, for no crime exists that is not in essence disobedient. "Disobedience" thereby unveils nothing of the interior of such criminality, referring not to a particular crime but only to the mechanistic possibility of specific misdeeds; it merely affirms, that is, ethical subjectivity as originating through the clip—the rupture from and thus instituted relation to a differentiated yet simultaneously instantiated value. Consequently, the reading of Ham's crime as "disobedience" effectively mimics the folding of the inaugurating violation back into the origin of ethical commencement whereby the subject emerges through a defiling stain that, as *also* the universal condition of its formation, forecloses from the start any undefiled existence that criminality *could* stain. Put otherwise, defining this violation as quintessentially rulebreaking or affective disrespect of the force that imparts and authorizes the rule—God, rational agents, the city/state, etc.—promulgates as the substantive transgression merely the space of criminality that the narrative already outlines.

To posit the father, in this case Noah, as the governing representative of the inviolable code anthropologically situates, in these more modern interpretations, philosophical ethics through the trope of family relations and discourses of "law." In this more secular landscape, then, Ham's crime violates not any particular law but law itself, producing the paradox of the indefinable crime that defines all crime. If such an offense were in fact prohibited *by* the law, it would thereby take place *within* law rather than through and against it. Parricide, incest, thievery, mail fraud—any of these could be said to found *a* law, even an entire set of codes, yet this construction already misleads by suggesting intrinsic meanings to these deeds that only the prohibitional command and nominalization can provide. "Murder" and "incest," for example, are thus conceivable as such only as what the law has already thematized as perceptive possibilities. If, therefore, the law does not merely judge these acts as crimes but simultaneously and actively "founds" them, this could occur only via the identification of phenomena as criminal within an existing economy of value. Moreover, even if a crime or its anterior prototypes *could* generate directly a law it still could not found *the* law: that which remains, despite its post-Hegelian popularity, a vast yet shallow procedural technology whose manipulability—that by which one could think and act "outside" or against the law—confirms it as an inessential apparatus rather than the worldly expression of value.

The crime of Ham does not receive from the law a name upon its commission, but, if anything, disputes the ghostly origin from which those names purportedly and solemnly issue. The transgression does not violate a rule, formula, or principle but rather strikes at the very source or possibility of rulemaking, threatening the assemblage of the law-producing machine. In this respect, Ham represents an acephalous or perhaps nonphallic power enabled not by the discipline and order (and neither thereby resistance and subversion) said to fund the law but by features of invocation, arbitrariness, and presentiment that comprise an "anti-power" alternatively known as fate, sorcery, or black magic—means by which power is not so much redirected as it is enchanted in its effects. In a drunken display of indiscretion, the law, like Noah, lies exposed; but this revelation in which there is nothing to reveal is necessary for its acquisition of a "body." The stain of value, that is, generates discovery of the "body of law" in its naked or pure state of "natural law"—a nakedness covered and defended by its progeny who must invoke routinely that unstained purity as the law's original and authoritative subjectively constituting force.

The Deed as Evidentiary

If reading Ham's crime as a first-order human disobedience reenacts rather than illuminates the narrative's sleight of hand, an alternative collation of interpretations posits the crime as the exceptional deviance of a unique individual rather than a universal violation. These allegations, belonging mostly to the earliest recorded set of explanations, speculate Ham to have engaged his father sexually, either in fellatio or anal intercourse, with the occasional charges of incestuous relations with his mother, miscegeny with a descendant of the "marked" Cain, or bestiality with various animals on the ark.[11] Related conjectures aver that Ham renders Noah impotent, often imagining a violent scenario of castration upon the sleeping father. In these depictions the criminal deed is explicit, extreme, and impassioned.[12] Contemporary texts categorize these medieval charges of Ham's rape of Noah as "homosexual" while characterizing his fornication with his mother as "incestuous." The anachronistic "homosexual" here implies not a "family" crime but one outside all relations save gender, thus posing a special threat to the future of human history and inheritance. This presumptive incompatibility of homosexuality and genealogy—which reflects, again, a *contemporary* understanding of these centuries-old recitations—is thus analogous to these same texts' rejection of criminal inheritability, both of which—homosexuality and criminality—are imagined to encompass intrinsically their own compensatory punishment as self-contained, nongenerative, nontransferable, and thus, ultimately, self-destructive. Such synoptic opiates offer a moral failsafe in their fantastical assurance that homosexuality and criminality end with the deviant subject's death as what cannot carry over into succeeding generations. The sexual deviant thus characterizes an ahistorical and always arbitrary mutation of its natural origin, in this case the heterosexual drive, insofar as the presumptive nonreproducibility of homosexuality means that the homosexual exists always in isolation, unable to establish any legitimate genealogical (i.e., kinship) relations. "Moral heterosexuality," taken as what creates and sustains life, is immortalized in contrast through the presumption *of inheritance*—that is, as the connective link that holds together not merely one generation to the next but the entirety of "humanity" as itself a coherent genealogy. Such are the modern investments in reconfiguring, then disputing, the arguably more ambitious and serious anterior accounts.[13]

Hypotheses of extravagant scenes of sexual violence may appear dubious in their extremity yet their graphicness is justified by a demand for a crime sufficiently symmetrical and extraordinary to warrant an equally decadent curse.[14] This obligation is recognized as well by those who envision the crime as that of disobedience, which remains open to extreme forms and, as the generic form of all crime, does not oppose these more lurid portrayals. The salient distinction between these two interpretative approaches hinges, therefore not on any degree of extravagance but on the premise that crimes of sexual violence leave evidentiary stains or scars—a criminal writing whose legibility survives the absence of the perpetrator. This detail, though not mentioned in any of the thorough compilations of historical exegeses of this passage, would seem nevertheless crucial for making sense of another curious omission of the biblical passage at issue: "Speculation by biblical exegetes as to what happened to the drunken, naked Noah in the tent has been whetted by the enigmatic statement that Noah, upon awakening from his stupor, 'knew what his youngest son had done unto him.' Apparently, more than Ham's voyeurism is involved, but precisely what is not amplified by the narrator."[15] The problem (and potential) of the unseen gaze of the voyeur as well as the words of the storyteller is that they leave behind no criminal trace, a central element of the narrative for which such scopophilic and discursive misdeeds of seeing Noah's nakedness and publishing it to his brothers cannot account. For Noah "knows" the crime committed against him not through its being conveyed to him by others (a retelling that would comprise a sub-narrative within the story itself) but as an immediacy that he grasps "upon awakening."

What generates Noah's knowledge that a crime has "happened" at all? Such immediate cognizance requires Noah's recognition of an alteration between the state of affairs prior to his unconsciousness and that attending his regained awareness. Upon awakening, Noah perhaps grasps the covering of his body as not of his own volition (in the unlikely case that he remembers in what fashion he passed out), yet this addition indicates no obvious malfeasance. Noah revives alone, in isolation, the perpetrator long since vanished; for all this, he "knows" that something has changed in this tented dwelling: his place of abode, the seat of power, the paternal house, the manor of civilization—now, suddenly, a crime scene. This crime goes unwitnessed by Noah but not therefore undiscovered. But to what could this knowledge be attributed other than an evidentiary mark, a remnant that, more than clue or data, illuminates an entire system of embodied significations that originate through this valuated deed? The early hypotheses of Ham's sexual contact with and/or castration of Noah, although too circumscribed to actuate criminal genealogy alone, nevertheless provide this catalytic element in their speculations by insinuating a material trace by which Noah gleans the alteration the crime effects. As with Oedipus, Noah must apprehend here the scarring remainder of the past as the stain that betrays what has been done to him. He awakens to an already executed deed; the violation, the forging of the blemish or wound, the alteration that cannot be undone, is complete. In his inebriated slumber, he misses his own marking; yet while not consciously "present" at the formation of the stain, Noah, unlike Oedipus, perceives it instantly.

The premise of the evidentiary trace does not vouch for allegations of Ham castrating or sodomizing his father. One need not presume stains of semen or blood to render the dynamic of the mark; all that is necessary here, following these interpretations, is a "carnal" knowledge that, while forwarded most frequently as a sexual intimacy, signifies at its most basic embodied self-consciousness as a function of evaluative knowledge. These interpretations thus read a materiality in Noah's acquisition of the knowledge of good and evil, wherein what becomes central in his realization of what his son "has done to him" is not the violation itself but that fact that it was done to a fleshly being of appetites, passions, and pleasures, and that this being is *himself*. Noah divines in that moment, then, not merely the abstract state that "a crime has been committed" but a corporeal self-identity that can become the wounded *object* of vice and immorality.

Ethical Knowledge as Carnal

The tripartition of body, value, and knowledge that characterizes modern thought estranges these relations so as to appear nonintersecting and incommensurable. But such ready compartmentalization of epistemic and evaluative knowledge seems not to undergird premodern accounts, where the business of discovering knowledge depends in part on establishing just these relations. Corporeality, in these cases, is not self-evidently a *thing*—that is, a materiality no different from any other object in the world that can be bracketed therefore as one of multiple and indiscriminate potential sources of phenomenal input. The indissociability of the epistemological, evaluative, and material is expressed in these analyses as the *carnal*, where "carnal knowledge" indexes simultaneously: the experience of a primal violation, recognition of the self as "flesh," awareness of the natural evaluative relations of beings and things, the translation of intuited percepts into knowledge as *ethical*, and the apprehension of a dynamics of secrecy and disclosure by which all meanings and values abide. Furthermore, carnal knowledge signifies the discovery of one's location within an inheritable line through which this knowledge passes, a knowledge that apprehends its own comparative quality and distinction from other constitutive ethical genealogies. Carnal knowledge, in these discourses, is the *only* mode of knowledge available—there is no other. The comparative inattention by modern readers to the Hamitic crime and the narrative feints it executes indicates less a shift from the religious to the secular than, as the exegeses of the crime offered by Saint Augustine and Philo illustrate, a shift in the logic of ethical knowledge that leaves contemporary interpreters of embodied value bereft of a mechanism even to venture a meaningful analysis of such formations.

St. Augustine admits to the reader straightaway that the real story of the Hamitic crime goes untold, though not for him because of any textual omission but rather because the tale and its elements are primarily "prophetic"—prefiguring the rise of the Church, specifically, but also relaying a divine message that does not emerge from a resolution of the text's literal criminal dilemma. Instead, the truth of the story belongs to its "hidden meanings" that one must uncover through symbolic analysis: "[T]he vineyard planted by Noah, the drunkenness resulting from its fruit, the nakedness of the sleeping Noah, and all the other events recorded in this story, were laden with prophetic meanings and covered with prophetic veils."[16] Nothing in the story is what it appears; at the same time, everything that the story *is*, the passage contains already—not as a cogent, linear narrative but as fragmentary pieces of evidence (i.e., clues, traces, signs, etc.). Thus the primordial crime does not represent for him a missing piece that would restore coherence and closure to the passage, insofar as all of the elements of the story—the vineyard, inebriation, nakedness, et al.—are themselves component pieces that have no uninterpreted significance. They are, he writes, "figures of speech known as 'part' for 'whole;'" where the meaning of the "whole" of that synecdoche has not yet come into historical existence.[17] The story of the crime is composed for Augustine, then, through textual marks that must be interpreted figuratively and proleptically, with an eye toward "the posterity of the sons" who will bring this prophetic inheritance into being. Hence what the passage hides it hides in plain sight; there are no missing words that would more effectively realize the crime—the concealment belongs to language itself as signs that, like Oedipus' mark, exist from the beginning, but whose meaning stays veiled until their anticipatory historical fruition has come to pass—that moment when, Augustine writes, "the things that were concealed have been abundantly revealed."[18]

Augustine places little emphasis on Ham's commission of the crime, describing Ham as the sinner "who had not covered the nakedness of his sleeping father, but instead had called attention to it."[19] Expounding briefly a bit later, he contrasts Ham's "external" dissemination of what occurs in the tent as a narrative in which Ham does "not understand . . . the sounds [he] utters." Ham speaks, but knows not of what he speaks—he is a mimic, iterating not lies but symbols and marks the prophetic meanings to which he has no access. The significance of the passage for Augustine lies more in Noah's transformation in becoming "drunk" and "naked": the moment, Augustine writes, in which "was derived the flesh," which is to say, that reveals Noah to himself as corporeal. This self-consciousness borne of the "flesh" designates for Augustine a "carnality" encompassing both the mental and physical. Opposing the idea that one could have a life of the "spirit" outside of carnality, Augustine asserts that the origination of the "flesh" is nothing other than the birth of "man." In making this clarification Augustine offers his theory of prophetic synecdoche: "It is on these lines that we interpret this passage, 'And the Word become flesh,' that is, 'became man' ... and similarly we have the 'whole from part' figure when 'flesh' is mentioned, and 'man' is meant."[20] Accordingly, carnal knowledge does not indicate the dualistic opposition of material to cognitive knowledge; citing St. Paul, Augustine affirms that this carnal self-consciousness reflects as much the "faults of the mind" as those of the body.[21] More precisely, "flesh" indicates not the "embodied" quality of the mind but, as fundamentally figurative, signifies all of humankind in its full scope of psychic processes.

Although Augustine harbors no doubt that this carnality expresses the evaluative failure or "fault" of humans, he notes that the "corruption of the body, which weighs down the soul, is not the cause of the first sin but its punishment." The *cause* or crime itself, Augustine thus implies, instigates and precedes human nature as embodied self-awareness and as "flesh." Because for Augustine all bodies are corrupted, there can be no embodied "human nature" outside of value and criminality. Rather, he remarks, human nature refers to the corruption of the good expressed as a "blemish" or "wound," anticipating already modern ethical subjectivity as stained and scarred from the start.[22] Accordingly, prior to the onset of the crime that arouses his carnality, Noah constitutes neither human being nor soulless body but a pure potentiality symbolizing its future incarnation—a "figure of speech" for which the "word" has not yet become "flesh." The "Noah" who plants, drinks, and lies uncovered in his tent remains a prophetic trope up until the transformative violation.

On this account, ethical knowledge surfaces as carnal self-awareness, where carnal knowledge designates both sensitization of the flesh or appetites as well as recognition of that sensitization; as knowledge, it attests to an affective grasping of the material self that, like a fixed stain, cannot be forgotten or unlearned.[23] Noah's awakening thus simultaneously signifies his enlightenment, for in that acquired self-consciousness is disclosed materiality as itself ethical—that is, a comprehension of the natural ethical order of the world. Ethical knowledge, for Augustine—rather than an epistemology that divulges matrices of fundamental violations or tables of commandments, principles, rules, and formulas—expresses itself as a semiotics of value within which phenomena appear as differentiated not only in kind but in worth, or more precisely, differentiated in kind as a function of worth.

Ethical Knowledge as Silence

Philo of Alexandria, the first-century scholar who provides early Christianity its Greek philosophical justification, declares this onset of value-differentiated knowledge a mode of "gnosis" by which he affirms Noah's transformation as occasioned through his grasping the vast geography of good and evil.[24] Upon awakening, Philo holds, Noah seizes ethical knowledge as who he *is* as embodied and thus what relations he bears to others; he then can unleash the curse as a means of ushering into existence the proper and organic relations between beings. In this respect, the curse for Philo obtains not as negative retribution or sovereign restitution but as a creative actualization of the corresponding arrangements through which entities realize their true natures in virtue of their evaluative organization. Noah's imprecation, that is, does not impose upon "neutral" genealogies an arbitrary ethical ranking wrought in a fit of blind anger, as is generally assumed; on the contrary, it dictates through recitation divinely established distinctions conjugated by evaluative difference. This articulation of hierarchical lineages does not bear upon them from the outside but gives rise to them through a definition of their innate and comparatively qualitative essences, affirming both that it *is* the case that certain lineages compare unfavorably to others *and* that this relative inferiority governs the identity of each.

In Philo's interpretation, Noah's soul is what grasps knowledge as *gnosis*; upon returning to sobriety, his soul achieves "clarity of vision" and "at once perceives"—clearly and distinctly—the wickedness that transpired in the tent. Such mental sobriety for Philo accompanies a higher form of a physical sobriety—that which excludes disease, the passions, and improper nutrition—and thus readies the soul's capacity for "sober understanding," a state of pure reflection on ideal forms unimpeded by "[external] objects of sense."[25] According to Philo, then, the soul ascertains the proper evaluative and natural relation of things in the world prior to and apart from intuitions of those phenomena; only when "aroused" from this contemplative state to one of decision-making—that is, when awakened into action by some external malfeasance—does evaluative knowledge or gnosis actualize as deeds.[26] For the sake of retaining ethical knowledge as prior to action, then, Philo must break into the Hamitic narrative to secure a space for this purely contemplative state between the moment of Noah's awakening and his apprehension of the natural ethical order of the world.

The logical problem of this proposed intercession is again that of the hypothetical "not-yet" as a sanctum of formal and interior self-reflection untainted by "external" impressions. Philo resolves this by holding that although Noah remains cognitively unaware of the crime's commission during his sleep his soul remains awake and absorbs all that transpires, knowledge that then pierces the mind upon regaining consciousness: "when the mind becomes sober, it must follow that it at once perceives the former doings [of Ham] . . . which in its drunken state it was incapable of comprehending."[27] As a result of its ethical arousal, Noah awakens into a mode of consciousness that, from this point on, necessarily formulates its experiences and past memories evaluatively. This conjecture allows Philo to argue that Noah "knows" what Ham did to him when he awakens insofar as, prior to this ethical illumination, Noah's perceptions were distorted and "drunken" representations that, lacking the form of value, could not constitute true knowledge. On the one hand, then, criminal knowledge—that is, entry into the semiotics of value—"must" transparently invest itself "at once" and "instantaneously" to consciousness. On the other hand, such an entrance must be breached by the interlude of the not-yet of nonevaluative contemplation if self-consciousness is to precede the embodied awareness that implicates it from the start within these evaluative relations. Thus while immediate ethical knowledge is essential for ascertaining and distinguishing phenomena in their individuated and proper relations in the world, its status as pure contemplation is nevertheless dependent upon an evidentiary trace of a "crime"—an already evaluative mark—that thereby contaminates from the start any possible inuslarity.

The contradiction persists into Philo's articulation of Ham's specific transgression: that Ham would "loudly proclaim what ought to be passed in silence, [and] expose to public vew what might well be hidden in the secrecy of the home and never pass the boundaries of [his] inward thoughts."[28] This reading of Ham's crime anticipates Augustine's interpretation of it as a discursive misdeed. Critically, however, Augustine's characterization of Ham's crime as that of mimicry means that it cannot serve as the first or primal violation that forges the scene into which Noah emerges from his slumber. But if not Ham's, then, what criminal offense sparks Noah's carnality and, thereby, the emergence of "flesh" as "mankind"? While Philo, like Augustine, finds Ham to transgress by immediately "publicizing" after leaving the tent the ethical knowledge that transforms both he and Noah "inside," he does not thereby exempt Ham from instigating this carnal criminality. Like Augustine, he does not refute that which Ham relates as false or non-knowledge but objects to its acquisition through an unauthorized transgression of "boundaries." Having slipped into Noah's tent—an entrance into discourse and representation— Ham is confronted by a scene that, once perceived, he ostensibly should have mentally shunned, preventing it from becoming actual *knowledge.* Instead, Philo claims, this stained knowledge becomes conducted through him, his father, and out to the world. Indeed, depending on how one reads Philo's complaint, this carnal knowledge should never have transitioned in Ham from perception to self-consciousness (i.e., passed from the exterior realm of the senses into the reflective interior) or been broadcast to others (crossed from reflective cognizance into that of circulating signs). In either case, criminal knowledge finds in Ham a virally contagious host.

But while Augustine fails to identify the crime that does instigate carnal knowledge, Philo's story configures that crime as an effect without cause. Reminiscent of the obligation to ethical ignorance implied by the Edenic prohibition of knowledge of good and evil, Philo's exegesis similarly erects as a "boundary" not to be "crossed," the very knowledge of which forges a "silent" break or rupture between (preethical) perception and ethical self-consciousness. His faulting of Ham's blathering indiscretion thus cautions the reader in like fashion; to cognize the crime properly requires a noiseless approach to it through a kind of peripheral apprehension that never comes into actual contact with the center of consciousness and thus is neither acknowledged nor explicitly narrated. Philo thus perpetuates the first feint of the narrative by rationalizing his omission of the phenomenal content of Ham's narrative to his brothers as evidence of his (Philo's) own performance of sacred silence. That the Hamitic passage insinuates the crime as what the reader can intuit becomes in Philo's exegesis the very condition and obligation of ethical readership: for the text to narrate this crime would be to reenact that indiscretion; the reader, therefore, *must* intuit this knowledge not only because the text would, in that retelling, betray its authority to share such knowledge, but also because the reader *ought* do no more than *intuit* the origin of evil, and resist thereby the crossing of that boundary into a knowledge still tainted by its generative criminality. The crime, literally, must go without saying, and it is as a pact of silence kept with the passage that Philo would justify his own refusal to cross this boundary into representation.

Philo's interpretation of Ham's crime as initiating and illegitimately simulating the formal structure of ethical knowledge makes it a seemingly discursive rather than evidentiary or material violation, yet such discursivity remains in his version contingent on the embodied quality of evaluative deeds. Recall that Ham transgresses here not by telling a falsehood but by sharing ethical knowledge that, while "true," is nevertheless not to be disclosed *to* or *by* him. That this knowledge and its differentiating enactment of valuated identities are not intrinsically bad is demonstrated by Noah's repetition of Ham's "criminal" action: upon being "disclosed" to him, Noah similarly exits the tent and immediately "shares" through his ordination what has been illuminated through the crime. Noah's postrevelatory entry into discourse—his own "public" enunciation that brings about the true and proper relations between bodies in the world—signifies doctrinal rather than inadmissible language, despite being sourced by the same criminality that Ham dishonorably allows to penetrate him. The qualitative distinction between the historically founding narrative and the criminally unrepeatable deceit, then, turns on the evaluative "body" from which it emanates. Were the violation merely discursive it would be so independent of the means of its transmission; Noah would have committed thereby the same criminal act as Ham. But consistent with the hypothesis that the definition and nature of any discrete act remains indissociable from the evaluatively embodied context of its performance, the criminal distinction between Noah and Ham that Philo sustains is far from independent of the value of those figures. Stated from the parapet of ethical late modernity: if the descendants of Ham prefigure what will come to be "black bodies" it is not as a consequence of that lineage being stained through a primordial violation but in its coming to occupy a carnality criminally predisposed to exceedingly "loud" exclamations—an ancestry capable only of enunciating their own volubility, where what is shouted slips already voided into a inaccessible continent.

Secret Passages

In the work of St. Augustine and, more prominently, that of Philo, self-conscious recognition emerges in criminality, a criminality that disseminates carnal knowledge. Accordingly, this criminality risks thereby the dissemination of speech that threatens the implication and infection of others as potential listeners and speakers—those incorporated into the ethical by loudly exclaiming into a void or by passing in silence that which goes without saying. It is in this context that the biblical story of Ham stages its transmission of ethical knowledge to the reader prophylactically, protecting it from miasmic consummation by inducting it into a pact of the silent unsaid. The following chapter explains how this criminal semiotics instigates ethical history; for now, however, one last orchestration of the first feint awaits—one that prophetically implicates the biblical narrative itself.

Philo's interpretation of the Hamitic passage aims to model the silence by which one properly enters the pact of ethical knowing that allows cognizance of the stain without becoming stained oneself. But among whom is this hushed complicity demanded? Need everyone within this evaluative community share this "secret knowledge," or is this a pact that initiates only the select few? Note that the pact of silence shrouding the narrative feint of a primordial crime does not designate an *aphilosophical* ignorance. Even the ignorance advocated earlier by Jocasta and Georgiana presumes a witting, philosophical savvy as to the nature of the pact and reasons for hiding what does not exist. Philo is himself complicit in this ethical sleight of hand that fabricates an ignorance as if there is something (the inaugural, foundational crime) about which to be ignorant, thereby producing the illusion of an a priori transgression. The narrative of Ham functions then to reframe as "unspeakable" what is in fact metaphysically and logically untheorizable— that is, the first crime-in-itself—and makes that silence "golden" as a witting virtue of self-discipline. The strategy bears sharp resemblances to a discussion in Plato's *Republic*, one that appears, at first, equally as explicit and unapologetic about the pact of secret knowledge as an active deceit necessary for the structural emergence of value (in this case as "justice"). Indeed, Philo's overt dependence on Plato's explication of this deceit in his reading of the Hamitic story also illustrates the mechanism of inheritance by which the pact of silence—and thus the strange confluence of storytelling, criminality, and carnality—moves across individuals and generations.

The *Republic*'s proffering of this deceit arises in the drafting of the educational program for the ostensible philosopher-guardians of the just city, when Socrates frets that the standard diet of fables and myths as the first stories consumed by children will corrupt their souls, being tales that routinely provide "a bad image of what the gods and heroes are like . . ."[29] For Socrates, defining a just city has come to depend upon the worth of such exemplars insofar as he has hung the possibility of civil justice on a tenuous analogy with the "just individual." For this reason he must govern the translation of civil justice into embodied characteristics, substituting for the definition of justice the identification of *just bodies*—bodies he defines as incapable therefore of performing vice.[30] Hence, Socrates must invest in the claim that such archetypes of virtue do exist, a commitment that obliges a procedure of stain removal upon those gods and heroes whom he recruits for this purpose. Thus his concern must go deeper than the worry about the "bad images" of gods and heroes in myths and legends; first and foremost, he must affirm that such unflattering portraits of gods and heroes are *false*. Socrates accordingly delivers the remarkable declaration in which narrative, value, and representation converge in a manner later internalized by monotheism and modern philosophy—that "a god must always be represented as he is," a claim he then syllogistically completes in the assertion that "a god is really good ... and must be described as such."[31] Tales of the improprieties of gods, he stresses, *must* be false insofar as gods and heroes are incapable of "mislead[ing] ... in words and deeds."[32] Such stories thus constitute character defamations of those a priori "good" bodies, becoming implicitly for Socrates the *first* crime.

Accordingly, the obligation to "supervise the storytellers" becomes the inaugural practical imperative for producing the just city—a supervision that will constitute the crux of this aspirational justice. Yet the objective of that supervision, it will turn out, will not be to filter and eliminate fiction from fact, untruth from truth, as Socrates initially implies, but to ensure that certain myths—or, more precisely, what is ethically unrepresentable and unknowable—be presented as unspeakable ethical knowledge. While referring to the myth of the god Uranus' castration by his Titan son Cronos— a scene of phallic and paternal vulnerability strikingly similar to the early exegeses of Noah's encounter with Ham—Socrates provides a major caveat to, without actually recanting, his adamant rejection of criminality by a god or hero. He abruptly concedes that the stories he has scorned heretofore as perjuries *may* be true, yet grants this hypothetical possibility on the formation of a pact of secrecy about such crimes from which certain storytellers are implicitly excluded: "But even if [such criminality] were true, it should be passed over in silence ... [and] if it has to be told, only a very few people— pledged to secrecy ... should hear it." He then explains why, outside of this ruling coterie, a lie about the untarnished virtue of gods and heroes must continue to be told to youth as well as to the general citizenship: "Falsehood, though of no use to the gods, is useful to people as a form of drug ... [and] if it is appropriate for anyone to use falsehoods for the good of the city ... it is the rulers. But everyone else must be kept away from them."[33]

Had the nature and origin of justice been resolved prior to this, one might study this falsehood as strictly a question of moral conduct (e.g., whether justice legitimates or even requires that those in power sometimes disseminate inaccurate information to the public). Because, however, there is as of yet no definition of the good or justice—and thus no ethical knowledge—such falsehood cannot be said to hide the nature of justice but must participate, in some fashion, in the founding of the good. Part of the lie's objective, then, is to fabricate the idea that it comes *after* the discovery of the truth of value— that it stains and obscures a preexisting good when, conceptually and narratively, it emerges in relation to and in tension with the concept of "good" as representational truth (to portray gods as they really "are"). Indeed, to pursue the question of the sovereign right to lie as if it were other than the question of the origin of criminality and ethical knowledge is to be taken in by the lie itself. To unfold the mechanics of this subtle displacement, one might return to the notion of "supervision" called for. As a formative rather than constraining notion, such supervision signifies not the curtailing of the "free speech" of citizens; to "supervise" in this context, rather, suggests the imperative of "oversight" in two senses. In one, "oversight" describes a structural ignorance whereby one must "overlook" the absence of an original transgression or, what is the same thing, overlook that the narrative transmission of the crime, as in the Hamitic story, stands in for the inaugural crime itself. For the sake of founding ethical knowledge one turns a blind eye to what cannot be seen.[34] When Socrates asserts the necessity of the lie, there is, as yet, no "truth" for which a lie could have any meaning but only mythic accountings. In other words, as with the Hamitic crime, the pact of secrecy here does not "hide" a truth under silence but rather *creates* the illusion of a knowable but unspeakable and forbidden evaluative truth upon which an evaluative order is predicated. The Platonic narrative feigns replacing truth with a lie, but in actuality constitutes *both* the truth and the lie through a federation of a "secret pact" that for the sake of preservation must be committed to iteration and thus storytelling.

It is to this need for iteration and storytelling that the other sense of "oversight" speaks, designating a mode of education and training, an escorting into the techniques of pedagogy. In this respect, the call to "supervise the storytellers" indicates apprenticeship more than censorship insofar as the directive is not to conceal true ethical knowledge from citizens but to groom storytellers to produce that knowledge by preserving the secret of the indeterminacy of criminality. While Socrates appears, then, to be "silencing" the storytellers, he is, rather, insisting upon their mentorship into the shared silence of the ethical pact. The need for supervision signifies that the pact cannot be sealed and forgotten; new storytellers must inherit and reiterate the story of dichotomous value, of the pure good as representational truth. Accordingly, the "pact of silence" preserving what is to be "passed over in silence" must be continually reiterated. Socrates thus issues two seemingly contradictory imperatives: to keep silent about *and* incessantly reiterate the secret of an unspeakable and hypothetical criminality, where that retelling takes the particular form of exchange expressed as supervision or oversight. Specifically, then, one satisfies both imperatives by "passing over" unanalyzed the unspeakable primordial crime; it is a transfer accomplished not via anonymous or public broadcasts but through the intimacy of a handing over to another who thus comes into ethical knowledge as a recipient or beneficiary. Hence the demand to "pass" the crime in silence signifies the duty both to preserve this criminal secret and to "pass along" this secret down the line, as it does, for instance, from Plato to Philo. Such is the task of the supervisor/overseer—to pass along its own sovereign secret such that one leaves behind in "passing" only that which one confers upon another in a genealogical emission.

No one escapes this conduction of criminal value or goes through empty-handed; the secret, passed over in silence, bypasses no one.[35] Everyone becomes an inheritor in this ritual transfer; that no one stands outside of this secret signifies its inability to produce the distinction between those individuals entitled to criminal knowledge and those paternalistically "protected" from it (i.e., that political parsing of rulers and the general citizen). Accordingly, the secret only simulates the cloaking of the answer to Glaucon's original question of "what justice is and what its origins are," suggesting the function of the pact of secrecy as other than an invested rigging of who will and will not inherit this "knowledge" and thus accede to sovereign rule.[36] What would emerge from this "pact of secrecy" that *must* be circulated would be, instead, an understanding of differentiated inheritable relations as natural-ized and ordained. The power of the lie inheres not in *what* it passes on (e.g., the reigns of social control) but in its productive naturalization of compara-tively legitimate and illegitimate lines of ethical descent along which the secret becomes passed.[37]

The Semiotics of Value

Noah, as opposed to our moderns, does not seek to erase his indelible mark; he does not curse his own curse. At the same time, he does not seek to live "lightly" with its consequences, as if the scar were the accidental stain of just any crime among others, or as if he could willfully, by dint of the power of self-definition, refashion the blemish into a beauty mark or brand. Instead he translates that criminal marking into a reiterative and dynamic stain that issues in histories of responsibility.

This is the second feint. The text would have us believe that the cursing by Noah is the origin of the ethical stain—that the malediction produces the first mark, and, moreover, in designating Canaan, initiates the metonymic movement of the stain from parent (Ham) to child (Canaan) believed to reproduce itself in perpetuity. The curse communicates itself as a pointed reckoning for a particular crime, but only on the premise that such a crime has occurred, as the curse can render its mark only in conjunction with another mark, specifically, the criminal trace that serves as the origin of ethical knowledge. But while the existence of such a crime necessitates the trace or evidentiary mark, it cannot be that this evidentiary mark signifies a specific, even extraordinary "crime." Specifically, it cannot indicate any single, "first" crime outside of an economy of value. If synecdoche is what is at work here, as Augustine proposes, the evidentiary mark stands not for the "entirety" of the primordial crime of which it is a part but for the entire system of evaluative marks. Cognizance of or "speaking" the crime would entail a language, a dynamic apparatus of evaluative relations within and for which a crime could surface. According to the conditions of any such system, however, no individual mark or crime could arise on its own as a strictly "first" mark or transcendental signifier—certainly not one that could metonymically bring about a comprehensive order of ethical knowledge. Thus the difficulty of identifying the substance of Ham's crime lies not in the discovery of a content that could be made present but in the impossibility of the emergence of any *nameable* crime outside an inheritable language of comparative worth. What *can* be said to open up in this moment instead would be a semiotics of value; in other words, "criminality" rather than "crime." Indeed, the common criticism that no single offence could warrant such an expansive curse is accommodated by this regard of the "crime" as "criminality"—that is, not the recitation of fundamentally transgressive actions but the forging of subjects in various kinship and communal relations differentiated through disparate valuations. If what the curse configures is this criminal difference rather than some capital crime, then what this second feint achieves is the illusory substitution of a constituent crime for what is, in the end, the emergence of criminality.

The curse, neither reactive nor retaliatory (as no crime exists for which it could be a proper response), stipulates the worth of the Hamitic line not as absolute but as comparative. As a complex of values set in relation to those of other inchoate lines of descent, this "relative" worth thus disburses as familial dividends. Like race, the curse articulates and formalizes an economy of ethical subjectivity whose constituting force is attributed to what escapes representation. Both the theological and secular versions of the inception of human taxonomies, in effect, locate behind a temporal and conceptual veil a predifferentiated yet elusive state characterized as unified, organic, and non-relational. In the first, the fantastical interior of Noah's tent hosts the rupture that pluralizes man into families; in the second, social scientific model, a strangely cultivating yet inconsistent climatology variously ripens unmarked prototypes into disparate races. In each case, stratification subordinates to and emerges from an occluded state of unmarked nondifferentiation; and yet, the intelligibility of this ethical order, and in particular of the unalloyed, incomparable state as other than those disparately stained and thereby individualized, comes only through knowledge that this subordination produces.

This hypothesis invites a more detailed consideration of how the narrative cloaking of the Hamitic crime returns in the representational invisibility of Kant's natal prototype. "To be sure," Kant explains, "we cannot hope any more to come upon the unaltered original human form anywhere in the world."[38] The statement posits original humans as unmarked ethically and racially while also explaining why no evidentiary residue of their existence remains. But is the lack of evidentiary trace a consequence of the extinction of such beings or because such beings in their undifferentiated purity would exhibit, by definition, no marks by which any perceptual recognition of them could take place? Kant portrays this slippage of our carnal ancestors into an unrecuperable anthropological past as a happenstance feature of natural history; as with the Hamitic crime, it is characterized as an event that, had certain random variables been otherwise, would have readily provided the link between a notional pure human existence and the disaggregated corporeal beings descended from it. The beholding of the unraced being is for Kant a narrowly missed encounter, a result of historical chance. Yet this phantom stem formation is no more the key to racial difference than is the particular crime against Noah to ethical difference.

Because race for Kant signifies deviation from the primary, unstained paradigm of the original stem formation, it serves thereby as a measurement as well; the differential variety of races is a function of the distance each stands from the organic ground zero represented by the unmarked human prototype. To the extent that the stem formation is, as Kant conceives of it, an ontological anchor, racial deviations register as absolute values, revealing at one stroke our location within an evaluative genealogy and the proximity of that ancestral line to ethical exemplarity. The figure of the organic prototype of humanity corrupts into differentiated racial lineages, records Kant, as a consequence of the interaction of metaphysical and empirical forces, specifically, the impact of climatological features upon predispositional potentialities. Kant's account of natural history, apart from certain questionable assertions, may nonetheless denote a critical philosophical advance in dismissing all premodern models predicated on "superstitions," the passing of "secret" knowledges, and "criminal" explanations of the formation of ethically embodied genealogies. In turn, his employment of race to connect the stem formation of humanity to its corporeal instantiations is today characterized as a similarly irrational and unscientific myth, the rejection of which we hail as another philosophical advance. It is a mistake, however, to imagine such logics inessential to the conception of value; they are, rather, the means for producing embodied value as the causal aftermath of a prior, preethical world. They actively fabricate the illusion of preethical beings—Ham and his brothers before the crime, the original, unmarked Kantian humans—who then, by some unrepresentable event, emerge as evaluatively distinct lineages. Contrary to our prevailing ethical and racial reasoning, then, the curse and race are what make possible the concept of the "human" as an individually responsible agent. Accordingly, "humanity" for Kant has meaning through its materialized, racial instantiations, indicating that "race" neither opposes nor negates "humanity" but designates the mode of its apprehensible representation. One thus captures "humankind" as a "kind of human"—*through*, rather than beyond, the language of race, which is to say, through racial knowledge. (How, otherwise, could the trope of "human race" not contradict itself? In this expression "human" is dependent upon, as defined through, the "race" presumed as its derivative, even though "race" is arguable a more expansive term, allowing for, say, the notion of a non-human "alien" race.) "Race" does not come into being as a solitary index of difference—as a mark placed on the subject after or on top of those prior marks that distinguish it as human, as the feint would suggest. It is not, indeed, itself a mark at all but, like criminality, a figural function from which emerges embodied, ethical subjects whose practices are constituted within an evaluative field.

If the only humans available to perception are those stained through the semiotics of ethical markings like race, how might one identify their authentic and individual unmarked qualities? Despite Kant's remark that we can no longer hope to come upon the original stem formation, hope is exactly what the stem salvages as the specter of a possible and desirable return to the undifferentiated immediacy of ethically and ethnically cleansed bodies. That humanity is not the realizable unity that race shatters and betrays but instead what is concurrently effected by means of racial knowledge does not make race a starting point or conceptual firmament but rather underscores it

as figural. Hence the carnality that Augustine introduces as synecdoche finds
its complement in Alain Locke's articulation of race as "idiomatic," a definition according to which race functions, coordinates, individualizes, and characterizes but *is* nothing, not because it does not "exist," but because in being
bound up with the very terms of historical existence attests to the always *pecu-
liar, localized, nonreferential form* of embodied expression.[39] Thus the common invocation of "humanity" as generic, universal, and referential—and
therefore as what can be spoken and known outside of ethics and race—must
simultaneously invoke, like criminality, a marked or scarred body as its particular, presumptive representation. In Kant's theory, whiteness assumes this
double role as the "closest" to the original stem formation, serving as both the
generic, universal "human" as well as the instantiated racial deviation. Even
so, other races are called for, as the stem genus cannot sustain the valorization
of whiteness on its own terms, for that privileging would require whiteness to
measure itself favorably against what remains inaccessible to representation.

The ethical category of human serves as both origin and ideal by which
differentiated criminalities and racializations achieve their subordinate and
deviant statuses, a subordination that, again, both descends from as well as
gives intelligibility to this category through corporeal and ethical marking.
Ethical and racial knowledges do not depend for their introduction upon the
performance of crime or fantasized encounter with an unraced everyman.
In our altered, already racially and criminally differentiated circumstance,
such knowledge comes upon us, as with Noah, as a seizure of our own stained
corporeality.

Missing the Mark

Here we reach the third and most seductive feint: that the contradictions and
omissions of the passage designate narrative imperfections the correction of
which would reveal more clearly the story's moral lesson as a parable. The
text, in its expository directness, seems to solicit these resolutions as those
it has implicitly provided, tasking the reader with restoring the passage's eli-
sions and untwisting its coils, as if retracing the partially faded characters of
an original script. This process of restoration, in addition to solving the crime
and affirming the moral significance of the passage, includes drafting hypotheses of how early redactors attempted to reconcile disparate versions of the
tale that, for instance, disagreed as to whether Ham or Canaan committed
the crime, or that imagined a fourth son of Noah's to be involved. To synthesize these renditions inflected through local traditions back into an original,

monolingual voice and logic continues for many scholars as the theopolitical objective and challenge of the story.

The feint, however, exploits precisely the literary expectations that inspire such strategic interpretations. For what these strategies miss in their creditable reconstruction is the possibility that the "problematic" textual gaps of the passage do not omit what the reader would reasonably infer but fashion those absences as omissions. On such an interpretation, the exclusions enact a creative rather than depreciative textual function, such that the purported lack of detail and description signify an active silence dissimulating as void, and therefore a constructed (though not calculated) stain of transparency. The passage thus would configure the stain not to paper over a real event—a crime, a name, a motive—but to draw the eye into seeing nothing at the very moment that the deception takes place: not elsewhere, not hidden *behind* a blanket or tent, but at the forefront of our depth of field, as what is closest to us and thus what we oversee. Hence the "loss of meaning" that the lack connotes facilitates rather than hampers or ruptures the function of the narrative. In this case, the omission of Ham's crime that provokes its hermeneutic reconstruction insinuates as self-evident that the perpetration of a singular deed, unwitnessed and unnamed, results in ethical difference that originates comparative social worth. Moreover, by producing not the inaugural deed but its purported cavity, the negative impression of its presence, the Hamitic myth premises ethical causality on a deed that goes without saying, the incontestable existence of which is maintained by perpetual oversight. The success of this sleight of hand is borne out in the near unanimous belief that ethics begins always and only with respect to a deed both evaluable and subjectively attributable that, like a spark, instigates a chain of rewards, punishments, gifts, and responsibilities.[40]

One can, however, "pull focus" in order to bring oversight itself into the field of vision. In this manner, the narrative recedes as an enigma that obligates either the conjuring of the unsolved crime or its affirmation as eternally unspeakable, exhibiting less the characteristics of the moral parable than of the genre of founding myth. That is to say, rather than a lesson to internalize or a secret to puzzle over, the story provides an explanation, in its very construction, of the nature and origin of knowledge as ethical. All that the narrative "hides" is the simulation of hiding itself, which, as a simulation, thereby remains in plain sight throughout. What appears to have been left or "cut out" has not gone missing but actively produces the moment of the seizure of differentiated and thus evaluative being.

Viewed from this angle, the narrative exhibits neither the incompleteness nor understatement regularly accorded it; its only "lacks" reflect the ciphers internal to and conditional for writing itself. Bowdlerization is no unwitting or intentional culprit in this account. Knowledge begins with the cognitive seizing of the stain or trace, marks that customarily and linguistically indicate the prior presence of other, more stable and pure phenomena but here are beholden to no such generative source as deed or *logos*. The feint, the simulacrum, the deviation, and the double do not obscure or conceal knowledge in substituting themselves for what we purport to be the primary and real elements of ethics: the human, the crime, purity, innocence, and transparency. They do not bar us from learning the true origin of ethical knowledge—metaphorically, of what occurs "inside the tent"—but, if anything, are elements by which the notion of an origin of ethics maintains itself.

Thus while anathema to the plot, the overt inconsistencies, apparent logical contradictions, and discretionary lapses of the passage are essential for establishing the nameless crime as that imaginary force of relation between the subject as historical materiality and as the autonomous site of evaluative worth. The Hamitic narrative has long resisted beyond conventional reason multiple attempts to correct its form and supplement its "missing" content and thereby stabilize its meaning. This resistance suggests that what appear as haphazard incongruities and absences, limitations readily overcome in other texts, here flexibly and resiliently sustain a historical mobility beyond any purported racialized intentionality. This mobility expresses itself not only through the secularized version of the ethical subject born innocent only to be immediately stained by crime but also, as offered in the following chapter, in the perpetuation of the curse as the ethical conduit of that marking.

Through these three feints the story of the crime of Ham has been mined with an eye turned not toward a reenactment of the scene's missing fragments but toward the mechanics of meaning through what is and is not given. In this the passage provided less a detailed transcript than a frugal montage, one irreducible to a single source or authoritative version and thus a text bereft of any clear prescriptive or political objectives. Unmoored from these authorial motives, the passage wants neither legibility nor meaning, offering up a seductive and savvy morphology of evaluative knowledge and its actualization in phenomenal bodies. The story recounts "knowledge of good and evil" as an effect of criminality itself, evinced by trace or scar; moreover, this criminal knowledge is grasped not self-reflectively or dialogically but instantaneously and carnally. Such immediate illumination signals a comprehension of the differentiated markings by which things acquire both identity and relationality. It is through this general mastery of the natural ethical order of the world and its objects that the taints of various categories or "families" of ethical subjectivities come to light.

This stain by which the crime, or rather, criminality, is immediately "known" by Noah (and simulated as known to the reader) depends for its meaning upon that other mark of the embodied, inheritable stain—that is, the curse as the production of the everlasting signifier of criminal subjectivity that inaugurates the dissemination of human history. Rather than two separate events, the criminal staining and curse serve as nodal elements in the unfolding of a semiotics of value, and therefore, as Ferdinand de Saussure contends, as marks that secure meaning through repetition and convention rather than as antitheses or points of origin.[41] Formative and informed, constituting and reconstituted, those stains that we have referred to as "permanent" thereby symbolize not fixed or immutable marks—stains that have set—but ones that reinstitute or "reset" themselves as continual rather than continuous. Accordingly, as illustrated in the next chapter, the stain does not fade in its cursed passage through ancestral lines but, in reproducing and reenacting itself in that descent, executes itself repeatedly as a fresh wound that signals the historical entrance of the ethical subject.

4

Cursed Inheritance

Every assignation of an inheritance harbors a
contradiction and a secret.

JACQUES DERRIDA, *Echographies of Television*

THE PREVIOUS CHAPTER examined premodern mythical structures
by which various primordial crimes have been said to come into existence.
Although focused on the particular biblical narrative of an encounter
between Noah and Ham, the larger argument questioned the philosophical
plausibility of any principle, rule, or misdeed not enmeshed within a semiotics of value, as that which enables both embodied self-consciousness and
the phenomenal experience of relational objects in the world. This examination generated the hypothesis that expressions of value begin not as crime
but in "criminality," a dynamic effected and perpetrated in part by illusions
and concealments that constitute the subject as differentially marked and as
the inheritor and purveyor of ethical knowledge. The question of "the crime"
gave way, that is, to the language of criminality—in particular, to the tropes
and metonymic devices by which ethical knowledge is kept in play as necessarily carnal and thereby always threatening the corruption of the subject
entrusted with that knowledge. The emphasis on the structural role of value
in representation and embodiment, however, would remain incomplete and
misleading without a complementary consideration of the temporality and
historicity of value. To stress the semiotic function of value may unwittingly
foreground the synchronic over the diachronic, as if the necessarily evaluative relations within which phenomena appear resist rather than coordinate
perceptual shifts over time. The constitution of ethical subjects through
inheritable value, however, could not occur outside of histories of responsibility through which those inheritances pass. Indeed, the previous chapter's
examination of "crime" could hardly bracket that analysis, even provisionally,
without frequently invoking the temporality expressed through the curse.

Having thus attempted to articulate value in its more "structural" or "syn-chronic" aspects, this chapter turns explicitly to the element of the curse, that by which value expresses itself not merely as a condition of difference but also as "movement." At issue here are the mechanics by which those evidentiary marks by which the ethical subject knows itself and is knowable to others pass through genealogical descent. Chapter 2 advanced a general theory for this movement of value as an initial response to Alain Locke's quandary on the feasibility of raced subjects inheriting "scars and traces" within a "social heredity," one wherein those marks serve as legible signifiers of value for mul-tiple subjects. It was proposed that this movement was consequent upon the structural nonidentity of bodies and thus of the mark itself (such that Frantz Fanon records his body and deeds as both his and not his own). The theme of nonidentity continued into the previous chapter via the functions of narra-tive feints, "overseeing," and metonymic figures of speech.

In shifting to interrogate the particular coinage of the curse, this chapter will elaborate on value in light of these various aspects of representation and language. Its systematic objective is to elucidate in greater detail the temporal features of the stain of ethics and embodiment (i.e., of carnality) through the story of Noah and Ham, not, once more, because this story possesses any exclusive or privileged truth but because its robust and premodern configura-tion puts in greater relief for contemporary philosophy the synthetic opera-tion by which these evaluative relations effect themselves. But the purpose of the subsequent pages is not to demonstrate ethics and race as merely beholden to and illustrative of the general conditions of signification and meaning; it is not to present a case study of applied theory that would reaffirm value in its current status as secondary to and parasitic of a more primary force of meaning. This chapter, rather, attempts to establish the function of inherit-able value as a catalyst for history as movement. The animating thrust here will be, in concert with the entirety of the book, to reorient ethics as value in its formative rather than *deforming* capacity. To this end, it will examine the curse as a means of contemplating ethical subjectivity as bereft of any "hidden" ethical content, whether envisioned as a "content of character," pure potentiality, biological materiality, affective sensation, or as morally intuitive, "secret" knowledge preserved in the silent recesses of the mind.

The task here, it should be clarified, is not to make these claims of foun-dational content disappear; the goal, rather, is to demonstrate that "founda-tions" are such insofar as they remain perpetually unmoored and contingent, as a "certain uncertainty" in Fanon's words. One could describe the following chapter as an explication of the conditions of this "uncertainty" within which the "certainty" of ethical individuation becomes possible, whereby value does not "fix" or inhibit subjectivity but animates and propels it through inheritable lineages. Such an argument leaves behind as shrapnel from the "theory wars" of previous decades fearful refrains of "doing away with" the subject. No final destruction or "deconstruction" of metaphysics is sought here; there is, instead, an appreciation of affordances that usher the subject into criminal associations, associations that by turn spark the dream and nightmare of sovereign and isolable self-identity.

Taking seriously the concept of the curse will require, first, its more substantive definition; the subsequent section thus sketches the generic parameters and features of the curse as a brand of punishment through a contrast with punishment in its standard usage as a penalty or correction. Unfolding from this broader survey will follow a closer treatment of the curse issued by Noah and its unique relation to criminality. Although by convention all punishments in essence respond to and depend upon the transgressions they address, the curse, it will be shown, suspends any peremptory and unilateral causal determination, instead activating value as a propellant or force of movement. The proposition requires a return to the scene of the Hamitic crime as well as a revisiting of the "figures" of the story, both of characters and of speech. In revisiting Philo and St. Augustine once more the curse is explicated not as something placed upon the subject but as criminal subjectivity *in motion*. The closing section then takes up Augustine's emphasis of the *name* as a predication that animates rather than inhibits the development of the ethical subject. The term *denomination* will come to stand for this theory of the necessarily evaluative and situational quality of nomination, as well as for how the subject is anticipated by its ethical appointments. Throughout, the discussion of the curse will further illuminate the guiding themes of the book: the syncretic function of race, the conditional possibility of representation upon value, and the identity of deeds as contingent upon the performing body.

The "curse," or the inheritability of ethical marking, persists even now as both necessary *and* impossible: necessary because the emergence of subjectivity presumes already a criminal stain, and impossible because to be "stained," ethically or physically, suggests a distortion or defect precipitated by a causal relationship incapable of being transferred and thus inherited. In the notion of the curse, then, we find both the knotting of genealogical and "cultural" inheritance that so disturbed Locke, but also the logic by which subjects become *effects* of historical, criminal value while simultaneously retaining responsibility as those who prophetically and reiteratively beget and give life to this criminality. At stake here is the power of the curse to instill and perpetuate an array of qualities *conceived of and executed in proper association* with those who *emerge in their very being as entitled to this evaluative status* and who, as noted by Locke, "could in no way either determine the period of those inequalities or their eradication."

The Logic of the Curse

The curse has been loosely referred to so far as a kind of punishment, but this characterization begs the specificity of its distinction from common moral and juridical languages, those compared to which it appears grotesque and absurd. Most important for this distinction is that the curse not represent an exaggerated or extreme penalizing measure but a qualitatively different mode of disciplinary reasoning. Without attempting any exhaustive definitions, we can view punishment in its standard and philosophical usages as a carefully weighed and circumscribed response to a codified offense—a "correction"— from punishment as inheritable criminal markings through which subjects and deeds become available as already valuated objects of consciousness—a "curse."

To begin, corrections impose compensatory values, services, or incarcerations of a specific amount or duration. They are finite: a prison sentence, indentured servitude, lashes, a fine, loss of license or employment, etc. Corrections imply a fixed point after which no additional suffering or compensation is to be extracted, however extreme the charge (inordinately large fines or consecutive jail terms that exceed life expectancy, for instance, represent abstractly viable closures prohibited from realization only by limits physical and economic). By this formula, the penalty to which the convicted is sentenced carries its own internal conclusion—even the penalty of death provides a limit-point signifying the discharge of a criminal debt. Curses, in contrast, stipulate a potentially infinite duration of bondage. They may break off after the satisfaction of some specified condition, as instanced by the "spells" of fairy tales, or effect a chain of events that augurs a particular outcome, as a kind of omen. Alternatively, they may be open-ended, as an ellipsis stretching into the future, and thus need not proleptically forecast any termination point. In such a case, the sentence of "infinity" that the curse delivers (even that of eternal damnation or suffering) is not one of determinate duration but of indeterminacy, wherein the latter does not oppose or exaggerate the term of a finite sentence but signals a disanalogous constellation of punishment. To read the infinite as quantitative would be to give fixity to the curse and thus circumscribe its tractability and movement, thereby curtailing the anxiety and malaise produced from the inability to anticipate its conclusion. The cruelty of the curse, that is, resides in its expiration belonging to the unpredictable vicissitudes of fate.

In the economic relation between the criminal and aggrieved in cases of correction the conditions of imprisonment or fine abolish the liability that the crime incurs. Accordingly each day of penance or partial repayment incrementally reduces proportionately the stain of the infraction: as Nietzsche details, this notion of crime coincides with the failure to fulfill a contract or promise regarding labor or goods. Because the body served originally as the promissory note for the transaction, he argues, it belonged from the start as a legitimate and extrinsically valuable source from which to extract payment, if forcibly, that would settle the sworn agreement. The demand of an "eye for an eye" becomes possible by regarding the body as initial capital, a deposit that vouches entry into the social. Here the body signifies a repository for future potential wealth and suffering, an engine that generates and reproduces compensatory labor, goods, or pain by which personal and communal accounts may be settled. From this, he proposes, the restitution of a penalty became, in effect, the payment of one's "debt to society."[1]

In contrast, curses defy a market economy by lacking a determined conclusion. As immeasurable, the unspeakable crime, for instance, does not submit to the order of quantification and thus escapes the accounting ledgers of the creditor/debtor. The labor and suffering extracted in these instances, then, do not exhibit commercial value or meaning; they bring the end of the curse no closer. The barometer of this suffering labor registers not temporal or monetary increments, or degrees of corporeal perversion and sacrifice, but regenerating cycles of grief. The myths of Prometheus and Sisyphus provide examples of torments the agony of which comes both from the particular tortures each endures as well as the awareness that the "conclusion" of that torturous endurance—the tearing out of one's liver or the raising of a mammoth boulder—coincides with the renewal of the same process. In contrast to the model of criminal debt, nothing is paid off at the beginning of each cycle and the punishment no nearer to its expiration. Even after innumerable iterations of the punitive burden the crime becomes no more distant; each cycle recommences the punishment as if for the first time. Finality, if it comes, does so not through the corrective practices of the criminal but through events external to the crime, as happenstance or as consequence of a seemingly unrelated narrative that entwines with and reshapes the curse. The result may improve one's condition (as in Prometheus's case, whose tormenting bird Hercules slays as one of his twelve tasks) or worsen it (as in the case of Atlas, whose "eternal" punishment to shoulder the heavens ends with his transformation into mountainous stone). In these relations the body bears the curse but is not simultaneously a power for its alleviation; its actions neither reduce nor release it from its criminal state .

According to the logic of the curse, punishment does not "fit the crime." Curses are not typically symbolic reversals of or restitutions for the offense or perpetrator—they do not rectify an imbalance—but dramatic and poetic trials that appropriate the body and place it in a kind of ritualistic animation, "compelling" its performance of actions that therefore both are and are not their *own* deeds. The body participates here not as a commodity or resource "owned" by the subject in the closed, reciprocal market of ethical debtor and creditor but as a figure of criminality in an open, nonreciprocal economy of value whose fluctuating and iterative processes render it incompatible with a morality predicated on compensatory justice. Moreover, in the correction economy the body operates as a generative yet depreciating value-machine that incurs debt (through its own criminal volition or in its intrinsic responsibility to others) and consequently the obligation to settle these accounts (even if this guarantees, as post-Kantian continentalists aver, a permanent state of arrears fostering in the subject an unshakeable "guilt").

The offender conceived as a discrete entity thus defines the limit of punishment as correction, insofar as corrections are *made to* the criminal (in the hope, say, of rehabilitation). Corrections can be imposed up to the entirety of the subject, exhausting it if necessary for the sake of justice. Michel Foucault may be right that such totalizing examples of criminality have all but disappeared over the past few centuries, eliminating the figure of the "monster" or wholly evil being as well as those disciplinary techniques (public shame, torture, forced confession, etc.) that sought as reprisal the complete extraction of moral malignance.[2] Nonetheless, such instances of consummate depravity and retribution also reflect punishment as a productive correction that forges ethical subjectivity in isolation, according special status to the criminal as breaking with the human, whether as the demonic that solicits exorcism or as the subhuman that requires moral education. The common thread is the belief in some remnant of the subjective psyche that is not irrevocably corruptible and which thus preserves the potential for moral improvement. This point is underscored by Foucault's discomfort with Nietzsche's notion of inheritable descent (*Herkunft*), a more substantive discussion of which takes place later in the chapter.[3] For now, however, it is sufficient to identify this residue of "resistance" as a preservation of unstained subjectivity representative of corrective punishment.

With the curse there exists no "fragile inheritor" who retains a remainder one might salvage or tutor. It does not condemn or attack the criminal as a subject; in a way, one could view the curse as indifferent to subjectivity insofar as subjectivity, if anything, owes its identity to the curse rather than the reverse. The parameters of genealogical inheritance do not isolate the criminal, holding it aloft for all others to see—it does not use the criminal to set an example, either as a warning or success story—again there is no moral lesson here to be learned, at least not in any traditional sense—rather the curse links the subject within the reproductive arcs of its relations. This genealogical structure of the curse neither "exceeds" the subject, such that the lineage of responsibility overdetermines being, nor is exceeded by it, on the ground that the subject must be more than its circumstances. To compose the subject as of either limited or overabundant potentiality—as overwhelmed or underwhelmed by the criminal environment within which it emerges—would be to set the subject *in relation to* value rather than as differentiated through it. Subjectivity is not installed here as the settled product of a single history of responsibility but designates an ongoing profusion of innumerable (though not equally informing) iterative formations of embodied worth.

The depiction of the curse thus far has focused on its extension into the future, not only in the repetitious aspects of its sentencing but also in the context of the signifying stain that appoints progeny within evaluative associations. The curse contains, however, the critical feature of "reciprocal implication" as well, by which shifts in value can reiterate and reshape genealogies "upwards" as well as "down." What descends through cursed lineage does not play out an already given arrangement; instead that descent simultaneously reconstitutes the meaning and worth of the ancestral symbols and figures that "prophesize" and "originate" what is to come. Noah, for instance, marks the line of Canaan, but is himself also marked by his offspring, aside from and in addition to anything Ham does to him in the tent. Hence the name "Noah" designates not only the builder of the ark, the chosen one, the mortal whom God spared and bound in a resurrective pact, but also signifies a worth indexed to the fortunes of those names to which it is tied through descent. Thus the curse places the criminal subjectivity of Noah, no less than that of his sons, at stake in the interpretation of the Hamitic passage. Noah's identity can have no security so long as criminal instability plagues his reputed descendants: this is the legacy that his offspring bequeath to *him*, for Noah's death does not cement his ethical station; rather his comparative value remains beholden to the fates of those understood as the contemporary inheritors of his blessings and curse.

In its modern expression, this reciprocal implication of the curse means that while raced subjects inherit the scars and traces of those who have come before them, the symbolic worth of that ancestry—of laws, deeds, lands, and qualities—that is, *who they were*—alters in accordance with the criminal dispositions of their imagined successors. The past, that is, possesses no immunity from the mutability of the mark any more than what is still to come. This mutability prevents, for instance, a history of early "Africa" from coalescing as a chain of objectively discernable events whose philosophical and cultural import remains to be definitively established. On the contrary, any such history operates at most as an ongoing thematic of "Africa" whose topography reshapes itself in conjunction with the relative worth of its perceived representatives. Accordingly disagreements on "Africa's" contributions to global intellectual and technological history that appear to hinge on the tracing back of certain ideas and objects to a precolonial origin simultaneously configure the idiom of "Africa" through those determining assessments. (W.E.B. DuBois provides the example whereby artistry influential to "civilization" was said to indicate a priori its *non-African origin*, meaning either that the *true* origin of such knowledge was as yet undiscovered or that those credited with developing such knowledge thereby proved themselves non-African. By such logic, he writes, "Egyptians" and "North Africans," for instance, become "Mediterranean" or "Middle Eastern," which is to say, "familiarized" within ethical genealogies appropriate to those tendencies.)[4] Accordingly even as the "origin" of inheritable transfers of ethical subjectivity, the Hamitic crime is not an immutable starting point but a continually recast, retroactively installed fantasy whose contours and meaning answer to contemporary representation.

Correction, finally, as distinct from the curse, implies a causal chain of crime and punishment whose links remain exclusive and nonintersecting. Crime in this model is sourced by the subjective interior expressed as compulsion, inclination, motivation, or decision, whether instinctual, biological, or willed. Its retribution issues as a temporally derivative, reactive, and repressive force that the subject experiences as the "other" of normative institutions or of internalized "laws" of the tiered psyche. Here the crime must be limned as clearly as possible insofar as proper punishment is imagined as what maps itself mimetically onto the given shape of the transgression. That ideal punishment "fits" the crime means that correction at its most elemental aims to annul criminal history, to settle all accounts back to a zero balance, achieving complete stain removal and thus the reconstituted state of original innocence that the violation shattered.[5] The curse, however, does not succeed and respond to a hermetically distinct crime but provides the generative context in which criminality emerges. Accordingly the curse becomes no less the "causal origin" of the crime—that is, the crime is less what brings about the malediction than what corroborates and confirms its prophetic authenticity. One is cursed because one transgresses but also transgresses because one is cursed; there is no way out of the "infernal circle," as Fanon remarks. Here, punishment is as anticipatory of the crime as the crime is indicative of the punishment; their relation is thus neither causal nor linear but biotic.

The Unaddressed Curse

Noah's malediction commands a servitude that appears to fall, without explanation, on Canaan, Ham's son, rather than on his father. Yet the meting out of this transgenerational disfavor includes concomitant blessings of fortune for Shem and Japheth that thereby incorporate all of Noah's sons into the scope of the curse:

> So he said, "Cursed be Canaan; A servant of servants He shall be to his brothers." He also said, "Blessed be the LORD, The God of Shem; And let Canaan be his servant." "May God enlarge Japheth, And let him dwell in the tents of Shem; And let Canaan be his servant."

The curse cannot motivate or elicit anything if thought of as what attaches to a particular subject or object, that is, as fixed to and limited by a preexisting materiality, for in such a case the curse, like correction, would terminate upon the death or destruction of that entity and could not exercise its inheritability. As what must engender and reproduce itself, the curse cannot parasitically corrupt or poison its host; such corruption would degrade the person of Canaan were he indeed the innocent victim of his father's crime and illegitimate recipient of punishment. If, on the other hand, Canaan rather than Ham commits the offense, then, aside from the narrative problems this substitution would create, his punishment would appear warranted.

From the standpoint of moral philosophy, the story presents an ambiguity regarding the one to whom the curse belongs; either Ham or Canaan, it seems, must serve as the intended recipient. Noah's statement "Cursed be Canaan" offers one of the only seemingly indisputable facts of the passage, as if to leave no doubt as to who bears fault here, yet nothing latent in the

story links Canaan directly to what transpires in the tent or its fraught expo-
sition to others. Indeed, his existence *within* the diagetic world of the other
characters begins only in that moment of his cursed naming. Without even
circumstantial evidence of Canaan's participation in the crime, then, his
punishment as a corrective response, interpreters agree, has no justification.
On this account, the passage has no truck as a *moral* allegory without the
imputation of an instigating deed by Canaan.

That the story maintains an indeterminate "object" of the curse (Ham,
Canaan, Canaanites, etc.) is troublesome only insofar as curses must fall *upon*
some subject or ancestry. On the contrary, if curses do not fall *upon* anything
but instead *establish* criminal affiliations, then this indeterminacy, rather
than textual defect or flaw, attests to the curse as well as its historical ana-
logues, like race, not as a contaminating predicate that clings to phenomena
but as the naturalized conditions of passage by which anything could be said
to *descend* from another. As the possibility of descent, the curse generates
elements that in their constant evolution or devolution exhibit the quality
of *motion*. The curse thus designates a fortune that could never belong to a
single individual because "belonging" in this sense signifies the naming or
appointment into a variety of blessings and curses that actuate the tethering
marks of kinship.

If the curse alights on neither Ham nor Canaan but instead identifies
these names as figures in evaluative relation, it follows that neither comprises a distinct subject in its own right, a conclusion drawn by both Philo
and St. Augustine in their clarifications of the passage. Whereas interpretations that dismiss the curse outright as illegitimate and untenable do so on
the presumption that Ham and Canaan must stand for fully individuated
characters outside of any possible history of responsibility, those of Philo
and Augustine propose theories of ethical descent and kinship the expressed
members of which represent different historical instantiations of a comparative criminal lineage. Neither interpretation, however, presents this inheritable ancestry as without subjects who author and realize crimes: descendants
in these exegeses are not simply left holding the bag for the criminals who
preceded them—rather their criminality reflects their participation in and
reconstitution of that heritage. For Philo and Augustine, criminality is both
a familial and figurative operation in which different genealogical positions
(ancestor/descendant, father/son) never actualize as fully differentiated and
independent ethical actors. Whereas for modernity that individuation, represented by the proper name (Noah/Ham/Canaan), is where responsibility
begins and ends, these premodern exegeses of the Hamitic passage show how

responsibility passes through such proper names, and thus how, in modernity, racial subjectivity can hold the individual responsible as precipitating an act that it has also inherited.

Notional Motion

For Philo, the criminality that marks Ham and Canaan, far from accident or political malfeasance, discloses not two discrete ethical agencies but variant expressions of the singular force of wickedness: "Ham . . . is a name for vice in the quiescent state and . . . Canaan for the same when it passes into active movement."[6] In this Aristotelian division the soul grasps virtue and vice at rest—as "potentiality"—while the body represents those forces in motion. Only in the latter phase for Philo does one become a proper object of praise and punishment; until this implementation by the body, however, those "who possess knowledge and nothing more, and are not actually doing anything remain in peace."[7] Philo thus contends that Noah rightly curses Canaan rather than Ham, as "Canaan" designates the explicit conjugation of Ham's potential wickedness. Ham and Canaan accordingly represent for him not distinct and incommensurable individuals tied through blood; they are not, foremost, anthropological beings at all, but complementary signifiers of criminality and crime: where Ham encompasses the pure potentiality of disembodied vice, Canaan represents evil actualized as historical events, wherein the body provides a means for "the soul . . . [to] burst into flame" given real world opportunities.[8]

The reasoning Philo offers for how Ham and Canaan both come under the curse appears to sacrifice ethical autonomy. Yet in rejecting Ham and Canaan as separate beings, Philo views them as together comprising "a single subject . . . presented in two different aspects," his solution yielding "one" subject that maintains two ethical identities: one ideal and the other worldly and embodied.[9] Cursed descent refers thus to a hereditary expression that occurs "within" the subject, passed down not from person to person but from soul to body. Although for Philo the actions of the subject are constituted by and dependent upon inheritable and environmental conditions, he holds that true subjective worth lies behind and prior to those deeds. The challenge for such a proposition is, notably, how anyone—including the subject itself—could acquire access to this true worth except through a performance always distorted by external factors. As Philo himself admits, the socially interpreted behaviors of individuals can, in the context of inheritable conditions, demonstrate the *opposite* of the subject's intrinsic ethical proclivities.

Accordingly because the deed may not accurately reflect—indeed may wholly pervert and obscure—the subject's natural tendencies, such tendencies cannot be accessed by tracking the crime back to its point of original "motion."

What then could serve as a mark or clue to the subject's genuine criminal tendencies? In Philo's scenario, performative deeds function at best as ambiguous signifiers of authentic ethical identity; none can be trusted to reveal the ethical nature of the soul. Yet if expressions of the soul are not ultimately governed by it, can those performances count as those of the soul in motion? How might Ham and Canaan represent two stages of the "same" subject given that the introduction of so many mediating factors would produce an unbridgeable dissonance between them? On this view, there would seem no ground to sustain even the claim of an original resting "Hamitic" state insofar as that existence has no unmediated, recognizable expression. For evaluative perception there is only the subject that has already "burst into flames" in historic animation, as the inheritor of social and embodied indicators of worth.

In critical respects Philo's interpretation foreshadows Kant's hypothesis of a generic human potentiality or "stem formation," the actualized form of which varies according to the real world conditions in which it materializes. Like that secular account, Philo's version also envisions the instantiation of the presocial abstraction of the "soul" as dependent upon largely random environmental and situational factors. Specifically he asserts that expressions of virtues and vices are mediated through inheritable circumstances like family status, wealth, and bodily integrity, as well as the random chance afforded by what some today call "moral luck." Thus Philo remarks that for those denied social opportunities, virtuous potentiality will remain unknown and inaccessible "like gold and silver laid up in hidden recesses of the earth where none can use them."[10] (Recall Kant's similar remark in the *Groundwork*: "Even if, by special disfavor of fortune or by the niggardly provision of a stepmotherly nature, [a good] will should wholly lack the capacity to carry out its purpose . . . then, like a jewel, it would still shine by itself, as something that has its full worth in itself.")[11] While this impoverishment prevents some from flourishing, Philo observes, similar conditions conversely prevent wicked souls from catalyzing in evil actions. In either case, he remarks, material and social circumstances may go so far as to induce performances contrary to the subject's ethical dispositions (offering, as an example, that while physical disability might compel a virtuous person to beg for food, it may force a wicked one to show humility). Accordingly, embodied and environmental differences for Philo routinely obstruct and corrupt the intrinsic qualities of the soul such that the "innately" virtuous can behave wickedly and vice versa.

In that respect, we could all claim descent from Canaan in that our actuated behaviors as inflected through physical and social conditions would disclose nothing about our true, organic worth.

The foremost point, however, is Philo's unsuccessful attempt to synthesize the concept of the autonomous subject's preexisting evaluative worth and the necessarily sociohistorical meanings of bodily acts. If the "Canaanite" expressions of "Hamitic" potentiality always stain and pervert that potentiality, how could one even posit the existence of that potentiality? Philo can thus theorize the genealogical movement of value through the name only by effecting a self-erasure of the first of its nominal terms (Ham). From Philo we nonetheless receive the insight that any genealogy of value, and thus the criminal stain, would have to pass *through* the entirety of ethical subjectivity, and consequently through any modern version of "potentiality" including those of "intention" and "motive."[12]

Perpetual Motion

In contrast to Philo, St. Augustine presents Ham not as a static and structural abstraction but, like Canaan, as an incarnate subject in perpetual motion. Such motion for him *is* wickedness, however, as well as the hallmark of divine disfavor occasioned through sin, a conclusion derived in part from his etymological reading of that proper name: equating "Ham" with "hot," Augustine profiles a character epitomized by inherently disruptive movement. In contrast to the Kantian newborn who breaks *in* to the world, disguising its criminality amongst legitimate members of the moral community, Augustine's Ham consistently breaks *out of* proper relationships and social contexts: "separat[ing] himself from both [brothers]" by his criminal activity, Ham breaks his fraternal and familial bonds; as excessively garrulous, he breaks the silence and "peace of the saints"; as restless and ablaze, he exhibits "impatience" in his "breast." Most detrimentally, like his forefather Adam, he breaks from the pure goodness that is divine. For Augustine, the subject does not descend or "fall" into criminality; rather, criminality refers to the turn or "fall" from good itself. That "the will does not fall 'into sin' [but] falls 'sinfully'" signifies wickedness not as what one moves *towards* but motion *itself.* Evil begins as "movement," such that the value of a deed is not internal or external to it as a separate yet linked feature but that by which any deed is itself a "movement" as a kind of effecting force.

Philo's division of Ham and Canaan as potentiality and actuality respectively disintegrates in Augustine's notion of carnality. As clarified in the previous chapter, Augustine argues against the idea of human nature as a prehistorical and nonmaterial ethical potentiality. "Humanity" has no nature that precedes criminality, he contends, but refers instead to a nature borne through the corruption and transgression of embodied movement. Accordingly human potentiality is, by definition, stained from the start through movement and consequently inseparable from its phenomenal "actuality" in embodied experience. Augustine remarks that the "motion" that inaugurates the criminal "turn" begins not as a notional will-to-evil but as a "movement of disobedience in [the] flesh."[13] To imagine instead that criminality begins with a stirring of the nonmaterial will that is subsequently activated through the body, he contends, would be to equate the criminal "human" with the purely good "soul," and thus human subjectivity as complete and whole prior to any corporeality. He accordingly mocks Platonists (and by extension Philo) for deeming materiality inessential to the formal truths of "man" while simultaneously asserting as eternal the cosmos and incarnate gods.[14] While other strands of Augustine's theology arguably uphold the distinction he criticizes here (e.g., his contrast of a "city of spirit" and "city of flesh"), his rejection of a noncarnal human "prototype" offers a fertile interpretation of radical criminality whereby genealogy is not what punishments fall *to* but is itself a fall (as cursed descent). Moreover, Augustine proposes, in falling humans turn "away from the unchangeable Good" and thus abandon the stability of the absolute, ensuring the perpetual movement of ethical subjectivity as what commences and remains in continuous flux.[15] The ethical worth of humanity vacillates in accordance with its distance from this original harmony with the good, a good it can never recover insofar as what "humanity" means for Augustine is precisely criminal being, with the first crime "so great that it . . . transmitted to posterity . . . a propensity to sin," affirming for all humans the predilection for transgression as its inexorable inheritance.[16]

Augustine places great weight on proper names in his interpretation, understanding Ham and Canaan as embodied "figures of speech"; such characters signify for him not fixed beings but representations whose meanings emerge and change through their metaphoric relations to past and future names. Whereas recent linguistic theory defines this motion of differential value as "play," Augustine conceives of it, in the vein of punishment, as "work." Thus he declares Canaan not only the "work" of Ham's reproductive labor but deports the name Canaan as "fitly interpreted 'their movement,' which is nothing else than their work."[17] Augustine's reading emphasizes the material conditions of language as a way of situating all activity that subjects experience as "exertion"—not as voluntary or involuntary, conceptual or physical, but as punitively carnal. Accordingly, Canaan is properly destined for Augustine to the continual motion of the forced laborer not in the guise of the slave or indentured servant (though these become possible formations as a result) but as one cursed with historical movement such that his words, intuitions, reflections, alliances, bodily "schema," and narrations—all that by which he might hope to acquire rest or security in the knowledge of himself as a self—can offer no respite or harbor. As a prosthetic extension of Ham, Canaan labors as "the boy, or slave" to his brothers "in the person of his son (i.e., his son)." "Canaan," that is, preserves as carnal reproduction Ham's lineage as the past that necessarily inheres in any new genealogical "citation." And in this, Augustine clarifies, Canaan anticipates the criminal subjectivity of future instantiations of the curse, those whom "it is possible and reasonable to regard Noah's middle son [Canaan] as typifying . . . [in that they] live scandalous lives," a hereticism perpetuated not via biological reproduction but through criminal and carnal inheritance.[18]

As a further effect of criminality as genealogical movement, Augustine suggests that every figural subject, as named and embodied, is prophetically preceded and anticipated (that is, *pre*figured) through signs that forecast one's character in advance. When correctly interpreted, Augustine remarks, those signs disclose the ethical subject to come, despite the indicators often being overlooked and the mark missed. In either case, he states, the figurative foreshadowing of the ethical subject precedes any physical "birth." In the Hamitic passage, the prophetic and criminal prefiguration of Canaan occurs just prior to the original violation as an anticipatory citation, repeated soon after, that ascribes primordial criminality to a figural relation rather than to an individuated subject:

> "Now the sons of Noah who came out of the ark were Shem and Ham and Japheth; and Ham was the father of Canaan. . . . Then Noah began farming and planted a vineyard. He drank of the wine and became drunk, and uncovered himself inside his tent. Ham, the father of Canaan, saw the nakedness of his father, and told his two brothers outside.

The announcement of Ham as "the father of Canaan" forges the paternal/filial bond as a criminal relation. It is not that Ham is the father of Canaan *and also* one who will shortly perform the violation initiating a cursed genealogy. He will, instead, enact this deed in his own name as well as in the

name of his son; or, rather, *as* his son, for whom he serves as proxy and guar-
antor, invoking the Fanonian paradigm by which such actions are "his own"
only insofar as they belong simultaneously to those who share that inheritance. Accordingly, Canaan's arrival in the diegesis is not only heralded by
his anticipatory citation as Ham's son but also announced in the guise of
bodies to come. In that sense, the story Canaan enters is one that, in retrospect, had always been a story written for and in expectation of his arrival.
He thereby appears not *after* but *at* the scene of the crime ("Ham, *the father of
Canaan*, saw the nakedness of his father, and told his two brothers outside"),
an entrance or staged break-in that criminally implicates him in his narrative
arrival, itself a criminal break into the secret pact of ethical knowledge.

The Blessing as Curse

This semiotics of the curse whose logic includes the subterfuges of secret
knowledges and illusory disclosures similarly constitutes the logic of the
"blessing." Accordingly, histories of responsibility prefigure ethical subjects
not only in relation to other delinquent ancestries but also to favored lines
of inheritable worth. Hence, the curse ordained through Noah enacts more
than the condemnatory sentencing of Ham and Canaan, effecting as well
the "blessed" ordinations of the "families" of Shem and Japheth ("Blessed be
the LORD, The God of Shem; And let Canaan be his servant." "May God
enlarge Japheth, And let him dwell in the tents of Shem; And let Canaan
be his servant.") Not external to the curse, such blessings constitute rather
those ancestries through which the Hamitic line represents a comparatively
deficient descent. The families of Shem and Japheth are not spared the consequences of the crime, though as "blessed" they receive a different fortune: one
an unadulterated "blessing," the other an "enlargement" more fortuitous
than a cursed existence yet not as exalted as the "tent" in which it dwells.

Ham's brothers do not come by their blessings through any pretense of
"good deeds," and so their inheritable ethical chosenness, as Cain Hope Felder
argues, may be unwarranted: "the people of Israel exhibit no extraordinary
attributes of values by which they objectivity merit Jahweh's election. . . ."[19]
The criticism, however, presumes with most interpretations that inheritable
blessings, like criminality, must originate from definable, preethical acts,
and furthermore, that blessings are not themselves a kind of criminality. On
the contrary, insofar as value expresses itself, like race, as a deviant mark, it
will do so even when that deviance is comparatively favorable (i.e., white). In
the same way that whiteness serves as the evaluative context within which

certain qualities become recognizable and anticipated, blessedness, rather than the product of good deeds, names that genealogy through which the deeds of ethical subjects actuate as comparatively favorable practices. The blessing thus surfaces within the structure of the curse and inheritable value rather than against it; as such, it is no more inescapable or liberated than a "cursed" lineage, nor is one freer for it. "Is it not true," Kierkegaard observes, "that the one whom God blesses he curses in the same breath?"[20] In that whiteness, as no less a stain than blackness, risks always a further "descent," the blessed are so only in relation to the criminal brethren they deign to supervise and overlook, and thereby remain at similar risk of their own decline as a cursed lineage, a threat no genealogy can escape. As whiteness curses its formation through blackness, the blessed curses its provenance of impurity and corruption. This instability or risk at the heart of the blessing—as what partakes necessarily in deviant and stained affiliations—is, one could say, the *price* whites pay for being *so valuable*.

The curse propels not universal "humanity" but, as with race, an ethically differentiated arrangement of genealogical descents, as witnessed in the verses preceding and following the short passage on Ham. The scene of the "crime" interrupts an earlier exchange in which God establishes a covenant with Noah, one provision of which is a guarantee of the postgenocidal restoration of humanity.[21] Just before the story of the crime comes a sentence that appears to transition into the institution of this provision: "*These three [were] the sons of Noah, and from these the whole earth was populated.*"[22] The narrative expectation produced by this is the consequent genealogical roll call of those first familial networks—that is, the entrance of descendants onto the world stage. Yet this dizzying register of prodigious offspring ("The sons of Japheth; Gomer and Magog, and Madai, and Javan, and Tubal . . ." et al.) is abruptly preempted; it hangs in suspension until the opening of the following chapter. Instead the declaration of Noah's sons as the source of world repopulation shifts suddenly to the account of Noah's experience with fermentation and the transgression and curse that follow. Only subsequent to this does the interrupted narrative of genealogical restoration recommence, not as a new verse but as the opening "chapter" of humankind. The curse functions thereby as what both concludes the Hamitic passage and opens up the "proper" narrative of temporal history.

Noah's cursing of Ham thus brings to closure in a single enunciation the dual narratives of the criminal and genealogical, a pronouncement that at once *executes*—both enables and terminates—unmarked ethical subjectivity. What otherwise might have transpired as a solemn, ceremonial speech act or deathbed ordination summoning into existence the proliferation of a people (Let Procreation Begin!) here takes the form of a juridical sentencing, the terms of which extend through eponymous lines in perpetuity.[23] It is through the linguistic enunciation that humanity and historical time emerge, both engendered by a curse that, in the same instant, overwrites them: humanity by a tiered fracturing into filiations, and historical, "mortal" time by the infinitude of the everlasting stain. As the culminating action of the story, Noah's ordination births not any single newborn but the concept or category within which every newborn is a particular, manifested instance; it is, more precisely, a resurrection of a categorical way of being that had been "washed clean" by the flood of prior criminal markings that could not otherwise, it would seem, have been erased.

Denominated Subjectivity

The chapter that immediately succeeds the articulation of the terms of the curse makes no overt reference to the event:

> May God enlarge Japheth, And let him dwell in the tents of Shem; And let Canaan be his servant." Noah lived three hundred and fifty years after the flood. So all the days of Noah were nine hundred and fifty years, and he died.
>
> [10] Now these are *the records of* the generations of Shem, Ham, and Japheth, the sons of Noah; and sons were born to them after the flood. The sons of Japheth *were* Gomer and Magog and Madai and Javan and Tubal and Meshech and Tiras. The sons of Gomer *were* Ashkenaz and Riphath and Togarmah. The sons of Javan *were* Elishah and Tarshish, Kittim and Dodanim, [et al.][24]

An unadorned series of names, these generational "records" precede the reanimation of any narrative action, as if providing a theatrical list of players, a role call of *dramatis personae* who will shortly, but not yet, perform the deeds by which they will demonstrate their virtues, vices, beneficence, and malfeasance, gradually disclosing their comparative worth. This coronating antechamber houses not subjects who reside in the space of possible actions but spectral prototypes and potentialities that resemble in their not-yet state the ethically embodied characters they promise to become. This citational introduction thus figurally denotes unmarked subjects still unscarred by evaluative and embodied predicates, where pure being is rendered solely by illocutionary utterances: "[Let there be] Gomer and Magog . . . Ashkenaz and Riphath . . . Elishah and Tarshish. . . ." The text would be said to offer, then, characters without characteristics whose ontological identities—the preethical truth of who they "are"—not only precede the introduction of the stain but purportedly provide the foundation or template upon which the scars and traces of evaluable deeds subsequently will inscribe themselves.

This enrollment of new lineages begins as faithfully silent in accordance with the conditions of the pact of shared ethical knowledge. Prior to this purgatorial theatrical state, however, Noah has enunciated already the relative worth of these names. His curse and blessings, traversing death, pass unbroken to his progeny, revealing Noah's recitation as simultaneously an incantation or raising of the dead through language, whereby each new generation finds itself resurrected through the anteceding criminal charge or movement of their accorded ancestors. This is possible only because the curse, once more, does not *place* a mark and fortune upon a given subject but enacts a naming that establishes and *transforms* subjectivity (consider, for instance, the common use of "curse words" as a slander or swearing that reconstitutes ethical identity, for example, the declaration of one as a swine, wretched beast, or any well-worn and cherished sexual or racial epithet that rechristens as much as revalues affiliated worth). The curse, as a mythical formulation, does not fabricate a value that becomes sutured to a name but rather bespeaks nominalization as always and necessarily evaluative.

Hence what appears a mere prefatory list of ethically unmarked names—placeholding ciphers that simulate in advance "real" biblical characters—is more pointedly a "program" made available to the reader and spectator that, in the dual senses of the term, prophetically prefigures those names so as to "program" or "schematize large families and alliances" and their "conflicts and factions."[25] Noah launches three lines of descent through an oration that is inaugural but also final, being both incontestable and, not insignificantly, the last recorded words he speaks. This conjunction of his sons with their ethical fates through performative incantations (akin to the playwright's *didascalia*) metonymically prefigures those "proper names"—Shem, Ham, Japheth—as inchoate ancestries, genealogical and qualitative citations of characters yet to enter the diagesis of mortality. Each recited name becomes thereby a titled heritage: through the curse, Ham signifies the "line of Ham" as, mutatis mutandis, does Shem in being "blessed," and Japheth "enlarged."[26] In that value conducts this metonymic translation between proper name and history of responsibility, this titling is more accurately an *entitling*, by which the name expresses not merely genealogical location but, in addition, the qualitative characteristics that comprise the differentiated worth of that association, and thus what is owed to and expected from any subject in virtue of that standing. Such entitlements *belong* to the subject not as the reward for performed deeds or the satisfaction of earlier, proprietary claims but in virtue of an endowment that confirms the name as an affiliative legacy. The subject comes into being insofar as it comes into fortune, entering like Oedipus with a mark that makes the future a birthright, whether known or unknown. History thus emanates through a decree that *denominates* in its nominations. It may suffice, in fact, merely to posit that there are *only* denominations, insofar as "denominating" signifies both "giving an appellation to"—in particular, through the act of "calling"—and designating the gradational worth of a thing or kind within a system of value (weight, money, etc.). The assertion that the nomination is a de facto denomination makes linguistically explicit the contention proposed in the first two chapters that value conditions the determination of what an event or action "is" for all representational percepts. This premise cuts against the depiction of existence as planar, which is to say, that diagrammatic resolve that receives the first question of being as intrinsically nonnormative.

Foucault, Genealogy, Value

The name as fortune and future does not predetermine specific behaviors of marked subjects, nor does it prophesy the tenor of events that will befall them (even the purportedly "blessed" are not spared episodes of subjugation). It denotes ethical subjectivity not as compromised by the name but as invested through it, an investment by which the subject becomes creditable within circuits of value as an "individual" producer and object of worth. The postdiluvial resurrection of humanity for which the curse functions as prolegomena cannot commence, therefore, from a mere roster of translucent, preethical entities whose proper names designate disparate individuals. It proceeds, rather, from a recitation or program that unveils an initial series of entitled iterations that the curse as movement and difference puts into play.

The covenant between Noah and God that ordains the repopulation of the world achieves itself in the carrying out of a criminal sentencing. Once the first round of humanity is wiped out through the flood, the (biological) clock stops. To be restarted, it must be rewound to produce a "secondary" originating offense. Another "fall" becomes necessary, for it seems that there can be no genealogical descent that is not propelled by an ethical descent. To envision genealogy as precipitated by value is already to reject the model of history as the mere unfolding of a sequential series of events, much less as that which disseminates through concentric rings of heterosexual reproduction. But it is also to reject ethics as genealogical networks of value that run parallel and external to genealogies of knowledge. Were ethics a metacommentary that ordered and ranked modes of behavior and ways of being, it would be on the premise that the relations, actions, and comportments to which value affixes could be conceptualized and enunciated prior to that entrance of value. This, however, would mean that embodied ways of being, as well as discursive formations themselves, owe for their emergence nothing to historical relations of value.

To hypothesize instead that value initiates and propels genealogical history, wherein the subjects of that history arise as "effects" of their qualitative, embodied inheritances, is nothing other than to say that genealogy has no movement without value. It is not by chance, therefore, that Foucault turns to Nietzsche to animate his static archaeology of knowledge into a mobile theory of genealogy. Yet in extracting the notion of "power" from "will-to-power," Foucault not only excises the vestigial metaphysics of the "will" but also expels from "power" the very engine of transvaluation that drives it. Foucault's contrast of "dominant" and "subjugated" knowledges denotes, however, an *evaluative* distinction, where value refers to the comparative, differentiating force by which knowledges could be asymmetric and thus "rise" or "fall." It is through *valuation*, as Nietzsche discloses, that truth has both identity *and* historical movement. "Power," accordingly, can neither dispose of ethics nor "expose" it as a disingenuously metastasized politics. Thus Foucault's theory of genealogy hesitates before Nietzsche's critical notion of descent or heritage (*Herkunft*). Foucault recognizes that descent for Nietzsche does not express the transmission of particular qualities but rather structures "affiliation to a group," yet he characterizes these affiliations as transmitted by "subtle, singular, and subindividual marks" that do not meaningfully signify racially or ethnically.[27] Foucault is understandably wary of the racial implications of descent, and thus reluctant to think the subject in a manner that would "map the destiny of a people" as well as "[impose] a predetermined form on all its vicissitudes."[28] It is specifically Nietzsche's association of descent with "inheritance" (*Erbschaft*) that for him renders the notion a "dangerous legacy." Such anxiety, however, mistakes inheritable genealogies as constrictive channels that flow just under the surface of disciplined subjectivity, currents constantly tugging the subject into streams of fated identities. Because on this view value is not a disciplinary force the pull of those legacies cannot be said to productively constitute subjects but only threaten them as "fragile inheritors."

Foucault sees descent as exposing "[the] errors, the false appraisals, and the faulty calculations that [give] birth to those things which continue to exist and have value for us."[29] He effectively critiques descent as an "evolution" that predetermines a fixed ranking of peoples; moreover, in redefining descent as a series of discrete "accidents" and "errors," he also rejects the theory of Augustine that the present is prefigured in the past through interpretable signs. For Augustine, however, recall that most signs remain overlooked until their prophecies have come into existence. In other words, descent for him provides not so much the knowledge of how things will or should be than the knowledge that allows one to retroactively understand how what exists was always destined to be. Inheritance, working backwards, does not constrain future selves but confirms, as with Canaan, the truth of the present. To avoid the (racial) danger of inheritable value, Foucault stresses that genealogy does not "demonstrate that the past actively exists in the present, [or] that it continues secretly to animate the present." How, though, could it *not* do this? How might the present be conceptualized except as what continues or alters the past, and thus what carries the past with it? Why, furthermore, should we take this "secret animation" to mean that the past predictably determines the present (in the vein of certain Marxist and psychoanalytic theories) rather than that the present is thinkable only through its production of a past? As suggested by Plato and the premoderns, the origin of value that propels inheritable descent is secret *because* it is not static but an always reconfigured and reiterated sign, as the secret aims not to hide a determining crime but to feign such an origin as the basis for any "group affiliation."

For descent to "give birth to value," it must partake of the concept of inheritance that Foucault wishes to separate from it. It does this through none other than "errors, false appraisals, and faulty calculations," for what are these other than little crimes that "give birth to" new historical paradigms, new genres of identity, and new conditions of speech? These "faults" are the "secrets"—signs disclosed to the genealogist in retrospect—that produce the faultlines of dominant and subjugated knowledges.

That genealogy is *necessarily* ethical does not make it an available object for ethical inquiry in the vein of a "history of ethics"; rather genealogy as ethical expresses the necessarily evaluative constitution of power relations as well as historical, discursive knowledges. There could be, that is, no discursive knowledge outside of an asymmetric force of value unless one imagines such knowledge as first congealing and then, under some secondary operation, taking on a relative valence. Genealogy, as Foucault and others have insightfully argued, commences not with a singular, irradiating event of history (discovery, logos, revelation, etc.) but with structural difference (signified by "power," "interpellation," "alterity," "writing," et al.); if so, value as the necessarily qualitative aspect that mediates difference as such remains its permanent stain.

The Parsing of Ethics and Genealogy

As entwined, the two themes that conclude the ninth chapter of Genesis— one of transgression and punishment, the other of genealogy regenerated— produce something greater than either would alone. Yet bothersome for many scholars is that an infraction could ignite a curse so potent as to prophetically prefigure ethical subjectivities in a manner that the singular will of the individual or even its involuntary "resistance" could not break or transcend. Accordingly, one interpretive strategy advocates disjoining the two narrative threads that comprise the passage in an effort to separate the ethical from the genealogical; Ephraim Isaac, for instance, affirms the passage's "idea of *moral* chosenness" as a means of differentiating people but contends that this division has no implications with respect to "biology," arguing that the story reinforces the core premise of "human dignity and . . . equality."[30] Cain Felder takes a somewhat different tack, voicing no objection to either narrative on its own but rejecting a consolidation that would sanction "a primeval rationale for differences in the destinies or fortunes of certain groups of persons."[31] Felder views Ham's violation as a matter "far less complicated"; his "solution" to the dilemma of the passage imagines an original, divine version that holds the two narratives apart, a division later compromised by a worldly, "politically motivated" merge.[32]

Felder's effort to decouple value and genealogy in these passages, and his suggestion that the authenticity (or "sacredness") of the two thematics rest on this separation, bespeaks broader theoretical tenets that similarly disaggregate culture from biology, ethics from epistemology, and value from interpretation. Through such dualistic partitioning, punishments remain strictly commensurate with individual agents while genealogical lines, ancestries, and bodies remain value neutral. Occluded here, however, is how worth tracks through primary designators of "who we are" (e.g., class, residence, profession, race, gender, age, size, etc.). Assuredly, acute awareness of subjugations based on these classifications leads one to shrink from sanctioning such markers as evaluative, any concession to which, it is feared, constitutes the first step to instigations of systematic cruelty. Moreover, as Stephen Mulhall clarifies, the notion of original sin or, here, the inheritable ethical stain, "violates a variety of interrelated and central Enlightenment precepts. It is fundamentally offensive to any conception of morality that places human autonomy at its heart [as well as being] offensive to reason."[33] In reaction, the subject becomes home for a kind of responsibility that, philosophers insist, does not and cannot be transferred through shared identities, and which properly attends only to the subject's prescriptive possibilities. In this an affirmation of the original neutrality of being is rationally commanded as the departure for the practice of ethical philosophy. Indeed what otherwise would prevent a Canaan and all his posterity from bearing the burden for a father's misdeed—without recourse, without appeal, without end?

The curse's negation of an exclusive correspondence between doer and deed creates the potential for a "single" crime to produce an inexhaustible number of criminals, each one absolutely guilty for the entirety of the original act. Canaan receives, importantly, not merely the punishment for Ham's misdeed but the blame for it as well. This blatant transference of responsibility not just as a "debt" inherited from another but as the reinstitution of that performative autonomy raises objections from those who wish to fix that criminal responsibility to ethical individuality. But if, as Alain Locke proposes, the critical error that led anthropologists to reaffirm existing racial hierarchies was their confidence in the fixity of qualitative characteristics, perhaps criminal responsibility, like race, is best regarded not as a burden that stains and stabilizes subjectivity but as relations that facilitate its evolving expression.[34]

Having detailed the curse as the premodern structure by which subjects are conceived as responsible actors of deeds within comparative and inheritable genealogies of value, we might now ask what features of that dynamic have persisted in modernity, not only through the concept of race but, more generally, in theories of subject formation. If denomination conscripts the subject into its comparative ethical appointments, how have contemporary theories of the subject represented, or perhaps tried to circumvent, these entitlements? Additionally, if value so centrally informs not only subject formation but representational meaning, should it not figure more prominently in precisely those postmetaphysical accounts in which historically situated consciousness presumably displaces the authority of the atomized individual? How would the curse, as what previously governed the determination of criminal subjects and actions, manifest in contemporary theories that appear, at first glance, to give no heed to such premodern structures? The next chapter thus directs the arguments so far pursued in this book to bear on more recent theories of subject formation in order to support the claim above that all genealogy is ethical genealogy. Opening with a reflective assessment of the general skepticism or "suspicion" towards relations of embodiment and value that arise through modernity, it proposes that the curse, reconfigured as "criminal suspicion," does not cede to the disenchantments of modern scientific logic but remains at home within it. Focusing on late Sartrean ethics and Althusserian ideology, the chapter articulates how criminal genealogy as "suspicion" continues to animate contemporary readings of the origin of embodied subjectivity.

5

Criminal Suspicions

> Do the ethics of suspects.
>
> SARTRE, *Notebook for an Ethics*

PHILOSOPHY TELLS THAT modernity commences with ontological doubt, a doubt recognized as "good" suspicion by all accounts, forthright and avuncular. Without this suspicion, would truth ever have been subjected to such thorough inspection? Similarly, if truth did not exhibit criminal tendencies—in league, specifically, with evil demonology—would Descartes have forcibly stopped and searched it, stripping it of external appearances, and systematically interrogating it? But this, again, all to the *good*, both for philosophy and truth itself, for doubt justifies itself in just this way: only that which conceals something dangerous—disorder, failure, incoherence, deception—need fear its scrutinizing and invasive procedures. Or so it is contended. Traipsing around in its dreamcoats, truth long disguised and inflated itself to the senses, passing in and out of all variety of costumes, preserving in these ways an awesome and inscrutable, and thus harmful mystery. With proper warrant then did Descartes remove it to an isolated cell and shine upon it a solitary, piercing bulb. In that type of setting, of course, everything appears only more suspicious, but this insinuation was necessary for truth's ethical liberation. Suspicion, then, ultimately allowed truth to *appear* as itself, a revelation by which it was *exonerated* as well from any intrinsic affiliation with evil. In other words, it was only those technologies of suspicion—science, systematicity, method, inquisition, etc.—that, in the capacity to state what *is* the case, could absolve a questionable identity *from* suspicion. Modernity may have applied doubt to truth, but the real triumph was that through doubt truth became *recognizable* as such, which is to say, shed at last its criminal suspiciousness.

The point has been made elsewhere that the modern turn of philosophy reflected not only a new set of representational relations between subjects and the world but also effected for those subjects "new" and multiple objects of inquiry.[1] The consequence, more than the development of a systematic and universal interrogative logic, was the initiation of an entire intellectual industry conjoined through specialized objects of knowledge, a burgeoning web of ateliers of esoteric investigation each constituted through the skeptical dissection of its object of concern. Suspicion guided each of these technologies of arrest and examination, demanding certain "violences"—the "thematization" of being, the contraction of *pharmakon* to "philosopheme," the formation of culture as epiphenomenal to nature—that promised, in the end, a plenitude of representation coincident with that specialized object's ostensible removal from doubt.

But this story of modernity originating with ontologically good doubt closed centuries later with "bad" suspicion—a *Nietzschean* suspicion—that placed in doubt not truth in isolation but truth as *value*. Unlike Cartesian doubt, this skepticism did not recuperate or exonerate, nor did it reveal meaning behind the veil; instead it doubted the beneficence of "good doubt" itself, wondering aloud whether philosophical knowledge was not a drive or force that just wanted to get its *hands* on something. Not truth but *truth-seeking* became thereby stained as an inherently *moral* endeavor, and not, in the end, to be trusted. As a consequence, truth sunk back into suspicious contingency regularized as "interpretive" and "perspectival," but not, this time, because of its own enigmatic machinations but because those Cartesians interrogators had neglected to first turn the spotlight on their own suspicious motivations. Thus while Descartes freed *truth* from suspicion, Nietzsche (followed soon by Freud) disclosed the philosopher or *truth-seeker* as a suspicious figure. Thus to this day, within and outside the discipline, while Descartes wears the mantle of the "productive" skeptic whose suspicions engender philosophical optimism, Nietzsche remains saddled (though with begrudging respect) with that of the "unproductive" nihilist whose legacy is the displacement of universal morality *by* ubiquitous suspiciousness (irony, simulacra, panopticism, performativity, etc.). The starkly disparate eulogies echo a reciped version of Western philosophy in which Descartes ultimately rescues metaphysics from the jaws of doubt whereas Nietzsche, anticipating an era of global spectatorship, provides colorful commentary on the savaging of metaphysics without the customary mantra of its inevitable rebirth.

If epistemology has managed to stitch itself back together since this dissolution, sometimes creatively, sometimes clumsily, through recourse to language and history—and, at its most voluble, to the biological sciences— ethics, on the other hand, has taken the hit rather poorly. Still actively mining the normative for the glint of an atomic element of value, ethics continues to circle in an eddy of loss and mourning, pursuing support for its principled weightiness. For unlike epistemology, ethics has struggled to configure itself through language and history without sacrificing what it imagines to be its sole philosophical and social contribution: the prescriptive declaration. Its throne of authority pulled out from under it, ethics' disclosure and denouncing of evil in a post-moral climate has becomes listless and predictable, as has its affirmation of the comparative moral superiority of various ideological relations, institutions, and cultural practices. But this sullenness is largely a factor of its having become separated in modernity from the discernment of truth and, subsequently, dependent upon the promise of epistemic certainty. Once ethics became formalized as a secondary procedure evaluating already vetted conceptual knowledge it could have no greater metaphysical legitimacy than the phenomena it assessed. In other words, as a subordinate attachment to phenomena, its own truth was necessarily predicated on the truth of that to which it was affixed. As supplementary valences placed upon or located within already given states of affairs, value was beholden to the limits of knowledge that circumscribed any possible representational truth. Accordingly, as epistemology came to concede the historical a priori and, additionally, the contingency and situatedness of mental states and knowledge formations, ethics as what drew its prescriptive authority from the epistemic firmament of modernity lost the ground of its legitimacy. While epistemology has weathered—and even flourished from—the shift from "Truth" to "truth," ethics has repeatedly faltered, in part because it is not clear whether historically contingent ethics can generate a prescriptive declaration, without which, according to its own premises, ethics would not *be* ethics; that is, it would no longer have philosophical *value*.

The cautionary and conflicted response of ethics has been to place chips on both the red and black, at once asserting the inviolable prescriptive through a virtual and classical "transcendental" (as rights, justice, dignity, plurality, etc.) while making a show of contingency, revisability, and negotiation as watchwords for a Nietzschean ethics of suspicion directed toward comprehensive and hermetic moral systems. Thus, for instance, Jacques Derrida issues a rhetorical extension of Nietzsche's castigation of "bad conscience," noting that one must simultaneously remain suspicious of "good conscience" as the attitude that one's inexhaustible responsibility to others could ever be fulfilled.[2] To stipulate in advance the boundaries of absolute duty, he suggests qua Kierkegaard, prevents openness to unanticipated and as yet inconceivable moral obligations still to come. Derrida thus situates ethics within the historical in the Hegelian sense that what the moral law commands is an open-ended evolution, yet maintains nevertheless the force of the pre-scriptive through declarations that subjects bear intrinsic "responsibility" for all others and that justice is "undeconstructable." Unlike his early writ-ings that strike precisely at metaphysical self-presence, in these texts Derrida indulges in bald pronouncements of first philosophy, as if the exclusive objec-tive of ethics were to discern humanistic, intuitive content. Michel Foucault accedes, too, to an ethics of suspicion in his late interviews on value. With his oft-cited remark that "[it] is not that everything is bad, but that everything is dangerous" he issues caution toward moral systems while distancing himself from the Nietzschean challenge to prescriptive self-determination.[3] The sum-mation leads him to the warrant of a "hyper- and pessimistic activism," a call to hesitant action that encapsulates the divided state of contemporary ethical thought, one unable to dispense with the imperative for dutiful interventions while simultaneously unable to draw them from incontrovertible truths on which value has come to depend.

The common complaint that Nietzsche delivers a purely "negative" approach to value finds no real contradiction here. Accordingly even an enthusiastic uptake of Nietzsche as decisively and unsparingly destabiliz-ing of moral certainty does not correspond to any revision of value as other than supplementary to and distinct from the production of knowledge. Consequently the "ethics of suspicion" as a strategy of cautious yet conscien-tious responsibility becomes one in which the "suspicious subject" is one who *wields* suspicion, applying it not only to phenomenal representations of the world but also, reflectively, to its own evaluations of those phenomena. It is to charge, in effect, that in addition to and *apart* from being a "thing" that thinks, the subject is a thing that "suspects," where suspicion denotes doubt in its ethical manifestation. Yet despite the profusion of interventions in the last several decades that have reimagined the subject as one effected by rather than possessing and wielding knowledge, not a single, sustained analytic has contemplated the "suspicious subject" in like fashion—*not*, that is, as the subject who responsibly engages in radical moral doubt but the subject who comes into being *through* criminal suspicion and thus *as a suspect* in name and identity.

In the same interview in which he recommends a course of "pessimis-tic activism," Foucault explains his concept of ethical subjectivity, per the absence of any "given" identities, as "much closer to Nietzsche's than to Sartre's," aligning himself less with an ethics of "authenticity" than of "cre-ativity."[4] Foucault's staging of Sartrean morality as a modernist and staid counterpoint to Nietzsche's bold theories of revaluation is not entirely without justification. Indeed, Sartre's most popular discussions of moral quandaries in which, as Foucault alludes, one strives for authentic subjectivity, provide an unlikely source for reconceptualizing value in light of Nietzschean skepticism. Yet a posthumous collection of Sartre's notes for an unfinished work on ethics offers a number of unexpected entries into such areas.[5] The collection of reflective, if often unfinished, apothegms and prolegomenas resembles Nietzsche's aphoristic style while its reading of ethical subjectivity as the product of a crime—more directly than most contemporary theory—ushers the reversal by which the subject who harbors suspicion becomes, in congress with Nietzschean revaluation, the subject *of* suspicion.

Marking Time

This chapter's epigraph—"Do the ethics of suspects"—appears in Sartre's *Notebooks for an Ethics* as a single, seemingly isolated imperative, specifically, as the fiftieth of sixty-eight numbered aphorisms in a section entitled "The Ambivalence of History and the Ambiguity of the Historical Fact."[6] The aphorisms surrounding the call for an "ethics of suspects" provide no overt context for or explication of it—not only is there no direct clarification of what an "ethics of suspects" might entail, nothing discloses to whom or in what modality the assertion is offered, whether as a rallying call to ethicists, a reminder Sartre gives himself with respect to the scope of his project, or a scratched enticement of a possible future line of inquiry.

Despite, however, its strangely severed immediate surroundings, multiple other passages in the notebooks offer tantalizing if inchoate counsel for articulating an "ethics of suspects." The most generous come early in the notebooks, where Sartre hypothesizes reflective consciousness and narrative history as both commencing through criminality. The passage opens abruptly and tumbles out in truncated prose, suggesting the preliminary and ongoing development of this thinking:

> The fault is not capricious. The historical act by which being negates itself into the For-itself is a fall and a memory of Paradise Lost. Myth of the fault in every religion and in folklore. . . . The appearance of the For-itself is properly speaking the irruption of History in the world. . . . Reflection originally springs up as an accessory to this since it is the creation of a new diaspora in the attempt at recuperation. But even then, as we know, it misses itself. Here, therefore, the possibility

of pure reflection arises as an admission of this missing the mark and as taking a stand in the face of it.[7]

Self-consciousness emerges here not with recognition of one's authentic mark or stain but with recognition that one has already, like Oedipus, *missed* the mark. Relational subjectivity "irrupts" or breaks into the world as history, and thus, as a genealogical entrance, through a descent or "fall." Two consequences follow from this primal crime: the first is a "diaspora" of being that, as a function of a "fault," generates a dispersion of fallen genealogies or "faultlines" whose relations are then predicated on and mediated through languages of origin "myths" and "folklore." The second is self-consciousness as an "accessory" to this crime and to the production of the consequent diasporas or faultlines. The "accessory" signifies self-consciousness as both an effect of the violation but also as what is present at the scene of the crime and thus at "fault" as a participant. Yet in keeping with the genre of origin myths in which the capital transgression defies and eludes representation, self-consciousness understands itself as an accessory only through a "memory." This memory, however, does not recollect the crime but the *missing* of the mark—that is, it "remembers" the preethical "paradise" as what is lost to it forever; it comes into self-consciousness through the reflective grasp of what it cannot bring into representation. But this missing of the mark could not have been otherwise for the sake of consciousness: the crime is not accidental or "capricious" but inevitable, yet the subject's relation to it remains clouded and unknown. Consciousness emerges in the shadows of suspicion and doubt—nothing, precisely, can be pinned on it, yet it is far from innocent.

This concentrated account in which Sartre pieces together value and consciousness offers no authentic subjectivity of the kind Foucault takes issue with in Sartre's other work. Here Sartre does not presume ethics as rules or guidelines by which some already formed being motivates or restricts itself, nor does he designate it a faculty or capacity by which a given subject can weigh possible future actions or retrospectively assess previous ones. The commencement of "pure reflection" discloses that, in the end, nothing in fact has been "lost" in that descent—certainly not any paradise—but only "missed." More precisely, the subject recognizes the "purity" of itself in recognizing that it has overlooked the impurity of its origin, signified by its everlasting stain.

Sartre goes on to theorize that this descent does not emanate from supposed preethical "animal" drives of the subject such as self-preservation or other "natural" inclinations: "My body, my sexual desires, my hunger, my sleep, and my death are first of all *me*, and they are also *values*. Finally, they are moments in the much vaster enterprise of my *action*."[8] Embodiment—desiring, breathing, sleeping, acting—is already ethical subjectivity, not in virtue of any prescriptive duty inherent to consciousness but because ethics names the differentiation by which subjectivity can reflectively identify something it understands as "itself," such that every "enterprise" of that subject acquires its meaning and identity—"what it is"—as a function of value. The history of philosophy has already, in its own way, demonstrated all of this: Plato on the appetites (hunger), Descartes on wakefulness (sleep), Freud on psychosexuality (desire), and Heidegger on death. In each case, the purportedly self-evident and purely ontological distinction—wakefulness/sleep, instinct/desire, existence/nonexistence, etc.—derives from a formalization and hierarchy that generates these elements in evaluative relation. Sleep, hunger, and other desires similarly take conscious form only in the context of material practices emergent within a "vast enterprise" of evaluative actions. But insofar as these actions are "me" they are not universal or stable "instincts," Sartre contends, but ways of being that are particular to the genealogical faultlines within which "I" fall. Following St. Augustine, he further proposes that our existential "situation"—the context that makes recognizable any possible action of that subject—is not what one *falls into* but what receptively *befalls* one as ethical history or descent:

> "What complicates the *situation* is that it is historical, that is, exactly the fact that it is already experienced and thought about by other For-itselves for whom I exist before being born and who make claims on my freedom. . . . [T]hese For-itselves have assigned me a future: they have already defined me as French, bourgeois, Jewish, etc.; they have already determined my earnings, my obligations, my chances; they have already made the world meaningful. . . . In a word, they have defined me as *nature*. I am born with my nature because other human beings came before me . . . [in being] Jewish, I am internally penetrated with a Jewish nature."[9]

The historical "situation" does more than effect ethical subjectivity through ongoing discourses of evaluative meaning; it indicates, more fully, that such ethical inheritances await subjectivity. Situatedness, Sartre implies, does not remain indifferent and unconcerned to what may be thrown into it, as a network of impersonal background forces that act upon whatever happens to fall within its relational field. Historical descent, rather, *anticipates* subjectivity, in its animated and captivating folkloric within which subjectivity reflexively apprehends itself as having missed the mark. Thus this descent reserves for being not simply a meaningful world but a world of meaning *personalized for that subject*.

Sartre's insight that "I exist before being born" encapsulates the "complication" of the subject in relation to its genealogical inheritances, which is also to say, the future "assigned" it predicated on its embodied and social affiliations. One might infer from this proposition that abstract qualities of the subject precede its concrete, material emergence, which is then drafted into its awaiting armature of meaning. Yet this picture mistakenly parses subjectivity and materiality in imaging birth as the commencement of material reality. Sartre's example of being "born" with a "Jewish nature" does not refer to an internal penetration that takes place on the maternity table but an array of bodily markings or stains by which a subject will already be recognized culturally and corporeally as "Jewish." In this respect, the anticipation of ethical inheritance has not only the characteristic of marking subjects but also, as Sartre asserts, of "marking time": in a conventional sense, history prepares for and awaits the subject, marking time until its arrival, but at the same time history is nothing but this anticipation in which nothing ever "arrives," bringing subjectivity into being precisely through those markings, such that birth does not signify the "beginning" of anything more than one temporal instance amongst several iterations of the ethical subject.

Time, however, not only marks for Sartre but is itself marked through subjectivity, being no less a consequence of criminal descent and thus relations of value. Sartre accordingly contemplates "Temporality conceived of as fallen, as decadent. . . . History is a *myth*. Or instead it serves to demonstrate the perenniality of certain institutions through their ups and downs. Time is essentially the time of repetition."[10] That time is a necessary condition of representation, as Kant argues, does not mean, as Sartre here suggests, that it is not also "fallen" or evaluative, or that the conditionality it sets for representation is not a function of that value. It may seem odd to imagine a transcendental aesthetic as "ethical," yet the point is not that time "is moral" or has ethical content but that, for instance, temporal marking—then/now, first/second, before/after, past/present/future—expresses itself through evaluatively differentiated terms. Furthermore, that Sartre cites institutions here rather than individuals as the vacillating expressions of temporal descent calls attention to the marking of the subject as funded not primarily by narrowly familial expectations and fantasies but complex and extremely specific *anticipatory* historical character formations. Such formations may be those that appear at the intersection of a variety of anxieties: the consumer whose ready access to cheap, processed foods makes every meal a dietetic battle with obesity; the techno-student neurologically geared toward virtually administered pedagogies; the Western laborer with a hundred-year life expectancy who must work until eighty-four to receive social entitlements—all historical figures anticipated through the shifting fortunes of institutional heritages.

In the above passages, Sartre explains history as what repeats itself as "myth," perpetuating at each iteration the structure of the fall and stain. At other instances in the *Notebook*, however, Sartre insists on the "separation" of "mythic" descent from "History," in which the latter continues to evolve alongside myth despite the "false representations of it." Furthermore, he writes, "History" also refers to the relation or struggle between these two representational means of temporal thinking: "the relation of History to the historical myth is itself History."[11] This "real" history, he continues, wins out over mythic history that is surpassed by "the progressive change in the essence of History" which "[t]oday . . . has regained its autonomy: it is the whole set of acts by which mankind decides about the essence of man for itself and for others in and through History."[12] Sartre thus seems to double back here and elsewhere on the hypothesis of ethics as the irruption into criminal history of suspicious subjectivity; in the comparative safety of these rough, unsigned reflections, he hedges on this grievous premise, returning to the commonplace view of criminal ethical inheritance as a isolated and mythic chapter in the story of humankind.

As Sartre's narrative of progressive History has it, the stain of ethical doubt and inheritance has been washed clean, allowing subjectivity to "regain" the prior "autonomy" of its modernist sovereignty that never truly disappeared but "fell" under the distorting, discoloring suspicions forged in mythic history. As a result of this triumph, humankind "decides" the destiny "for man itself and for others" (and it may be that the shape of this "deciding for others" is, paradoxically, the kind of formation that anticipates ethical subjectivity). But when, one might ask, did this victory of History over myth take place? Or, more accurately, what in the relation of "real" to "mythic" history ultimately allowed for the hegemony of the former? If ethics has found its footing today, that success would be recorded, according to Sartre, not necessarily in writings on moral theory but in that mapping of subjectivity as constituted through the dynamic between "real" and "mythic" historical representation.

This assertion that "the relation of History to the historical myth is itself History" bears a strikingly resemblance to Althusser's late-Marxian definition of ideology as "a 'representation' of the imaginary relationship of individuals

to their real conditions of existence,"[13] a proposition that also locates subjectivity at the representational intersection of real and mythic history. If the
criminal stain of modernity and premodernity comes to an end in the contemporary disclosure of the institutional production of ideology, as Sartre
implies, Althusser's theory of the interpellative formation of subjectivity
should serve as a eulogy to these fantasies of inheritable ethical embodiment,
releasing at last the subject from its criminal suspiciousness. To be sure, these
well-scavenged ideas of Althusser may seem unwelcome to considerations of
criminal *ethical* subjectivity insofar as one of the advantages of Althusserian
theory is thought to be its apprehension of subjectivity as a fundamentally
political entity and its consequent decentering of ethics as merely one of many
ideological formations. And yet, what contemporary theory better examples
a subjectivity that arises as a perpetual figure of criminal suspicion? If Sartre's
utterance "Do the ethics of suspects" is a prophetic prefiguring, Althusser's
theory of ideology and interpellation is its anticipated descendant.

Strange Subjects

> [Ideology transforms] individuals into subjects . . . by
> that very precise operation which I have called *inter-*
> *pellation* or hailing, and which can be imagined along
> the lines of the most commonplace everyday police (or
> other) hailing: "Hey, you there!"

> Assuming that the theoretical scene I have imagined
> takes place in the street, the hailed individual will turn
> round. By this mere conversion, he becomes a *subject.*[14]

Althusser describes the double constitution of subjectivity and ideology as
a "strange phenomenon" that epitomizes nevertheless the "commonplace,"
speaking of ideology and subjectivity as simultaneously unique and banal.
Strange also is Althusser's example of the "everyday" hail that incites this
double constitution—namely, a decidedly *uncommon* run-in with the author-
ities. In a footnote, Althusser admits that the police hail is a "special form"
of interpellation, again both anomalous *and* ordinary, though he does not
detail what sets it apart from other modes of hailing. By "special" Althusser
may be acknowledging that instances of interpellation by police in modern
civil societies are relatively rare for the majority, those who live without the
steady punctuation of such encounters. If so, the "special form" of the police

hail may warrant the categorization of those for whom such incidents *are* typical—immigrants, the homeless, "profiled" racial and ethnic classes—as *strange* subjects: atypical representatives of a common or universal subjectivity. From the start, Althusser's theory of subject formation seems attuned to the production of stained subjectivities as at once deviant and unmarked.

Althusser holds that the mode of ideological self-consciousness is recognition; but what is the proto-subject to recognize itself *as*? The strangeness of interpellation as both common *and* exceptional reflects the hail as constituting *two* rather than one "concrete" beings, with the other—the police officer—*also* a special or atypical figure (rather than an "everyman"). This suggests that the "specialness" of the subject constituted by the hail is also achieved through its manifestation as the "recognizable" complement to the specialness of the officer—the former the one who, in the given scenario, evokes the officer's criminal suspicion. But is the suspect the only subjectivity produced in this moment? The officer, it would seem, would also come into being in this exchange, as an effect of its own hail, insofar as the officer's identity as such depends upon its recognition by the suspect. Accordingly the officer need function here as no less a figure enabled in this relation, a figure whose "agency" only appears as such from the standpoint of the suspect, whereas, for the officer, the perspective is reversed: it is the suspect, or more precisely criminal suspicion, that summons it *as* a responsive figure of authority motivated or *moved* to action by that suspicion. The "specialness" of the subject, in contrast, attests to a uniqueness forging it as a figure of suspicion. The subject is suspicious *on its face*, which is to say in its very symbolic carnality.

Criminality does not "belong," then, to the suspect as a kind of property; rather it already *is* the context of the Althusserian imaginary; it has, and needs, no explanation. The preethical diegesis would accordingly be a preideological one, free of institutions and state apparatuses; thus to stage the scene as the coming to consciousness of an "innocent" individual would affirm ideology as a brainwashing or staining in the manner against which Althusserian theory is directed. That criminality provides the relational context that makes subject formation possible does not imply or obligate the naming of a primordial crime.[15] No transgressive content informs this relation, no information illuminates the doings of the one who is hailed. Accordingly, the ideological subject as suspect is neither innocent nor guilty—or, more precisely, such divisions are themselves derivative of, rather than what constitute, criminal responsibility. That "innocence" and "guilt" do become self-conscious, possible identities owes itself rather to theories of the ethical stain that insist upon a transgression imprinting itself on the unmarked and unaffiliated body. Such narratives can only gesture, like the Hamitic myth, to that preethical figure *through the stain*—that is, through the displacement of value as a secondary and occluding quality under the mask of which resides the unscarred and uninscribed prototype of the authentic, differentiated individual who simultaneously instances the universal genus-species.

Althusser does, to be sure, refer to "guilty conscience" as a consequent feature of criminal subject formation. Yet this guilt should not be thought of as what springs from a deep well internal to the subject or as a debt or penalty; such popular moral renderings of "guilt" strip ethical subjectivity of its embodied and genealogical criminal kinships. Instead, insofar as "guilt" functions as an expression of the subject's realization of the missed mark, that is, of the scars and traces, as Alain Locke writes, by which it is conscripted into a cursed inheritance, it cannot be the product of any nameable crime (certainly no crime against "humanity"). Such "guilt" would signify, then, not the Nietzschean notion of *schuld* as a responsibility incurred through the closed economy of the balance sheet (or even, as Derrida suggests, the open economy of the gift), but in the Fanonian sense of one's self-recognition through responsibility for the crimes of one's inherited lines of embodied relations and ancestors. Another way of saying this is that the guilt of the Althusserian subject is not that of one who has *committed a crime*, known or unknown, for this conclusion does not hold or suspend the line by which suspicion can persist—one who is guilty in this manner is no longer suspicious, no longer a continuing subject of investigation. The hailed subject, rather, is one guilty by association—that is, as Sartre writes above, as an *accessory* to the crime. Like Canaan, the interpellated subject is one *narratively placed at the scene of the crime*, even before its conventional "birth," and thus enters the world through implication as a suspicious subject.

Criminal interpellation cannot be accounted for by any particular violation out of which a crime might be construed, even though Western intellectual history seems rife with portrayals of ethical subject formation triggered by some such fractious event: a primordial violence, theft, or betrayal that initiates cycles of retribution; a battle of forces, wills, or bodies resulting in a victor and vanquished; a lie, deception, fantasy, or broken promise or pact that takes the subject out of itself and disguises its phenomenological oneness with others. Such origin narratives conjure a conflict designed to *explain* disparity, which is to say, to justify evaluative difference. (Consider that at stake in these familiar scenes of subject formation is not ontological recognition—that is, how these figures grasp each other as identical "human" entities capable of countersigning consciousness in the first place. What these accounts narrate, rather, is the emergence of hierarchical relations as mutually recognized within an already presumed single species; analogous to Kant's natural history, they thereby elucidate statuses or lines of embodied worth.) Althusserian subject formation, however, is not fabricated as the commencement of all subject formation—of life, sociality, institutions, history, etc., as a beginning that would require, thereby, a theater of the onset of criminality—but one that presumes, *in media res*, already ongoing criminal affiliations. Interpellation thus does not shatter and disperse a generic humanity along lines of ethical inheritance, thereby creating and explaining, for instance, class division; it does not give warrant to the dynamic of institutional agent and urban suspect. Without the conceit of an instigating crime, ideology theorizes a criminal subject formation that—in failing to posit universally innate qualities or teleological objectives of the species as generative, interpretable motives of its principle characters—suspends all naturalizing accounts.

Conjuring Origins

That no crime is named at the site of ideological subject formation does not ensure that the scene escapes, as it were, its own inheritance from those that have come before it—those, in particular, that consistently and, in some respects, necessarily, have conceived the origin of value through the metaphor of the stain. Althusser cautions, for instance, that his "theatrical" portrayal of the extraordinary yet banal formation of relational subjectivity not be mistaken as a referential event, aware that certain compositional conditions of representation, for instance, the necessary temporality in which the affair unfolds, implicitly suggest such historical actualization. One might point also to the "characterizations" of the officer and hailed "individual" whose mere naming implies an unstained mode of existence as they take their places in readiness for the drama that will constitute them. The conditions of representation demand that they narratively preexist—if only as a phantasm of the not-yet—the ideological transformation of subjectivity they exist to demonstrate, thus simulating a kind of human proto-consciousness that precedes its onstage entrance into historical and, here, ideological performance. Like the roll call of names that immediately follows the unveiling of the biblical curse, of stranded figures not yet galvanized by the narrative in their "roles," the mere citation of suspect and agent as those whom ideology *will* "befall" insinuates the mythic space of the unmarked.

Althusser attempts to address, however, the illusion of such pretext by having the reader resituate the scene distorted by these representational limitations: "what thus seems to take place outside ideology (to be precise, in the street), in reality takes place in ideology."[16] One thus must go beyond the allegory to understand ideology, a "moving through" that requires one take the additional step of psychically resituating the given scene of interpellation *within* the context meant to define it. This assignment to restage as *internal* to ideology what the allegory unwittingly if unavoidably presents as *external* to it—a procedure Althusser leaves for readers to effect through their own cognitive imaginary—would ideally counteract, for him, the incoherence of nonideological subjectivity. Moreover, this instruction aims, with a sharp eye on earlier origin myths, to break the allegory from its own inheritance as the latest in a long line of structural fantasies that found embodied consciousness through the stain. Althusser's supplemental directive to *reconjure* the backstage of this piece of theater—that which conventionally functions as the realm of unmarked pure potentiality—as already within a semiology of criminal relations can be read, in other words, as that which orders the shift from "myth" to "ideology." For Althusser to produce a theory entirely "within" ideology, then, obliges simultaneously its severing from forms of representation external to ideology as well as, thereby, a full liberation from and rejection of the prior intellectual heritage of allegories of subjectivity to which ideology would remain answerable.

In ideology, Althusser contends, the "question of the 'cause' . . . disappears."[17] This is because, he reasons, any "cause" of ideology would also operate *within* rather than outside the imaginary relation that "govern individuals." It would be, then, "this relation that contains the 'cause' which has to explain the imaginary distortion of the ideological representation of the real world."[18] Cautiously retaining the language of causality, Althusser's theory does not portray as missing the kind of "causal" explanation that would, for instance, unveil the "crime" by which the proletariat is thought to have earned its comparatively miserable existence, a revelation that could in turn be revaluated to confer upon that class an authentic moral superiority. For the ideological relation to contain any cause that may or may not found it is to suspend, in other words, causality itself; it is not to say that causality does not exist but that it can never be isolatable and external to the relationality it is thought to produce.

If the allegory does not symbolize the transition from an undifferentiated to a differentiated humanity—if it does not mark, so to speak, the beginning of the mark—what critical transition does it designate? Althusser describes subject formation as a "conversion" or "transformation," yet in this risks summoning an anterior mode of being that becomes thus "converted" or "transformed." If read as what converts the (purely potential) "individual" into historic "subjectivity," the allegory would fulfill its legacy as the contemporary instantiation of the demand for a logic that explains and legitimates differentiated lines of value within which the subject becomes recognizable. In contrast, if understood as what must be revisioned *within* ideology and thus as what disinherits the scene from a philosophical lineage of origin myths, the allegory would seem to eradicate the point of "transformation" or "conversion" at which ideology and subjectivity are said to be doubly constituted.

Althusser fabricates his conceptual narrative so as to unravel at the moment of transformation, and in this manner to effect a disinheritance at precisely that point of ethical transit. This disavowal means thereby to disown and disable the mise-en-scene of interpellation as "real" relations that ideological fantasy distorts; in that sense it rejects any means by which to legitimate an ethical genealogy (e.g., of gender, race, biology, etc.) as intrinsically determining and thus as prior to value itself. Facilitating this self-destruction is the "spontaneity" of ideological and subjective formation that for Althusser affirms the "always already" nature of ideology. As "spontaneous," subject formation, he seems to say, is atemporal—it does not, technically, "unfold" either as material history or within an imagined ideology. The scene is allegorical not merely as a generic extrapolation but also in presenting as a sequential event what occurs as a "vertical" rather than horizontal phenomenon as well as what has always already "happened." As "vertical," components of that formation—suspicion, the hail, the turn—have, "in reality," no discrete identity from one another, and thus have no correct or predetermined temporal order. As what has always already "happened," spontaneous subject formation is representable only through recollection, not as a historical moment of past experience but as a primal scene or fantasy that, again, the subject must itself "conjure." Moreover, if one follows Sartre's sketch of the formation of reflective self-consciousness, this conjured memory recollects not the criminal transaction—the "event" of the encounter with the suspicious agent—but its representational unavailability. As spontaneous, subject formation returns to inaccessibility merely in virtue of the conditional limits of its representation.

The spontaneity of subject formation designates an incommensurability with and impossibility of its narrativity, being a phenomenon without introduction, crisis, denouement, or conclusion. Even at its most irreducible, it defies the temporal differentiation required for narrativity. Hence, the recitation of any story, however abstract and metaphorical, about "spontaneous" ideological and subject formation, necessarily and formally betrays that spontaneity, substituting for it a temporal sequence in which that formation becomes implicitly the "transformed" effect of a prior, unconverted state through some causal agent. In Philo's discussion of the Hamitic myth, for instance, Noah's grasping of what had "been done to him" in the absence of a causal, criminal trace depended thereby on Noah being seized spontaneously by full ethical knowledge, a hypothesis that does not resolve the origin of value but plunges it into infinite regress. The impasse produced by this contradiction, however, indicates no flaw in the allegory that Althusser could have rectified but suggests rather that, as necessarily "storied," the fantasized relation—here, ideology—bespeaks its prior inheritance even in its attempt to break from it.

Recognition as Appointment

The Althusserian subject does not "need" or crave recognition; rather, recognition is always sufficient and in play for it, such that it makes no sense to speak of the subject in terms of degrees of self-consciousness. Recognition in this sense differs from the trope of "visibility" by which the comparative significance of subjugated identities in various social or textual settings are frequently graphed. Although a metaphor that perhaps oversells the value of presence, visibility conveys nonetheless the multiple contexts in which such disenfranchised bodies become mute or ventriloquized props of ideology, for instance, in Roland Barthes' analysis of the picture of the French-African soldier saluting the French flag.[19] Visibility, however, is not equivalent to or a mode of Althusserian recognition; on the contrary, visibility presumes recognition at all times. In that we "are *always already* subjects," Althusser explains, "[we] constantly practice the rituals of ideological recognition."[20] Recognition is not gradual but spontaneous; thus, even if socially "invisible," one does not have "less" recognition or become unrecognizable, insofar as recognition admits of no such increase or decrease. One's visibility, in contrast, can grow or diminish. Visibility, unlike recognition, remains fundamentally circumstantial—gendered, racial, and queer figures that recede into the background in some contexts stick out prominently in others, in ways, notably, that urge against any determinate assessment of "visibility" as "good." Here one must consider carefully the ways in which ethical genealogies configure the (criminal) appearance of especially "strange" and suspicious subjects— the question of visibility, accordingly, never being merely about appearance or disappearance but of what qualitative features bring the subject into visible relief. Recognition, in this sense, serves as the "background" against which visibility surfaces and recedes, constituting us as characters who fade in and out of public consciousness but to whom ISAs (Ideological State Apparatuses) and RSAs (Repressive State Apparatuses) are always attentive. As a "function of ideology," then, recognition has no quantitative articulation in terms of presence or nonpresence, or by that model through which a group logically could demand "more" recognition. That we are always-already subjects means that recognition, as those qualitative and embodied characteristics by which the subject may appear as such, obtains for the subject from the start as the very threshold of its being.

Recognition is not therefore immutable or universal in its expression but always of the "concrete" quality characteristic of genealogical legacies of responsibility. In a manner similar to Sartre's description of the historical "situation" that anticipates and "receives" subjects into their ethical "natures," Althusser explicates recognition by reference to anticipatory inheritances though which the subject appears in its "uniqueness." Building on a citation from Freud, Althusser articulates the always already quality of recognition through ethical markings that not only constitute subjectivity but do so in a manner that configures the subject as "irreplaceable":

> That an individual is always-already a subject, even before he is born, is nevertheless the plain reality, accessible to everyone and not a paradox at all. Freud ... [notes] the ideological ritual that surrounds the expectation of a "birth," that "happy event." Everyone knows how much and in what way an unborn child is expected ... it is certain in advance that it will bear its Father's Name, and will therefore have an identity and be irreplaceable. Before its birth, the child is therefore always-already a subject, appointed as a subject in and by the specific familial ideological configuration in which it is "expected" once it has been conceived. . . . [I]t is in this implacable ... structure that the former subject-to-be will have to "find" "its" place, i.e. "become" the sexual subject (boy or girl) which it already is in advance.[21]

Subject formation here does not grant intrinsic qualities that strive to flourish and develop through negotiation of disciplinary social forces; rather subjectivity signifies one's structural figuration into "preappointed" qualitative relations that neither mask nor corrupt an idiosyncratic "true" proto-being. These anticipatory "appointments" that condition the newborn's reception thus garner its "irreplaceability" as a differentiated and distinctly recognizable entity. That various expectations structure the newborn's arrival "once it has been conceived" underscores the indivisibility of subjectivity as a "psychic conception" in its Freudian sense—that is to say, as at once representational in its embodiment. In other words, the "conception" of the child is never simply a physical or material phenomenon but always and simultaneously a fantasmatic "concept" generative of those appointments. Accordingly, the quotational suspension of the notion of "birth" in the citation cautions, as does the Sartrean notion of historical "situation," against privileging the expulsion of the infant from the womb as an essential or even significant moment of subject formation. If this were the case, the delivery of the child, ideologically speaking, would be greeted not with exclamations of "Here it comes!" "Here it is!" but something along the lines of "Who is it?" "Who's there?" This scenario that Althusser uses to illustrate one's coming into relational consciousness does not reflect the classical struggle for recognition: in this "happy event" the subject faces no witting rival—no one challenges, threatens, or brutalizes it, forcing the subject to reappropriate, triumph over, or capitulate to that opposition, the outcome of which would determine its form of self-consciousness. Like the Augustinian theory of ethical inheritance, recognition according to Althusser is a joyous confirmation of what was always to be; it is never itself in contention but always what the subject is jubilantly escorted and fellated into. What has long been imagined as a stranger appearing on the horizon is in quite particular ways already very well known to us.

In his theater of the always-already subject above Althusser offers only two explicit examples of appointment: gender (its "place" as a boy or girl) and the paternal name (an entitlement that the child "bears"). That sexual difference and the denominative extension of a family history of responsibility reflect for him, presumably, the two clearest "concrete" anticipations or prophecies of ideological subject formation, discloses in turn his allegory as what itself has been interpellated and ushered into its conscription as a contemporary descendant of prior myths of the origin of value. Reflected in *its* appointments are the scenes that ideology rehearses and overwrites directly—namely, the two biblical myths of differential subject formation: the fall from the garden of Eden and the Hamitic curse, both parables in which criminality incites and affirms the irruption of inheritable and recognizable ethical markings as respectively sexual difference and genealogical families or lines of descent (what later will be expressed predominantly in terms of race). In addition, Althusser's theory of ideological anticipation regenerates ancient

and pre-Christian narratives of cursed subjectivities whose criminal knowledge passes down through an exclusionary pact as now an allegory of criminal suspicion "accessible to everyone and not a paradox at all." Finally, in its
production of an "abstract" scenario that yields "concrete" subjects, ideology nevertheless does not supply a means to "deracialize" Kant's depiction
of the translation of purely potential and unmarked humans into racially
embodied beings bearing inheritable evaluative qualities of disparate worth.
Instead ideology illuminates a figuration like race as a historical instance of
a denominating structure of inheritable appointments that comprises suspicious subjectivities, those constituted within that "special form" of criminal
relation as the "strange" exceptionality that personifies the "commonality" of
all ideological subjectivity.

For ideology to distinguish itself from the criminal knowledge of these
ancestral logics it must delineate itself through that provenance yet at the
same time mark its distinction from it. Althusser thus defines ideology as
explicitly and structurally separate from what "the ethnologist examines [as]
the myths of a 'primitive society,' " the latter as "world outlooks" that contemporary society refers to as "religious ideology, ethical ideology, legal ideology,
political ideology, etc."[22] Here Althusser dismisses prior myths as examples of
"so many" worldviews that the critic who "does not live one of [them] as the
truth" can dispassionately dissect.[23] Myths, he continues, are theories that
mislead through evocative sleights of hand, insinuating, like the Hamitic
narrative, the representational availability to the reader of the origin of value
and criminal knowledge, in which allusions and synecdoches "need only
be 'interpreted' to discover the reality of the world behind their imaginary
representation of that world."[24] Ideology thus affirms its disassociation from
myth in its emphasis on the spontaneous relationality of subject formation
that would contain any cause or origin *within*. Althusser's scenes of interpellation thus work to disown any genealogies to which they appear indebted
by taking on the stain as all that there is—by asserting, in other words, that
no purely good God or hero is brought down by the lie of the storyteller, that
no figure enjoys the splendor of a divine fellowship prior to a transgression
that spurs a tragic descent, and that no original and universal stem formation lurks behind the scarred racial body of modernity. Yet among the ways
that ideology strikes at the myth of the stain is the confirmation of how this
possibility of disinheritance remains contingent on a relation of inheritance
from which it aims to distance itself. For ideology, that affiliation is expressed
in the additional and final "step" that enjoins the reader who would grasp
the structure of subject formation to conjure privately a purely ideological

conceptual space, an instruction that participates in and passes on the secrecies and pacts of silence overseen by its predecessors.

The scenes of interpellative subjectivity need not refute all prior myths to succeed in demonstrating the subject as always already embedded in value in its embodiment and relations. As it is, Althusser's theory of ideology works against the consignment of ethics to the periphery of knowledge and cognitive formation in its insistence on the structural materiality or carnality of expressions of value—that is, Althusser submits here a critique of a *kind* of ethical philosophy, specifically, that which imagines itself as studying what transcends and remains external to the multiple appointments that comprise concrete subjects. It would be this kind of ethics as "worldview" that comes too late, seeking to "evaluate" what exists already through and in virtue of evaluative relations.

Inferior Ethics

"I advance it therefore as a suspicion only," writes Thomas Jefferson in his *Notes on the State of Virginia*, "that the blacks, whether originally a distinct race, or made distinct by time and circumstances, are *inferior* to the whites in the endowments both of body and mind"[25] From the standpoint of scientific inquiry, Jefferson's framing of the inferiority of blacks as "only" a suspicion demonstrates *good* doubt—a doubt that, unlike the Nietzschean version, offers itself thereby as the instrument that would liberate blackness from this cloud of suspicion. As "mere" hypothesis, the deficiency of blacks hangs in suspension as an undetermined possibility, an insecurity that functions as a condition for an eventual determination of the truth of the proposition, and thus for the permanent exoneration of blacks from ethical suspicion. Whether or not blacks are "inferior in body in mind," despite hinging on the definitions of its key terms, is for that no less a question *not* answerable by black people—it is not, properly, even a question *to* them—but resolvable solely by appeal to an epistemological method. To the extent that ethics communicates solely through the prescriptive declaration, it has no point of entry here. As what has sworn off its contributions to "what is" for dominion over "what should be" as a separate and secondary domain, it must await the work of skepticism in order to have leave to speak. The guise of a Nietzschean doubt as fostering an ethics of suspicion, in its turn, further sanctions this doubt in the demand to continue indefinitely the adducing of evidence for the sake of judgments that, as at most provisional and contingent, permanently preserve suspicions of inferiority.

The intervention ethics most frequently fantasizes is the declaration of innocence across the board, as an authoritative reprieve that pronounces as outside of and immune to suspicion certain "special" characters—the rational, the human, the family, the sentient, etc. Yet this exclusion has been logically inert from the start given its counterpart of a skepticism predicated precisely on illimitable doubt. Moreover, in failing to appreciate its determinative role in the qualitative formation of these special figures (of the rational, etc.) that postfoundational theory has since placed under suspicion, ethics could envision no alternative for itself but to slump into a prescriptive politics or crawl back into the shells of ancient philosophical and religious doctrines.

There is yet, however, the recourse to a further suspicion, specifically, that which doubts phenomenal representation as outside of value. It is a suspicion in which nothing is saved or salvaged, exonerated or immune. It is not a protest of sovereign innocence to the scientist, to the juror, or to the hailing officer but a voluble whisper to those to whom one is forever tied in the passing of criminal knowledge—those who embody the inheritable marks of appointment that no questioning will ever clear from suspicion. One might imagine that open secret as what David Walker conveys to Jefferson in the none-too-hushed response of his 1829 *Appeal*: "divested of prejudice either on the side of my colour or that of the whites, [I] advance my suspicion of them, whether they are *as good by nature* as we are or not."[26]

Conclusion

DREAMS AND NIGHTMARES

DREAMS AND NIGHTMARES
NIGHTMARES . . . DREAMS! OH!
DREAMING THAT THE NEGROES
Of the South Have Taken Over. . .
VOTED ALL THE DIXIECRATS
RIGHT OUT OF POWER—

COMES THE *COLORED HOUR*: . . .
IN WHITE PILLARED MANSIONS
SITTING ON THEIR WIDE VERANDAS,
WEALTHY NEGROES HAVE WHITE SERVANTS,
WHITE SHARECROPPERS WORK THE BLACK PLANTATIONS,
AND COLORED CHILDREN HAVE WHITE MAMMIES

LANGSTON HUGHES, "Cultural Exchange"

IN 1963, MARTIN LUTHER KING shares his dream of ethical sovereignty for the nation and the world. In this imagined future, individuals bear responsibility for the "content of their character" and not for their "skin." In so doing, King invokes the trope of the "dream" popular in discourses of racial reflection and activism of the time. The poet Langston Hughes, for instance, appeals often to "the dream" both to conceptualize an emancipatory space for African Americans and to galvanize others in the striving toward its realization. In 1932 he muses of the "Dream Keeper" who beckons "Bring me all of your dreams" in order to protect them "from the too-rough fingers of the world."[1] A few decades later, asking in "Harlem" the question "What happens to a dream deferred?" he wonders, against the earlier "Dream Keeper," whether and how long a "kept" dream can stay alive.[2] By 1961, in the poem "Cultural Exchange" above, the dream manifests as an inverted historical reality, one that does not gesture to an as yet unimaginable place of racial transcendence but prophecies a reversal of fortune in which blackness takes the place of whiteness.[3] Compared to the earnest tenor of the two prior "dream" poems, "Cultural Exchange" comes across as jocular and ebullient in imagining the switch that disenfranchises whites and places them in social and economic servitude to blacks. And why would this not be a source of pleasure? More specifically, not a *guilty* pleasure, but a right and just pleasure—an ethical pleasure?

Consider this, then, the new dream of racial "justice," imagined by Thomas Jefferson over a century and a half prior to Hughes's amusing reverie:

> "I tremble for my country when I reflect that God is just: that his justice cannot sleep for ever: that considering numbers, nature and natural means only, a revolution of the wheel of fortune, an exchange of situation is among possible events; that it may become probable by supernatural interference!"[4]

The "exchange of situation" that generates Jefferson's anxiety linguistically and hypothetically anticipates the "cultural exchange" that Hughes portrays; what is more, neither vision can denounce that racial exchange of status as an unequivocally illegitimate turn of events.[5] It *might* be a nightmare, but it also might be the dream of "justice." In both cases justice is of ambiguous origin; it is not clear that this state of affairs comes about because of or for the sake of justice. It instead may be that fortune, as what ceaselessly revolves, will always and eventually bring about an exchange of favor that produces an inversion of worth, and that justice is nothing but this permanent possibility. Such an exchange of favor may be brought about as well, suggests Jefferson, by a "supernatural interference" that, paradoxically, will be received as the outcome of "nature and natural means." An ethical "revolution," in other words, will always justify itself; it will become inevitable not only as the product of fortune but also as the consequence of intrinsic qualities of the blessed—say, as a result of a pact that promises divine favor or of an inheritable set of predispositions first acquired as a result of a benevolent topographical climate. To be appointed into a blessed inheritance is to take that favor as a testament to one's nature. In this vein, to study nature is not to deny the randomness of the origin of that favor, an accident that even Kant concedes in attributing favor to early environmental factors, but to find teleology in that inheritance. It does not question nature *as* value.

This is as much as nature can do given the wildcard of "supernatural inter-ference." As Philo notes, as long as fate (as divine will or happenstance) has a hand in the expressive possibilities of ethical subjectivity, no "true" ethical nature could be said to dictate that expression, in that the origin of embod-ied performance would not be traceable from its contextual enactment. It is this inability to exonerate, for instance, racial performativity from criminal-ity through a systematic accumulation of evidence that leads Kelly Miller to consider delivering himself and blacks to the mercy of this indecipherable force that may "predestine" a people to the "everlasting stain" of cursed inher-itance. Whether one attributes ethical favor and disfavor to cosmic interfer-ence, physiological natures or, as in the case of *Oedipus Rex*, an unnamed source that thereby admits no solicitation or appeal, the value of the subject will remain, in all such cases, a matter of permanent suspicion.

Justice, Jefferson writes, "cannot sleep forever." Perhaps, like Noah, drunk and slumbering in his tent, justice will awaken, spontaneously seized by the knowledge of the crimes that have been committed against it during its rest. It will draw itself up and put right in one declaration all that has gone wrong in the absence of its watch. But if justice can awaken this means it also falls asleep, again and again, so that after untold iterations wakefulness and sleep lose their distinction from the dream and the nightmare. To rouse themselves "awake" from the nightmare of racial subjugation, people of color have had to go *back* into the dream where they anticipate the ascent of their ethical and genealogical inheritance. Once it arrives—when? In the Colored Hour—the curse will have become a blessing and criminal racial nature will disclose itself as having *always been* "good." This hour comes in its own time, not in the recognition of the good works of people of color or in their convincing others that their actions are separate and distinct from their embodied ethi-cal associations. The hour does not come when people of color discredit white morality or succeed in having whites admit to their historical "crimes." It will come, rather, in the wake of prophesies and symbols that, in retrospect, will be recognized as having always announced its arrival.

No less significantly, the exchange will not emancipate anyone *from* inheritable value; it will not achieve a break from histories of responsibility. The line along which is passed the secret of criminal knowledge may become comparatively more or less favorable; additionally what *constitutes* the recog-nizable features of that line—how it appears as such—may assuredly alter. But this hour will not bring the means to secure ethical favor or self-identity by "passing" on this inheritance as a way to escape all such associations; at most, one will pass *into* other, presumptively more compensatory ethical lineages. In Nella Larsen's novella *Passing*, Clare Kendry pursues this route as one "determined to get away, to be a person and not . . . a daughter of the indiscreet Ham."[6] For Kendry, becoming a "person"—that is, achieving self-determined ethical sovereignty—takes place through an ethical descent into white genealogy, her refusal of African heritage contingent on the disavowal of ancestry as any kind of marking at all. That is, only by becoming white can she imagine herself as unmarked by genealogical inheritance and thus outside the racialized passage of histories of responsibility.

Hughes dreams of the coming of the Hour when people of color take their seats at the helm of social and institutional power. But if the colored hour is still *to come*, what is the racial and temporal quality of *current* ethical relations? Are they not colored and historical too? If criminality inaugurates embodied racial difference and genealogical descent, then the possibility of "uncolored" subjective relations, those unmarked by legible scars and traces, would be conditional on a correlative break from all "hours"—that is, from temporal history itself. In other words, uncolored or unmarked ethical subjectivity would not be what comes "in time" but outside of it.

To foresee the coming of the Colored Hour is to see that even this blessed turn of events would prove, like the inheritances of today, only temporary. This is because the "everlasting stain" does not, as Miller fears, fix the evaluative meaning of "blackness" or signify the term "race" as what will continue as a primary idiom for relations of embodied ethical subjectivity.[7] It signals, rather, that what is "permanent" are the idiomatic and allegorical modes of representation by which knowledge as already denominated will be grasped and disseminated.

"The whites want slaves, and want us for their slaves, but some of them will curse the day they ever saw us," vocalizes David Walker. "As true as the sun ever shone in its meridian splendor, my colour will root some of them out of the very face of the earth. . . . [I]f these things do not occur in their proper time, it is because the world in which we live does not exist, and we are deceived with regard to its existence."[8] The "truth" of value and thus of ethical subjectivity will not be disclosed by the extraction of the stain of race or of any other qualitatively affiliative and inheritable markings; rather it will be the mark or color that will "root out" value in its cursed materiality of affiliations and appointments. If we existed then as today within the dream and nightmare of inheritable ethical descent, then the colored hour will come. If it does not come in its "proper time," it will be the result of having missed the prophetic signs of its arrival, leaving us to mark time as a history of anticipation.

Ethics as Value

To conceptualize ethics as "value" is to understand phenomena as constituted in and through worth, and thus ethics as what neither begins nor ends with the prescriptive declaration. On this picture, the first question of ethics is how it is possible for anything to show up as "valuable;" how it is, in sum, that worldly objects and subjects resonate worth in their mere representation. This worth is not primarily divisible as "good" and "bad" but rather allocates and denominates things as they "are." Accordingly, value already inheres in and as the possibility of representational distinction: shape, size, extension, color, etc.; none attach separately or secondarily to consciousness, deeds, or objects but instead partake in rendering recognizable the elements of the conceptual and perceptual world. In particular, value accounts for the necessarily qualitative relations within which phenomena *can* appear in their associative affiliations with other phenomena. The differential relation and thus possibility of perception is the consequence, moreover, of marks that are always qualitative rather than "neutral." Thus the determination of "what" an object or deed "is" is itself an evaluative and thus ethical identification. This evaluation comes about not because one "attaches" an affect to what consciousness has presumably and implicitly intuited, as if the critique of the reception of the world logically could and did precede any analysis of "the value of the world," as Nietzsche holds. This is because any representation is made as a relative distinction *to* and *from*, a parsing that thereby presumes evaluable marks of affiliation and disaffiliation.

This suggests, furthermore, that self-consciousness emerges as well within and through expressive signifiers of worth afforded in its recognizable relations to others. As such, all subjects come into being *as* ethical, which is to say, as resonant of various dispositional qualities and tendencies. These qualities are neither *inside* nor *outside* of the subject as inherent moral nature or as externally applied characteristics; instead they configure subjectivity within an economy of value as that by which subjectivity is recognizable, not as what "possesses" characteristics but as a "character" or figure whose anticipatory and metonymic name is thus always and necessarily a denomination. The subject, therefore, does not enter or break "into" ethics or denomination through conscious action prior to which it preserves a preethical neutrality or innocence; rather it acquires its evaluative name through the prophetic and anticipatory appointments in which it is conscripted. These appointments designate various affiliative and institutional kinships (race, family, gender/sex, sexuality, etc.) the associative and expectational qualities of which descend through genealogical and thus ethical inheritances. Insofar as the subject is escorted into ethical knowledge as a descendant within these lineages it partakes of responsibility for those qualities and thereby for the hypothetical crimes said to originate those inheritances. What inaugurates and perpetuates ethical genealogies, however, is not crime but "criminality" in the guise of the curse, a conceptual "clip" that executes an initiation and termination of the ethical subject (as simultaneously the newest and final instantiation of that line) as distinct and differentiated and thus "individually" responsible while at the same time an *effect* of the relations of criminal value from which it descends. As an "accessory" of criminality rather than the direct perpetrator of a crime, ethical subjectivity perceives itself and becomes similarly perceived as suspicious. This suspicion represents the philosophical and ideological reception of all subject formation, wherein the possibility of subjectivity is contingent on the impossibility of exoneration, and thus on its continuation as an object of evaluative skepticism.

If the perception and representation of phenomena do not precede evaluation but presume it, the "stain" of value is neither epiphenomenal nor extraneous but intrinsic and formative. The stain would thus not distort or occlude but afford existence as already within differentiating and thus qualitatively evaluative relations. This does not mean that the colored or evaluative force of a representation refers to any innate qualities, as if the stain were itself an authentic and self-referential mark. It indicates instead that the meaningfulness of a mark presumes a comparative valence for the sake of its differentiation from other signifiers. Thus the "stain" of perception is nothing other than its representational possibility within value, which is to say that there is never, from the start, anything beneath or behind evaluation. "Value"— and its expression through the embodied concept of "race"—is not a "thing" but names dynamics of differential modes of relation by which "things" appear already within and through confederate qualitative associations and dissociations.

In that consciousness is embodied, evaluative signifiers can be said to mobilize as "scars" and "traces" that render the subject as carnal and figural, and thus as discernable markings that, through metaphor and synecdoche, disclose the "strangely" exceptional and "irreplaceable" figure as the "part" that symbolizes the "whole" lineage of criminal and genealogical descent. By these symbolic marks of ethical subjectivity, one oversees, as if from the view of a king, the allegorical flow of the criminal past and prophetic future of an entire natural history.

That ethical inheritance denominates the subject as an instantiated descendant and criminal accessory to multiple histories of responsibility, may seem, to many, more nightmare than dream. But before one seeks a way out, a path of disinheritance, an incontrovertible piece of exculpatory evidence—before, that is, one loudly declares an unwillingness to speak the criminal secrets of one's ethical heritage, and thus to pass the curse down the line—one might ask oneself whether this disavowal is not *precisely* the advancement of one's modern and *very* racial ethical inheritance. One might, that is, recognize one's ethical configuration as an executor of a fortune whose worth is continually revalued, an implication of the self eloquently relayed by James Baldwin:

> The custodian of an inheritance, which is what blacks have had to be, in Western culture, must hand the inheritance down the line. So, you, the custodian, recognize, finally, that your life does not belong to you: nothing belongs to you. This will not sound like freedom to Western ears, since the Western world pivots on the infantile, and, in action, criminal delusions of possession, and of property. . . .
>
> But the people of the West will not understand this until everything which they now think they have has been taken away from them. In passing, one may observe how remarkable it is that a people so quick and so proud to boast of what they have taken from others are unable to imagine that what they have taken from others can also be taken from them.[9]

Notes

INTRODUCTION

1. See Jacques Derrida, *Dissemination*, trans. Barbara Johnson (Chicago: University of Chicago Press, 1982).

2. See Jean-Paul Sartre, *Existentialism is a Humanism*, trans. Carol Macomber (New Haven, CT: Yale University Press, 2007).

3. Naomi Zack's *The Ethics and Mores of Race: Equality after the History of Philosophy* (Lanham, MD: Rowman & Littlefield, 2011) and Anna Stubblefield's *Ethics Along the Color Line* (Ithaca, NY: Cornell University Press,, 2005), despite their titles, focus exclusively on the resolution of racial disparities; in neither is there an extended discussion of "race" as an ethical "object," for the broader reasons discussed later.

4. Bernard Williams, *Ethics and the Limits of Philosophy* (Cambridge, MA: Harvard University Press, 1985), 72.

5. Immanuel Kant, "On the Different Races of Man," in *Race and the Enlightenment*, ed. Emmanuel Eze (Malden, MA: Blackwell, 1997), 48.

6. Kant's racial rankings are not consistent across his works or even within them: earlier in the same discussion Kant declares "the Negroes and Whites to be fundamental races" (42).

7. Hereafter the "*pre*-ethical" will appear stylistically as the "preethical," although what will be at issue throughout the book is the implausibility of the "preethical" as a coherent concept or phenomenal status, specifically, as what purportedly precedes yet remains "bound" to ethics from the start. It is thus requested that the reader retain, to the extent possible, the hesitation and tension of the hyphenated "pre-ethical" in their reception of the unhyphenated appearances of the term.

8. Friedrich Nietzsche, *The Will To Power*, ed. Walter Kaufmann (New York: Vintage, 1968), 260; Frantz Fanon, *Black Skin, White Masks*, trans. Charles Lam Markmann (New York: Grove, 1967), 109.

9. Linda Alcoff, *Visible Identities: Race, Gender, and the Self* (New York: Oxford, 2006), 199.
10. Ibid., 7.
11. Ibid., 180.
12. Ibid., 202.
13. Ibid., 196.
14. Ibid., 204.
15. Ibid., 204.
16. Ibid., 180.
17. Ibid., 185.
18. Ibid., 181.
19. Ibid., 204.
20. Alain Locke, "Value," in *The Philosophy of Alain Locke*, ed. Leonard Harris (Philadelphia: Temple University Press, 1989), 119.
21. Cornel West, *Prophesy Deliverance!* (Philadelphia: Westminster, 1982), 49.
22. Ibid., 47,
23. Ibid., 47.
24. West, 64. On the matter of "functionality" without telos, intentionality, or originating cause, Nietzsche observes that "the cause of the origin of a thing and its eventual utility, its actual employment and place in a system of purposes, lie worlds apart." (Nietzsche, *Genealogy of Morals*, 77). The function of a thing, he reminds us, is answerable not to its purported origin but to its "place in a system of purposes," such that "function" is not beholden to evolutionary and causal trajectories, those from which intentional purpose might be extracted. As we will come to see, this arrangement is complicated by the fact that even though no authentic or deliberate link binds origin and structural function—in this case, the conditions through which racial inequality emerges and the embeddedness of ethics and race in modernist projects of identification and classification—that path of historical and political lineage must always be theorized into existence. Consequently, the explanatory role of this lineage will be, as West himself alludes, metaphoric or idiomatic, which is to say, also an effect or function of racial difference.
25. West, *Prophesy*, 55.
26. Ibid., 58.
27. It is perhaps notable that the modern production of the observable and verifiable object is described by West, if slightly ironically, as the "breakthrough" of new paradigms while, by contrast, the evaluative paradigm of modernity is cast as "recovered" from a dead past. In subsequent chapters, the modern ethical subject will be reframed as what necessarily "breaks through" the paradigm of moral purity to recover or inherit its "dead" genealogical past.
28. As cited in West, *Prophesy*, 56.
29. Ibid., 56.
30. Ibid., 47.

31. As cited in West, *Prophesy,* 54.

32. Alain Locke, *Race Contacts and Interracial Relations*, ed. Jeffrey C. Stewart (Washington, DC: Howard University Press, 1992), 3. See also p. 42 of the same text where Locke hypothesizes that "if there has been anything that has hindered the observation of the phenomena of race contacts it has been that unscientific point of view which has colored, favorably or unfavorably, the facts so that it has been almost impossible to extract any clear scientific attitude or scientific result from the process."

33. Susan E. Babbitt and Sue Campbell, eds., *Racism and Philosophy* (Ithaca, NY: Cornell University Press, 1999), 1.

34. There are too many such writings to list here: examples include Bernard Boxhill, ed., *Race and Racism* (New York: Oxford University Press, 2001); Marshall Cohen, Thomas Nagel, and Thomas Scanlon, eds., *Equality and Preferential Treatment* (Princeton, NJ: Princeton University Press, 1977); and Lawrence Blum, *"I'm Not a Racist, But . .". The Moral Quandary of Race* (Ithaca, NY: Cornell University Press, 2002)

35. Charles Mills, "Racial Liberalism," *PMLA* 123, no. 5 (2008): 1382.

36. John Rawls, *A Theory of Justice* (Cambridge, MA: Harvard University Press, 1971).

37. Rawls, *Theory of Justice*, 15; for Mills' statements affirming his (conditional) support of Rawlsian theory, see Carole Pateman and Charles Mills, *Contract and Domination* (Cambridge, UK: Polity, 2007) and Mills, "Retrieving Rawls for Racial Justice? A Critique of Tommie Shelby," *Critical Philosophies of Race* 1.1 (2013): 1–27.

38. Mills, "Racial Liberalism," 1383.

39. Michael J. Monahan, *The Creolizing Subject* (New York: Fordham University Press, 2011), 221.

40. Agnes Heller, "The Role of Interpretation in Modern Ethical Practice," *Philosophy and Social Criticism* 17.2 (April 1991): 83–101.

41. Ibid., 85.

42. Ibid., 98.

43. Ibid., 86.

44. Williams, *Ethics and the Limits of Philosophy*, 116.

45. Ibid., 118.

46. Ibid., 118.

47. Ibid., 118.

48. Ibid., 118

49. Alcoff, for instance, takes the fact that "there is a newly emerging biological consensus that race is a myth" as proof that race is not "real," granting authority thereby to naturalistic explanations of race over nonnatural ones (181; see also 198). Monahan's objection to this common turn to biology for "real" answers about race is herein shared: "[T]he 'naturalism' underlying much of the literature on race, prevents it from being truly and radically rigorous . . . [One] must raise the

question of why and how, for example, one might take biology to be determinate of racial membership, and what that implies about our sense of the meaning and significance of race" (16–17).

50. For further discussion of this point see Michael Thompson, *Life and Action: Elementary Structures of Practice and Practical Thought* (Cambridge, MA: Harvard University Press, 2008).

CHAPTER 1

An earlier and much different version of this chapter first appeared as "Stain Removal: On Race and Ethics" in *Philosophy and Social Criticism* 33.4 (June 2007): 498–528.

1. Martin Luther King, Jr., "I Have a Dream," in *A Testament of Hope: The Essential Writings and Speeches of Martin Luther King, Jr.*, ed. James M. Washington (New York: Harper Collins, 1986), 219.

2. For an excellent discussion of Descartes' narrative practices, see L. Aryeh Kosman, "The Naïve Narrator: Meditation in Descartes' *Meditations*," in *Essays on Descartes' Meditations*, ed. A. O. Rorty (Berkeley: University of California Press, 1986).

3. Immanuel Kant, *Groundwork of the Metaphysics of Morals*, ed. and trans. Mary Gregor (Cambridge, UK: Cambridge University Press, 1997), 41.

4. Kant, *Groundwork*, 41.

5. See King, "Love, Law, and Civil Disobedience," in *A Testament of Hope: The Essential Writings and Speeches of Martin Luther King, Jr.*, ed. James M. Washington (Harper Collins, 1986), xx. That the freedom opportuned in this dreamscape cashes itself out against the body is reaffirmed in King's view of moral justice as the "cash" due on a "check" or "promissory note" that secures "upon demand the riches of freedom" as payment for uncompensated contributions of labor to the nation. Yet he cautions that moral citizenship in this "rightful place" obligates "meeting physical force with soul force." Hence, it is at that point when racialized bodies melt into a universal "flesh" that all "shall see [freedom] together." The symbolic rejection of the body in "nonviolence," more than an astute political tactic, is the philosophical "means" that harmonize with the "ends" of an indifference to the body in moral judgment, where only the nonmaterial soul constitutes the object of evaluation. Kant himself details a similar negation ensuring the silence and transparency of the body, remarking that the law the subject gives to itself is necessary but not sufficient for sovereignty. One also must be, he writes, "without needs and with unlimited resources adequate to his will," which is to say, wholly self-reliant with respect to all personal and psychical developmental needs: nourishment, shelter, affection, care—as well as those instruments necessary to maximize one's gifts. True moral autonomy thus requires corporeal muteness, insofar as what inhibits moral sovereignty are those desires of the body that compel one to seek out another for their satisfaction. See Kant, *Groundwork*, 41.

6. West, *Prophesy Deliverance!*, 53.

7. Alcoff, *Visible Identities,* 184; see also 172–173, 196–199.

8. Michael Omi and Howard Winant, *Racial Formations in the United States* (New York: Routledge, 1994), 55.

9. Ibid., (italics theirs).

10. Ibid.

11. Ibid.

12. Lewis Gordon, *Existentia Africana: Understanding Africana Existential Thought* (New York: Routledge, 2000), 84.

13. Omi and Winant, *Racial Formations*, 55.

14. Jean-Paul Sartre, *Anti-Semite and Jew*, trans. George Becker (New York: Schocken, 1948), 19–20.

15. See Michel Foucault, *Power/Knowledge: Selected Interviews and Writings, 1972–1977*, ed. Colin Gordon, trans. Colin Gordon et al. (New York: Pantheon, 1980), 81–91.

16. Ibid., 82.

17. Kant, *The Metaphysics of Morals*, trans. Mary Gregor (Cambridge, UK: Cambridge University Press, 1991), 101; *Kant's Gesammelte Schriften*, Vol. 6, ed. Preukischen Akademie der Wissenschaften (Berlin: G. Reimer, 1914), 283.

18. Kant, *Metaphysics of Morals*, 139.

19. Ibid., (italics mine).

20. See ibid., 140.

21. See also his analysis of inheritance (ibid., 110–111; appendix 171–172), which reflects as well this dilemma of pure freedom. On the one hand, Kant recognizes that inheritance cannot mean the "empirical" transfer of objects, and thus conjectures that the "change of belongings takes place in one moment, namely when the testator ceases to exist (*articulo mortis*)" (110). This "moment," Kant continues, is not a unit of time, (otherwise the property of the deceased would be, if only for a fractional period, "ownerless"), but is "ideal." Yet this automatic and instant nature of the transfer means that the recipient of the legacy acquires that inheritance whether desired or not. Although Kant appears explicitly concerned with the transfer of objects in his first discussion of inheritance, the section immediately following this one, "Leaving Behind a Good Reputation after One's Death," treats moral worth as a possession or property that can be "stained" by others even after one's passing (specifically, he conjectures, through accusations of criminality). While Kant thus views the ethical subject's worth as that which, like material possessions, remains after the death of the individual, he stops short of including these qualities as inherited automatically by the heirs of the deceased. The consequence is then the opposite of the pure and free individual "not yet" burdened by value: the specter of ethical subjectivity without a body, a curiosity Kant accepts as a "phenomenon as strange as it is undeniable" (111).

22. Robert Bernasconi, "Kant as an Unfamiliar Source of Racism," in *Philosophers on Race*, eds. Julie K. Ward and Tommy L. Lott (Malden, MA: Blackwell, 2002), 149–162.

23. See Kant, *Metaphysics of Morals*, 139.

24. Bernasconi, "Kant as an Unfamiliar Source of Racism," 152. In his book *Kant's Impure Ethics* (New York: Oxford University Press, 2000), Robert Louden doubts Kant's anthropological theories as informing the moral writings on the basis that "the two bodies of work almost seem to be talking past one another—they often don't appear to link up" (63). Indeed, they *do talk past* each other and *don't appear to link up* in any obvious or unproblematic way. But one should read here a historical rather than natural incompatibility of these discourses as indicative of modernity's struggle both to integrate *and keep separate* the ethical and material, or as Louden outlines, the "pure" and the "impure." It is this impossible yet obligatory, syncretic function that race comes to provide for modernity. In a later essay, Louden reaffirms the "formidable conceptual gap between Kant's anthropology lectures and his ethical texts," suggesting that "the very idea of a *moral* anthropology hovers awkwardly between both fields; at home in neither." See "The Second Part of Morals," in *Essays on Kant's Anthropology*, eds. Brian Jacobs and Patrick Kain (Cambridge: Cambridge University Press, 2003), 63. Again, this "conceptual gap" between embodied genealogies and value reflects no natural incongruity but signifies precisely what is produced and defended for the sake of originally innocent, self-determining subjects. If "race" is condemned as an unstable, vagabond sign it is because, as idiomatic and "hovering," it preserves its indispensability as what brooks the passage between the artificially separated categories of the evaluative and descriptive. As an early example of a productive thinking together of Kant's anthropology with his *Critiques*, see Michel Foucault's (originally unpublished) translation and introduction to Kant's *Anthropology from a Pragmatic Point of View* in Michel Foucault, *Introduction to Kant's Anthropology*, ed. Robert Nigro, trans. Robert Nigro and Kate Briggs (Los Angeles, CA: Semiotexte, 2008).

25. Kant, "On the Different Races of Man," 23.

26. Kant, "Physical Geography," trans. K. M. Faull and Emmanuel Eze, in *Race and the Enlightenment*, ed. Emmanuel Eze (Malden, MA: Blackwell, 1997), 61.

27. Ibid., 61.

28. Kant, "On the Different Races of Man," 22; see also Kant, "Physical Geography," 61–62.

29. Kant, "On the Use of Teleological Principles in Philosophy," trans. Jon Mark Mikkelsen, in *Race*, ed. Robert Bernasconi (Malden, MA: Blackwell, 2001), 47.

30. Kant, "On the Different Races of Man," 20.

31. Ibid., 17.

32. Ibid., 20.

33. Kant, "Physical Geography," 61.

34. Kant, "Teleological Principles," 41.

35. This assertion, central to Kant's monogenic theory of race, occurs in several places. See, for example, "On the Different Races of Man," 19–20; "Teleological Principles," 41–49.

36. Kant, "Teleological Principles," 48, 42.

37. See Ibid., 47, fn. 4, 54–55.

38. Ibid., 40–41.

39. Kant, "Physical Geography," 60.

40. Kant goes some way toward acknowledging this parallel in "Teleological Principles" (37, 52). Here he equates, explicitly and implicitly, knowledge of freedom and morality with knowledge of race and natural history, contending both require metaphysical theories of purpose to structure experiential knowledge.

41. Kant, "On the Different Races of Man," 16–17.

42. Ibid.

43. Ibid., 23.

44. Ibid.

45. Kant, "Teleological Principles," 42. That whiteness deviates so minimally from original man presumably obviates the need, in Kant's eyes, for any equivalent hypothesis on the causes of white skin.

46. Fanon, *Black Skins, White Masks*, 110.

47. Ibid., 111.

48. Ibid., 110–111.

49. For a specifically Kantian reading of these passages, see Ronald T. Judy's "Fanon's Body of Black Experience," in *Fanon: A Critical Reader*, eds. L. R. Gordon, T. D. Sharpley-Whiting, and R. T. White (Malden, MA: Blackwell, 1996), 57–58.

50. Fanon, *Black Skins, White Masks*, 109, 112.

51. Kant explains that continued migration inhibited the full development of Native Americans, making them "unfit for any culture." See "Teleological Principles," 48.

52. Fanon, *Black Skins, White Masks*, 109.

53. Ibid., 112. Both Kant and Fanon thus view race as what inhibits motion—that which freezes and holds subjectivity in place, though for Fanon this takes place prematurely, indicating the suspension rather than completion of an actualizing process. Furthermore, both view blackness as a greater constraint than whiteness. It is this comparative mobility of whites, Kant offers, that has allowed them not only to occupy every corner of the world but also to "educate" and "control" its inhabitants ("On the Different Races of Man," 23; "Physical Geography," 64). For an excellent discussion of racial "fixing" as a photographic process, see David Marriott's *On Black Men* (New York: Columbia University Press, 2000). For a broader discussion of the "fixing" of racial representation, see Stuart Hall, "The After-Life of Frantz Fanon," in *The Fact of Blackness*, ed. Alan Read (Seattle: Bay Press, 1996).

54. Fanon, *Black Skins, White Masks*, 113.

55. Ibid., 112.

56. Teresa de Lauretis, "Difference Embodied: Reflections on *Black Skins, White Masks*," *Parallax* 8, no. 2 (2002): 57.

57. See Hall, "After-life," 20–21.

58. Fanon, *Black Skins, White Masks*, 112.

59. Ibid., 189.

60. Ibid., 111–114.

61. Frantz Fanon, *Peau Noire, Masque Blancs* (Paris: Seuil, 1952), 92.

62. Fanon, *Black Skins, White Masks*, 114 (amendments mine).

63. David Marriot writes of this scene that the "little French boy's combined fear and anxiety stain Fanon, mark him indelibly both within and without. The overwhelming alienation of the scene . . . remains traumatic for him." See *On Black Men,* ix.

64. Fanon, *Black Skins, White Masks*, 116.

65. Jean Laplanche and J.-B. Pontalis, *The Language of Psychoanalysis*, trans. Donald Nicholson-Smith (London: Norton, 1973), 118.

66. See Heller, "The Role of Interpretation."

67. Kant, "Teleological Principles," 46–47.

68. Such a reading might usefully be contrasted with the metaphor of "invisibility" often invoked to describe the multiple alienations experienced by people of color, of which Ralph Ellison's 1947 novel *Invisible Man* is a classic example. (New York: Vintage, 1990). A discussion of recognition as a condition for the trope of visibility/invisibility takes place in chapter 5.

69. With respect to the difference between "genealogical" and "biological" race, Richard Dyer writes that "the simple identification of bodily differences between populations [biological race] almost certainly predates constructing different lineages for them [genealogical race]." The contention here is that there is no such thing as a "simple identification" of difference if one means by this a preethical distinction; to "identify" different "populations" is precisely to "construct" "genealogical lineages." See Richard Dyer, *White*. (London: Routledge, 1997), 20.

70. Hawthorne, "The Birthmark," in *Mosses From an Old Manse* (New York: Modern Library, 2003), 40.

71. Ibid., 29.

72. Ibid.

73. Ibid., 32.

74. Ibid., 30.

75. Ibid., 32, 35–36.

76. Ibid., 42.

77. Ibid., 43.

CHAPTER 2

1. Kelly Miller, *Race Adjustment: The Everlasting Stain. The American Negro: His History and Literature* Series (New York: Arno, 1968), 97.

2. Compare the following from Booker T. Washington: "Many white people seldom come into contact with the Negro in any other capacity than that of domestic service. If they get a poor idea of our character and service in that respect, they will infer that the entire life of the Negro is unsatisfactory from every point of view. We want to be sure that wherever our life touches that of the white man, we conduct ourselves so that he will get the best impression possible of us." *Character Building* (Amsterdam, NY: Fredonia Books, 2002), 155.

3. Miller, "Race Adjustment," 91.

4. Ibid., 92.

5. Miller also proposes that the impact of religion offers a "sociological phenomenon . . . as easily measured as any other data" in order to promote religion as what can develop and alter ethical proclivities in a measurable way. In the next breath, however, Miller avers that religion achieves this effect due to preexisting racial dispositions: "The Negro as we know him in America is of a deeply religious nature. He is widely noted for his emotional and spiritual susceptibilities. His weird, plaintive, melodious longings are fraught with spiritual substances and meaning. . . ." ("Race Adjustment," 133) The mutability of behavioral tendencies is thus contained nevertheless within comparatively implacable dispositions said to be fundamental to the race.

6. W.E.B. DuBois and Augustus Granville Dill, *Morals and Manners among Negro Americans* (Atlanta: Atlanta University Press, 1914), http://docsouth.unc.edu/church/morals/dubois.html.

7. Miller, *Race Adjustment*, 85; 187.

8. DuBois and Dill, "Morals and Manners," 16.

9. Miller, *Everlasting Stain*, 3.

10. Ibid.

11. Ibid., 33.

12. Ibid., 3–4.

13. Ibid., ix.

14. Ibid., xii.

15. Ibid., xiii.

16. Josiah Royce, *Race Questions, Provincialisms, and Other American Problems* (Freeport, NY: Books for Libraries, 1967), 32–33.

17. Ibid., 33.

18. Alain Locke, *Race Contacts*, 3.

19. Ibid., 4.

20. Ibid., 10.

21. Ibid., 13; see also 10.

22. Ibid., (my italics).

23. Ibid., 5.

24. Ibid., 7.

25. Ibid.

26. Ibid.

27. Ibid., 8.

28. Ibid., 11.

29. Ibid., 7.

30. As an example of this evaluative distinction of the biological, see Linda Alcoff's justification of sexual difference as predicated on physiologically significant traits and racial difference as predicated on physiologically insignificant ones. *Visible Identities,* 164–166.

31. Locke, *Race Contacts,* 11 (bracketed text original editorial addition).

32. Ibid., *Race Contacts,* 12.

33. Ibid. 12.

34. See Kant, *Groundwork,* 41–48.

35. Ibid., 46.

36. Onora O'Neill, *Constructions of Reason* (Cambridge, UK: Cambridge University Press, 1989), 9–13.

37. One would do better to read "instinct" in the textured ways it appears in both Nietzsche and Freud, where it also signifies by turn "habit," "drive," and "second nature." On Freud's complex use of "instinct" in particular, see Jean Laplanche, *Freud and the Sexual: Essays 2000–2006,* ed. John Fletcher, trans. John Fletcher, Jonathan House, and Nicholas Ray (International Psychoanalytic Books, 2011) and Teresa de Lauretis, *Freud's Drive* (New York: Palgrave MacMillan, 2010).

38. See Jerry Miller, *Philosophy and Social Criticism* 38, no. 9 (November 2012).

39. See, as an example, Charles Taylor, *The Ethics of Authenticity* (Cambridge, MA: Harvard University Press, 1992).

40. Kant, *Groundwork,* 8.

41. For an example, see Judith Butler's theory of ethical subjectivity as borne of "passionate attachments" animated by a spontaneous "conscience" in *The Psychic Life of Power* (Palo Alto, CA: Stanford University Press, 1997).

42. See Jean-François Lyotard, *The Differend: Phrases in Dispute,* trans. Georges Van Den Abbeele (Minneapolis: University of Minnesota Press, 1989).

43. See Soren Kierkegaard, *Fear and Trembling/Repetition,* trans. Edna Hong and Howard Hong (Princeton, NJ: Princeton, 1983) and Sigmund Freud, *Totem and Taboo,* trans. James Strachey (New York: Norton, 1990).

44. Kant, "Physical Geography," 61.

45. Genesis 9:18–10:1 (New American Standard).

46. Werner Sollors, *Neither Black Nor White Yet Both* (New York: Oxford University Press, 1997), 92–96.

47. On the colonial implications of the racialized story of Ham, see Philip S. Zachernuk, "Of Origins and Colonial Order: Southern Nigerian Historians and the 'Hamitic Hypothesis' c. 1870–1970," *Journal of African History* 35, no. 3 (1994) 427–455.

48. See Ephraim Isaac, "Genesis, Judaism, and the Sons of Ham," in *Slaves and Slavery in Muslim Africa,* vol. 1: *Islam and the Ideology of Enslavement,* ed. John Willis (London: Frank Cass, 1985), 77, 80.

49. See Gene Rice, "The Alleged Curse on Ham," in *Holy Bible: African American Jubilee Edition* (New York: American Bible Society, 1999) and Rice, "The Curse that Never Was (Genesis 9:18–27)," *The Journal of Religious Thought* 29, no. 1 (1972).

50. Some examples: David Aaron, "Early Rabbinic Exegesis on Noah's Son Ham and the So-Called 'Hamitic Myth,'" *Journal of the American Academy of Religion* 63, no. 4 (1995); David Brion Davis, "Jews, Blacks, and the Roots of Racism," *Midstream* (December 2001); David Goldenberg, "The Curse of Ham: A Case of Rabbinic Racism?" in *Struggles in the Promised Land*, eds. Jack Salzman and Cornel West (New York: Oxford University Press, 1997), 21–51.

51. Sir Thomas Browne, *The Works of Sir Thomas Browne*, vol. 3, ed. Geoffrey Keynes (London: Faber & Gwyer, 1928), 242–243.

52. See Stephen R. Haynes, *Noah's Curse: The Biblical Justification of American Slavery* (New York: Oxford University Press, 2002); William Kingsley, pub., "Slavery and the Bible," *New Englander* 15, no. 57 (February 1857), 104.

53. Sollors, *Neither Black Nor White*, 109.

54. Alexander Crummell, "The Negro Race Not Under A Curse," in *The Future of Africa* (New York: Scribner, 1862), 327–328. See also Edward Wilmot Blyden's 1862 essay "Noah's Malediction," *Slavery and Abolition* 1, no. 1 (1980): 18–24, as well as David Goldenberg's *The Curse of Ham* (Princeton, NJ: Princeton University Press, 2005), the latter noting that the racialized version that "entered the canon of Western religion and folklore . . . stayed put well into the twentieth century." (142)

55. Locke, *Race Contacts*, 12

56. See Plato's "Meno" in *Five Dialogues*, trans. G. M. A. Grube, rev. John M. Cooper (Indianapolis, IN: Hackett, 2002) and *The Republic*, trans. G. M. A. Grube, rev. C. D. C. Reeve (Indianapolis, IN: Hackett, 1982).

57. Another "mystery" regarding this round of frothy dismissals of the relevance of race to the Old Testament passage is the near complete absence in these discussions of *any* critical writings on race—in particular, references to and insights from the now substantive archive of Africana scholarship. Can a genealogically prescribed degradation of black consciousness be facilely and righteously discredited by those whose writings reproduce that worthlessness? Presumably, the historical functions and formations of race are sufficiently transparent as to warrant and normalize the ignorance of its disciplinary study in the production of an academic argument in which race is central. That is to say, it would be unwise to underestimate, even now, the stakes for intellectual custody of this "myth."

CHAPTER 3

1. Charles Mills, *Blackness Visible: Essays On Philosophy and Race* (Ithaca, NY: Cornell University Press, 1998), 9.

2. See August Nigro's *The Net of Nemesis: Studies in Tragic Bond/Age* (Selinsgrove, PA: Susquehanna University Press, 2000) for a discussion of how in *Oedipus Rex* "the symbol of bondage . . . is coupled with the symbol of defilement, the stain." (31)

3. Sophocles, "*Oedipus the King*," in *Sophocles*, ed. and trans. David Grene (Chicago: University of Chicago Press, 1954), 58.

4. Ibid.

5. Ibid., 19.

6. Ibid., 23.

7. Nietzsche, *Beyond Good and Evil*, 32.

8. James Baldwin, *The Evidence of Things Not Seen* (New York: Holt, Rinehart & Winston 1995).

9. Sollors, *Neither Black nor White Yet Both*, 96.

10. See Howard Eilberg-Schwartz, *God's Phallus* (Boston, MA: Beacon, 1994), 87; Cain Hope Felder, *Troubling Biblical Waters* (Maryknoll, NY: Orbis, 1989), 39–40; Rice, "The Alleged Curse on Ham," 130; Rice, "The Curse that Never Was," 11.

11. These charges of incestuous relations, Gene Rice explains, are "tempting" insofar as they are consistent with the suggestion of Leviticus 20:17 that "to see the nakedness of another leads naturally to sexual relations." See Rice, "The Alleged Curse on Ham," 136, and Rice, "The Curse that Never Was," 12.

12. See Isaac, "Sons of Ham," 84; Sollors, *Neither Black Nor White*, 97–102; Rice, "The Curse that Never Was," 11; and Steven Haynes, *Noah's Curse: The Biblical Justification of American Slavery* (New York: Oxford University Press, 2002), x.

13. On the matter of queer futurity, see Lee Edelman, *No Future: Queer Theory and the Death Drive* (Durham, NC: Duke University Press, 2004).

14. H. Hirsch Cohen, *The Drunkenness of Noah* (Tuscaloosa: University of Alabama Press, 1974), 13.

15. Ibid.

16. Saint Augustine of Hippo, *City of God*, trans. Henry Bettenson (London: Penguin, 2004), 649.

17. Ibid., 548.

18. Ibid., 650.

19. Ibid., 649.

20. Ibid., 549.

21. Ibid.

22. Ibid., 246–248.

23. Convention tempts the use here of "satisfaction" rather than "sensitization" to describe what these encounters of the flesh or appetites yield, yet "satisfaction" is too narrow a concept to account for cases in which carnal knowledge comes through events contrary to one's desires or affects.

24. Philo, *Philo:* Vol. 3, trans. F. H. Colson and G. H. Whitaker (Cambridge, MA: Harvard University Press, 1930), 458.

25. Ibid., 445.
26. Ibid., 445.
27. Ibid., 461.
28. Ibid., 447.
29. Plato, *The Republic*, trans. G. M. A. Grube, rev. C. D. C. Reeve (Indianapolis, IN: Hackett, 1982), 53.
30. See ibid., 55.
31. Ibid., 54–55.
32. Ibid., 59.
33. Ibid., 64–65.
34. The constitutional aspect of "oversight" intrinsic to supervision thus differs substantively from any theory of "perspectivism," by which the very possibility of "vision" presumes a subjectively limited viewpoint that thereby occasions "blind spots" of knowledge. In such a theory, those "oversights" in one's perspectival field are those that *could* be seen clearly by others or through a repositioning of one's own epistemological standpoint. The notion of oversight proposed here, on the contrary, does not imagine knowledge as preceding one's possible perception of it; rather "oversight" signifies the production of the illusory "blind spot" as the surreptitiously hidden or stained site of a presumptive truth.
35. See Augustine's reference to Matthew 26:39 in which Christ, the night of his arrest leading to crucifixion, makes the following appeal to God to spare him that fate: " 'Father, if it is possible, let this cup pass me by.' " (The request is repeated once more, unsuccessfully, in Matthew 26:42) *City of God*, 651.
36. Plato, *Republic*, 34.
37. Attesting to this organic emergence of genealogy through criminality is the curious locution of the "noble lie" [*gennaion pseudo*]. As Kateri Carmola explains, "The term *gennaion* means 'noble' in the sense of 'well-born' or 'well-conceived.' Its root, *gennaios*, refers to birth and familial background, and carries the connotation of something being 'suitable to one's birth or descent' . . . [rather than] *kalos*, which is to say aesthetically beautiful or fine." See "Noble Lying: Justice and Intergenerational Tension in Plato's 'Republic,'" *Political Theory*, 31, no. 1 (2003): 40. The revelation of the nature of justice is thus coincident with the revelation of one's birthright and line of descent. Yet this disclosure does not affix isolable and discrete ethical lineages but only affiliations that suffer both intra- and extrafamilial "tensions": "The first is the specific problem of parentage, embodied in the implied distinction between legitimate and illegitimate offspring. The second is . . . the problem of particular past generations for those who found new cities, begin new orders, or try to establish a new sense of justice—the inescapable (and tragic) hold of the past on the present." (41) Both "tensions" reflect one and the same dilemma of ethical knowledge, a "new justice" by which a "new order" becomes appreciable, whereby who and what "is" comes into being through the clip of evaluative relations.

38. Kant, "Physical Geography," 23.
39. Alain Locke, *The Philosophy of Alain Locke*, 1989, 213.
40. This includes the "deed" of inaction in the face of a duty or obligation.
41. See Ferdinand Saussure, *Course in General Linguistics*, eds. Charles Bally and Albert Sechehaye, trans. Roy Harris (Chicago: Open Court, 1986).

CHAPTER 4

1. See Nietzsche, *Genealogy of Morals*, 1989.
2. See Michel Foucault, *Discipline and Punish*, trans. Alan Sheridan (New York: Vintage, 1995), and Foucault, *Abnormal: Lectures at the Collège de France, 1974–1975*, eds. Valerio Marchetti and Antonella Salomoni, trans. Graham Burchell (New York: Picador, 2004).
3. Foucault, "Nietzsche, Genealogy, History," in *Aesthetics, Method, and Epistemology: The Essential Works of Foucault, 1954–1984*, vol. 2, ed. James Faubion, trans. Robert Hurley et al. (New York: New Press, 2001), 373–376.
4. See W.E.B. DuBois, *The World and Africa* (New York: International Publishers, 1989); see also V.Y. Mudimbe, *The Invention of Africa* (Bloomington: Indiana University Press, 1988), 13.
5. That the "punishment fit the crime" applies as well to those corrective dynamics in which additional "interest" is extracted from the criminal. Punishment need not operate as a literal, mirrored inverse of the offense (an eye for an eye) to demonstrate this equation. Rather, it need be understood only as a proper if also symbolic *compensation*. Justice thus can aspire to actuarial calculations, where the objective of punishment becomes its *precision*—that is, neither insufficient nor excessive but meticulously calibrated. As an example, see Jacques Derrida's call for such precision in institutional responses to criminality. "The Rhetoric of Drugs," in *Points . . .: Interviews 1974–1994*, ed. Elisabeth Weber, trans. Michael Israel et al. (Palo Alto, CA: Stanford University Press, 1995).
6. Philo, "*Philo*," 461, 467.
7. Ibid., 465.
8. Ibid., 467.
9. Ibid., 469.
10. Ibid., 465, 467.
11. Kant, *Groundwork*, 8.
12. Here one might add the unconscious drives of desire and inclination as well.
13. Augustine, *City of God*, 278. Augustine does not hold an exclusively uniform position here, as he elsewhere provides a more intentional origin of criminality, proposing that "a bad deed could not have been done had not bad will preceded it," a position that, depending on whether his idea of carnality refers exclusively to the will, complicates if not contradicts his critique (308).
14. Ibid., 282–284.

15. Ibid., 309; this "turning away" of the self into the self anticipates a similar critical move in existentialist theories. See Walter Kaufmann, *Existentialism From Dostoyevsky to Sartre* (New York: Plume, 1975), 13.

16. Augustine, *City of God*, 309, 295.

17. Ibid., 651.

18. Ibid., 650.

19. Felder, *Troubling Biblical Waters*, 44.

20. Kierkegaard, *Fear and Trembling*, 65.

21. See *Genesis* 9:1–16.

22. *Genesis* 9:19.

23. *Genesis* 9:12.

24. *Genesis* 9:18–27, 10:1.

25. Patrice Pavis, *Dictionary of the Theater: Terms, Concepts, and Analysis*, trans. Christine Shantz (Toronto: University of Toronto Press, 1999), 199.

26. See Rice, "The Alleged Curse on Ham," 131: "With the blessing of Japheth it becomes clear that we are not dealing with individuals alone but with groups of people and their political relationships to one another." The proposition here, however, is that something more fundamental than politics is at issue.

27. Foucault, "Nietzsche, Genealogy, History," 373.

28. Ibid., 374.

29. Ibid.

30. Isaac, "Sons of Ham," 79.

31. Felder, *Troubling Biblical Waters*, 39.

32. Ibid., 38–45.

33. See Stephen Mulhall, *Philosophical Myths of the Fall* (Princeton, NJ: Princeton, 2005).

34. In the work of early anthropologists, he laments, "there is not an anthropological factor which even shows a hint of becoming dynamic. All are static." Locke, *Race Contacts*, 6.

CHAPTER 5

1. The most notable examples of this may be Michel Foucault's *The Order of Things* (New York: Vintage, 1994) and Jean-François Lyotard's *The Postmodern Condition*, trans. Geoff Bennington and Brian Massumi (Minneapolis: University of Minnesota Press, 1984).

2. Jacques Derrida, *Aporias*, trans. Thomas Dutoit (Palo Alto, CA: Stanford University Press, 1993).

3. Foucault, "On the Genealogy of Ethics," in *Ethics: Subjectivity and Truth: The Essential Works of Foucault, 1954–1984,* vol. 1, ed. Paul Rabinow, trans. Robert Hurley et al. (New York: New Press, 1997), 256.

4. Foucault, "Genealogy of Ethics," 262. See also his description of his understanding of power as opposed to Sartre's in relation to ethics in "The Ethic of the Concern for Self as a Practice of Freedom," in *Ethics: Subjectivity and Truth: The Essential Works of Foucault, 1954–1984,* vol. 1, ed. Paul Rabinow, trans. Robert Hurley et al. (New York: New Press, 1997), 298–299.

5. Jean-Paul Sartre, *Notebooks for an Ethics*, trans. David Pellauer (Chicago: University of Chicago Press, 1992).

6. Several more unnumbered aphorisms follow the sixty-eighth in this section, as if even this elementary mode of categorization eventually collapses as a consequence of Sartre's own ambivalence and ambiguity.

7. Sartre, *Notebook for an Ethics*, 11

8. Ibid., 95.

9. Ibid., 57–58.

10. Ibid., 32–33.

11. Ibid., 33.

12. Ibid.

13. Louis Althusser, *Lenin and Philosophy and Other Essays*, trans. Ben Brewster (New York: Monthly Review Press, 1971), 162.

14. Althusser, *Lenin and Philosophy*, 174.

15. In this respect, Althusser's allegory resurrects the Oedipal myth's vernacular of an unconditioned criminality, one that no deed precipitates. Laius, the father of Oedipus, receives word of his curse that foretells his death at the hands of his son via an oracle who, we are given to believe, does not author the sentence and its terms but merely conveys them. The oracle says nothing of the source or motivation of the curse; moreover, nothing in the prophecy suggests the curse as a response to or punishment for Laius's criminal behavior of the past, nor, for that matter, do the characters interpret it as such: the news troubles Laius and Jocasta, assuredly, yet neither demands justification for this sentencing nor objects to it outwardly as unfair or unwarranted, even in their scheme to rewrite the future. The curse is not justified by the story but what justifies and generates it. Thus the play begins within the curse: at the opening of the first scene it has already long existed, and at no point does it become negotiable. Like Althusserian criminality, the curse comprises the relational background and propellant of the drama that has no representational or causal origin, and thus underscores its structural inability to be either "given" or "possessed" by subjects. The background of criminality that enables Althusserian subjectivity does not thereby denote an indifference to it any more than Laius and Jocasta can be said indifferent to the curse: it is exactly the unquestioning and unquestionable positing of Laius's curse by the oracle as "what is" that affirms the "givenness" of the inheritable criminal subjectivity of Laius and thus of his son Oedipus, a naturalizing codification of relations reflective precisely of ideology.

16. Althusser, *Lenin and Philosophy*, 175.

17. Ibid., 165.
18. Ibid., 164.
19. Roland Barthes, *Mythologies*, trans. Annette Lavers (New York: Hill and Wang, 1972).
20. Althusser, *Lenin and Philosophy*, 172.
21. Ibid., 176.
22. Ibid., 164.
23. Ibid.
24. Ibid.
25. Thomas Jefferson, *Notes on the State of Virginia*, ed. William Peden (Chapel Hill: University of North Carolina Press, 1955), 213.
26. David Walker, *David Walker's Appeal*, ed. Sean Wilentz (New York: Hill and Wang, 1995), 17.

CONCLUSION

1. Langston Hughes, "The Dream Keeper," in *The Collected Poems of Langston Hughes*, ed. Arnold Rampersad (New York: Vintage, 1995), 45.
2. Hughes, "Harlem," in *The Collected Poems of Langston Hughes*, ed. Arnold Rampersad (New York: Vintage, 1995), 426.
3. Hughes, "Cultural Exchange," in *The Collected Poems of Langston Hughes*, ed. Arnold Rampersad (New York: Vintage, 1995), 476–481.
4. Jefferson, *Notes on the State of Virginia*, 163.
5. Denouncements of this reversal, however, are not only a common reaction but have also rationalized the continuation of racial violence as a necessary defense against such an exchange. In *My Bondage and My Freedom*, Frederick Douglass decries the account of vindication provided to a plantation owner by one of his overseers who has murdered a slave:

   That very convenient covert for all manner of cruelty and outrage—that cowardly alarm-cry, that the slaves would *"take the place,"* was pleaded, in extenuation of this revolting crime, just as it had been cited in defense of a thousand similar ones. He argued that if one slave refused to be corrected, and was allowed to escape with his life, when he had been told that he should lose it if he persisted in his course, the other slaves would soon copy his example; the result of which would be, the freedom of the slaves, and the enslavement of the whites. I have every reason to believe that [the overseer] Mr. Gore's defense, or explanation, was deemed satisfactory—at least to [plantation owner] Col. Lloyd." *Frederick Douglass: Autobiographies*, ed. Henry Louis Gates (New York: Library of America, 1994), 202.

The exchange of fortune that for Hughes is both dream and nightmare is, for the overseer, a revenge fantasy in which the "freedom of the slaves" is logically of a piece with the "enslavement" of whites. The revenge fantasy, however, belongs not to the slave but to the master, as what narcissistically redrafts whites into the center of black fantasies of freedom. The conception of this revolution as a species of resentful desire, moreover, implies that while whites receive pleasure from the plurality of goods afforded by institutional favor—that is, in appreciation of the good fortune that is their due—the pleasure of black people in a similar position would derive from the suffering of whites. In its modern-day version, the revenge fantasy persists, as Douglass foreshadows, in the belief that people of color, as educationally and aesthetically disenfranchised, have become "sensitized" to obtain pleasure through negating and destructive cultural representations. On such contemporary racial reversals in ethics, see Reid Miller, "A Lesson in Moral Spectatorship," *Critical Inquiry* 34, no. 4 (Summer 2008).

6. Nella Larsen, *Quicksand* and *Passing* (New Brunswick, NJ: Rutgers University Press, 1986), 159.

7. From W.E.B. DuBois, *The World and Africa*, 227:

> "What in truth is going to be the future of black folk? Are they going to die out gradually, with only traces of their blood to remind the world of their former existence? Are they going to be permanently segregated from the world in Africa or elsewhere, leaving the white world free of its fear and repulsion? Or in some slow and fast intermingling of peoples will all colors of mankind merge into some indistinguishable unity? None of these solutions seems practicable or imminent for many a long day. And, after all, none would really solve the basic problem of the relations of peoples; for even if extremes of human differences vanish, there will always remain differences, and around them the problems of human living-together."

8. Walker, *David Walker's Appeal*, 20.

9. James Baldwin, *The Devil Finds Work* (New York: Dial, 1976), 139–140.

Bibliography

Aaron, David. "Early Rabbinic Exegesis on Noah's Son Ham and the So-Called 'Hamitic Myth.'" *Journal of the American Academy of Religion* 63, no. 4 (1995): 721–760.

Alcoff, Linda. *Visible Identities: Race, Gender, and the Self.* New York: Oxford University Press, 2006.

Althusser, Louis. *Lenin and Philosophy and Other Essays.* Translated by Ben Brewster. New York: Monthly Review Press, 1971.

Babbitt, Susan E., and Sue Campbell, eds. *Racism and Philosophy.* Ithaca, NY: Cornell University Press, 1999.

Baldwin, James. *The Devil Finds Work.* New York: Dial, 1976.

Baldwin, James. *The Evidence of Things Not Seen.* New York: Holt, Rinehart, and Winston, 1995.

Barthes, Roland. *Mythologies.* Translated by Annette Lavers. New York: Hill and Wang, 1972.

Bernasconi, Robert. "Kant as an Unfamiliar Source of Racism." In *Philosophers on Race,* edited by Julie K. Ward and Tommy L. Lott, 145–167. Oxford: Blackwell, 2002.

Blum, Lawrence. *"I'm Not a Racist, But. .": The Moral Quandary of Race.* Ithaca, NY: Cornell University Press, 2002.

Blyden, Edward Wilmot. "Noah's Maledicton." *Slavery and Abolition* 1, no. 1 (1980): 18–24.

Boxhill, Bernard, ed. *Race and Racism.* New York: Oxford University Press, 2001.

Browne, Sir Thomas. *Pseudodoxia Epidemica.* Vol. 3. Edited by Geoffrey Keynes. London: Faber & Gwyer, 1928.

Butler, Judith. *The Psychic Life of Power.* Palo Alto, CA: Stanford University Press, 1997.

Carmola, Kateri. "Noble Lying: Justice and Intergenerational Tension in Plato's 'Republic.'" *Political Theory* 31, no. 1 (2003): 39–62.

Cohen, H. Hirsch. *The Drunkenness of Noah.* Tuscaloosa: University of Alabama Press, 1974.

Cohen, Marshall, Thomas Nagel, and Thomas Scanlon, eds. *Equality and Preferential Treatment*. Princeton, NJ: Princeton University Press, 1977.

Crummell, Alexander. "The Negro Race Not Under A Curse." In *The Future of Africa*. By Alexander Crummell. 327–354. New York: Scribner, 1862.

Davis, David Brion. "Jews, Blacks, and the Roots of Racism." *Midstream* (December 2001): 5–7.

de Lauretis, Teresa. "Difference Embodied: Reflections on *Black Skins, White Masks*." *Parallax* 8, no. 2 (2002): 54–68.

de Lauretis, Teresa. *Freud's Drive*. New York: Palgrave Macmillan, 2010.

Derrida, Jacques. *Dissemination*. Translated by Barbara Johnson. Chicago: University of Chicago Press, 1982.

Derrida, Jacques. *Aporias*. Translated by Thomas Dutoit. Palo Alto, CA: Stanford University Press, 1993.

Derrida, Jacques. "The Rhetoric of Drugs." In *Points . . .: Interviews 1974–1994*, edited by Elisabeth Weber, translated by Michael Israel et al., 228–254. Palo Alto, CA: Stanford University Press, 1995.

Douglass, Frederick. *Frederick Douglass: Autobiographies*. Edited by Henry Louis Gates. New York: Library of America, 1994.

DuBois, W.E.B. *The World and Africa*. New York: International Publishers, 1996.

DuBois, W.E.B., and Augustus Granville Dill. *Morals and Manners among Negro Americans*. Atlanta: Atlanta University Press, 1914, http://docsouth.unc.edu/church/morals/dubois.html.

Dyer, Richard. *White*. London: Routledge, 1997.

Edelman, Lee. *No Future: Queer Theory and the Death Drive*. Durham, NC: Duke University Press, 2004.

Eilberg-Schwartz, Howard. *God's Phallus*. Boston, MA: Beacon, 1994.

Ellison, Ralph. *Invisible Man*. New York: Vintage, 1990.

Eze, Emmanuel, ed. *Race and the Enlightenment*. Malden, MA: Blackwell, 1997.

Fanon, Frantz. *Peau Noire, Masque Blancs*. Paris: Seuil, 1952.

Fanon, Frantz. *Black Skin, White Masks*. Translated by Charles Lam Markmann. New York: Grove, 1967.

Felder, Cain Hope. *Troubling Biblical Waters*. Maryknoll, New York: Orbis, 1989.

Foucault, Michel. *Power/Knowledge: Selected Interviews and Writings, 1972–1977*. Edited by Colin Gordon. Translated by Colin Gordon, et al. New York: Pantheon, 1980.

Foucault, Michel. *The Order of Things*. New York: Vintage, 1994.

Foucault, Michel. *Discipline and Punish*. Translated by Alan Sheridan. New York: Vintage, 1994.

Foucault, Michel. "The Ethic of the Concern for Self as a Practice of Freedom." In *Ethics: Subjectivity and Truth: The Essential Works of Foucault, 1954–1984*, Vol. 1, edited by Paul Rabinow, translated by Robert Hurley et al., 281–302. New York: New Press, 1997.

Foucault, Michel. "On the Genealogy of Ethics: An Overview of Work in Progress." In *Ethics: Subjectivity and Truth: The Essential Works of Foucault, 1954–1984*, Vol. 1, edited by Paul Rabinow, translated by Robert Hurley et al., 253–280. New York: New Press, 1997.

Foucault, Michel. "Nietzsche, Genealogy, History." In *Aesthetics, Method, and Epistemology: The Essential Works of Foucault, 1954–1984*, Vol. 2, edited by James Faubion, translated by Robert Hurley et al., 369–392. New York: New Press, 2001.

Foucault, Michel. *Abnormal: Lectures at the Collège de France, 1974–1975*. Edited by Valerio Marchetti and Antonella Salomoni. Translated by Graham Burchell. New York: Picador, 2004.

Foucault, Michel. *Introduction to Kant's Anthropology*. Edited by Robert Nigro. Translated by Robert Nigro and Kate Briggs. Los Angeles: Semiotexte, 2008.

Freud, Sigmund. *Totem and Taboo*. Translated by James Strachey. New York: Norton, 1990.

Goldenberg, David. "The Curse of Ham: A Case of Rabbinic Racism?" In *Struggles in the Promised Land*, edited by Jack Salzman and Cornel West, 21–52. New York: Oxford University Press, 1997.

Goldenberg, David. *The Curse of Ham*. Princeton, NJ: Princeton University Press, 2005.

Gordon, Lewis. *Existentia Africana: Understanding Africana Existential Thought*. New York: Routledge, 2000.

Hall, Stuart. "The After-life of Frantz Fanon." In *The Fact of Blackness: Frantz Fanon and Visual Representation*, edited by Alan Read, 12–37. Seattle: Bay Press, 1996.

Hawthorne, Nathaniel. "The Birthmark." In *Mosses from an Old Manse*. By Nathaniel Hawthorne, 28–44. New York: Modern Library, 2003.

Haynes, Stephen R. *Noah's Curse: The Biblical Justification of American Slavery*. New York: Oxford University Press, 2002.

Heller, Agnes. "The Role of Interpretation in Modern Ethical Practice." *Philosophy and Social Criticism* 17, no. 2 (April 1991): 83–101.

Hughes, Langston. "Cultural Exchange." In *The Collected Poems of Langston Hughes*, edited by Arnold Rampersad, 476–481. New York: Vintage, 1995.

Hughes, Langston. "The Dream Keeper." In *The Collected Poems of Langston Hughes*, edited by Arnold Rampersad, 45. New York: Vintage, 1995.

Hughes, Langston. "Harlem." In *The Collected Poems of Langston Hughes*, edited by Arnold Rampersad, 426. New York: Vintage, 1995.

Isaac, Ephraim. "Genesis, Judaism, and the Sons of Ham." In *Slaves and Slavery in Muslim Africa*, Vol. 2 of *Islam and the Ideology of Enslavement*, edited by John Willis, 75–91. London: Frank Cass, 1985.

Jefferson, Thomas. *Notes on the State of Virginia*. Edited by William Peden. Chapel Hill: University of North Carolina Press, 1955.

Jordan, Winthrop. *White Over Black: American Attitudes Towards the Negro, 1550–1812*. Chapel Hill: University of North Carolina Press, 1968.

Judy, Ronald T. "Fanon's Body of Black Experience." In *Fanon: A Critical Reader*. Based on the Eleventh Annual Symposium on African-American Culture and Philosophy, Held at Purdue University on March 23-24, 1995, edited by L. R. Gordon, T. D. Sharpley-Whiting, and R. T. White, 53–73. Malden, MA: Blackwell, 1996.

Kant, Immanuel. *Kant's Gesammelte Schriften*. Vol. 6. Edited by Preukischen Akademie der Wissenschaften. Berlin: G. Reimer, 1914.

Kant, Immanuel. *Metaphysics of Morals*. Translated by Mary Gregor. Cambridge, UK: Cambridge University Press, 1991.

Kant, Immanuel. *Groundwork of the Metaphysics of Morals*. Edited and Translated by Mary Gregor. Cambridge, UK: Cambridge University Press, 1997.

Kant, Immanuel. "On the Different Races of Man." In *Race and the Enlightenment*, edited by Emmanuel Eze, 38–48. Malden, MA: Blackwell, 1997.

Kant, Immanuel. "Physical Geography." Translated by K. M. Faull and Emmanuel Eze. In *Race and the Enlightenment*, edited by Emmanuel Eze, 58–64. Malden, MA: Blackwell, 1997.

Kant, Immanuel. "On the Use of Teleological Principles in Philosophy." Translated by Jon Mark Mikkelsen. In *Race*, edited by Robert Bernasconi, 37–56. Malden, MA: Blackwell, 2001.

Kaufmann, Walter. *Existentialism From Dostoyevsky to Sartre*. New York: Plume, 1975.

Kierkegaard, Soren. *Fear and Trembling/Repetition*. Translated by Edna Hong and Howard Hong. Princeton, NJ: Princeton University Press, 1983.

King, Martin Luther. Jr. , "I Have a Dream." In *A Testament of Hope: The Essential Writings and Speeches of Martin Luther King, Jr.*, edited by James M. Washington, 217–220. New York: Harper Collins, 1986.

King, Martin Luther. Jr., "Love, Law, and Civil Disobedience." In *A Testament of Hope: The Essential Writings and Speeches of Martin Luther King, Jr.*, edited by James M. Washington, 43–53. New York: Harper Collins, 1986.

Kingsley, William, pub. Special Issue: "Slavery and the Bible." *The New Englander* 15, no. 57 (February 1857): 102–115.

Kosman, L. Aryeh. "The Naïve Narrator: Meditation in Descartes' *Meditations*." In *Essays on Descartes' Meditations*, edited by A. O. Rorty, 21–43. Berkeley: University of California Press, 1986.

Laplanche, Jean. *Freud and the Sexual: Essays 2000–2006*. Edited by John Fletcher. Translated by John Fletcher, Jonathan House, and Nicholas Ray. International Psychoanalytic Books, 2011.

Laplanche, Jean and J.-B. Pontalis. *The Language of Psychoanalysis*. Translated by Donald Nicholson-Smith. New York: Norton, 1973.

Larsen, Nella. *Quicksand* and *Passing*. New Brunswick, NJ: Rutgers University Press, 1986.

Locke, Alain. *The Philosophy of Alain Locke*. Edited by Leonard Harris. Philadelphia: Temple University Press, 1989.

Locke, Alain. *Race Contacts and Interracial Relations*. Edited by Jeffrey C. Stewart. Washington, DC: Howard University Press, 1992.

Louden, Robert. *Kant's Impure Ethics*. New York: Oxford University Press, 2000.

Louden, Robert. "The Second Part of Morals." In *Essays on Kant's Anthropology*, edited by Brian Jacobs and Patrick Kain, 60–84. Cambridge, UK: Cambridge University Press, 2003.

Lyotard, Jean-François. *The Postmodern Condition*. Translated by Geoff Bennington and Brian Massumi. Minneapolis: University of Minnesota Press, 1984.

Lyotard, Jean-François. *The Differend: Phrases in Dispute*. Translated by Georges Van Den Abbeele. Minneapolis: University of Minnesota Press, 1989.

Marriott, David. *On Black Men*. New York: Columbia University Press, 2000.

Miller, Jerry. "(no relation)." *Philosophy and Social Criticism* 38, no. 9 (2012): 955–975.

Miller, Kelly. *Race Adjustment: The Everlasting Stain*. The American Negro: His History and Literature. New York: Arno, 1968.

Miller, Reid. "A Lesson in Moral Spectatorship," *Critical Inquiry* 34, no. 4 (Summer 2008): 706–728 [Editorial Correction, *Critical Inquiry* 35, no. 3 (Spring 2009): 727–728.

Mills, Charles. *Blackness Visible: Essays On Philosophy and Race*. Ithaca, NY: Cornell University Press, 1998.

Mills, Charles. "Racial Liberalism," *PMLA* 123, no. 5 (2008): 1380–1397.

Mills, Charles. "Retrieving Rawls for Racial Justice? A Critique of Tommie Shelby." *Critical Philosophies of Race* 1, no. 1 (2013): 1–27.

Monahan, Michael J. *The Creolizing Subject*. New York: Fordham University Press, 2011.

Mudimbe, V. Y. *The Invention of Africa*. Bloomington: Indiana University Press, 1988.

Mulhall, Stephen. *Philosophical Myths of the Fall*. Princeton, NJ: Princeton University Press, 2005.

Nietzsche, Friedrich. *The Will To Power*. Edited by Walter Kaufmann. Translated by Walter Kaufmann and R. J. Hollingdale. New York: Vintage, 1968.

Nietzsche, Friedrich. *Genealogy of Morals*. Edited and translated by Walter Kaufmann. New York: Vintage, 1989.

Nigro, August. *The Net of Nemesis: Studies in Tragic Bond/Age*. Selinsgrove, PA: Susquehanna University Press, 2000.

Omi, Michael, and Howard Winant. *Racial Formations in the United States*. New York: Routledge, 1994.

O'Neill, Onora. *Constructions of Reason*. Cambridge, UK: Cambridge University Press, 1989.

Patemen, Carole, and Charles Mills. *Contract and Domination*. Cambridge, UK: Polity, 2007.

Pavis, Patrice. *Dictionary of the Theater: Terms, Concepts, and Analysis*. Translated by Christine Shantz. Toronto: University of Toronto Press, 1999.

Philo. *Philo*: Volume 3. Translated by F. H. Colson and G. H. Whitaker. Cambridge, MA: Harvard University Press, 1930.

Plato. *The Republic*. Translated by G. M. A. Grube. Revised by C. D. C. Reeve. Indianapolis, IN: Hackett, 1982.

Plato. *Meno*. Translated by G. M. A. Grube. Revised by John Cooper. Indianapolis, IN: Hackett, 2002.

Rawls, John. *A Theory of Justice*. Cambridge, MA: Harvard University Press, 1971.

Rice, Gene. "The Curse that Never Was (Genesis 9:18–27)." *The Journal of Religious Thought* 29 (1972): 5–27.

Rice, Gene. "The Alleged Curse on Ham." In *Holy Bible: African American Jubilee Edition*, 127–143. New York: American Bible Society, 1999.

Rorty, Richard. *Contingency, Irony, and Solidarity*. New York: Cambridge University Press, 1989.

Royce, Josiah. *Race Questions, Provincialisms, and Other American Problems*. Freeport, NY: Books for Libraries, 1967.

Sartre, Jean-Paul. *Anti-Semite and Jew*. Translated by George Becker. New York: Schocken, 1948.

Sartre, Jean-Paul. *Notebooks for an Ethics*. Translated by David Pellauer. Chicago: University of Chicago Press, 1992.

Sartre, Jean-Paul. *Existentialism is a Humanism*. Translated by Carol Macomber. New Haven, CT: Yale University Press, 2007.

Saussure, Ferdinand. *Course in General Linguistics*. Edited by Charles Bally and Albert Sechehaye. Translated by Roy Harris. Chicago: Open Court, 1986.

Sollors, Werner. *Neither Black Nor White Yet Both*. New York: Oxford University Press, 1997.

Sophocles, "*Oedipus the King*." In *Sophocles*, edited and translated by David Grene. Chicago: University of Chicago Press, 1954.

St. Augustine of Hippo. *City of God*. Translated by Henry Bettenson. London: Penguin, 2004.

Stubblefield, Anna. *Ethics Along the Color Line*. Ithaca, NY: Cornell University Press, 2005.

Taylor, Charles. *The Ethics of Authenticity*. Cambridge, MA: Harvard University Press, 1992.

Thompson, Michael. *Life and Action: Elementary Structures of Practice and Practical Thought*. Cambridge, MA: Harvard University Press, 2008.

Walker, David. *David Walker's Appeal*. Edited by Sean Wilentz. New York: Hill and Wang, 1995.

Washington, Booker T. *Character Building*. Amsterdam, NY: Fredonia Books, 2002.

West, Cornel. *Prophesy Deliverance!* Philadelphia: Westminster, 1982.

Williams, Bernard. *Ethics and the Limits of Philosophy*. Cambridge, MA: Harvard University Press, 1985.

Zachernuk, Philip S. "Of Origins and Colonial Order: Southern Nigerian Historians and the 'Hamitic Hypothesis' c. 1870–1970." *Journal of African History* 35, no. 3 (1994): 427–455.

Zack, Naomi. *The Ethics and Mores of Race: Equality after the History of Philosophy*. Lanham, MD: Rowman & Littlefield, 2011.

Index

CPSIA information can be obtained
at www.ICGtesting.com
Printed in the USA
BVHW082106110219
540032BV00005B/11/P